THE *EAGLE* AND BROOKLYN

The new Brooklyn *Eagle* building in the 1890s.

THE *EAGLE*
and
BROOKLYN

A COMMUNITY NEWSPAPER
1841-1955

Raymond A. Schroth, S.J.

Contributions in American Studies, Number 13

Greenwood Press
Westport, Connecticut ● London, England

Library of Congress Cataloging in Publication Data

Schroth, Raymond A
    The Eagle and Brooklyn: a community newspaper, 1841-
1955.

    (Contributions in American studies, no. 13)
    Bibliography: p.
    1. Brooklyn eagle. I. Title.
PN4899.N42B77   071'.47'23   73-20972
ISBN 0-8371-7335-3

Copyright © 1974 by Raymond A. Schroth, S.J.

Library of Congress Catalog Card Number: 73-20972
ISBN: 0-8371-7335-3

First published in 1974

Greenwood Press, a division of Williamhouse-Regency Inc.
51 Riverside Avenue, Westport, Connecticut 06880

Manufactured in the United States of America

TO MY FATHER AND MOTHER

CONTENTS

LIST OF ILLUSTRATIONS

PREFACE

When the Brooklyn *Eagle* died, the community of Brooklyn—an urban center to which the word "community" really once applied —lost a key institution that dated back to the beginning of its history and played a major role in its self-definition.

This history of the *Eagle* will narrate and analyze the *Eagle*'s role in shaping Brooklyn's self-image. It is of necessity a limited work, and therefore cannot attempt to treat the whole 114-year history of the newspaper or of Brooklyn; but it will concentrate on several of the more interesting issues that seem to best exemplify Brooklyn's need to stress its independence of and even its superiority to Manhattan, its more powerful neighbor across the river. It will discuss those journalists, such as Walt Whitman, Thomas Kinsella, St. Clair McKelway, Harris Crist, H. V. Kaltenborn, Cleveland Rodgers, Edwin B. Wilson, and Frank D. Schroth, who best embodied what *Eagle* men and many Brooklynites often called the "Brooklyn" or the "*Eagle*" spirit. This study will also try to avoid what was sometimes an *Eagle* fault: an uncritical tone. There is reason to believe that by so stressing Brooklyn's positive qualities as a "borough of homes and churches" and by so concentrating its influence on its own list of "prominent citizens" the *Eagle* lost touch with a changing Brooklyn.

This account, therefore, of the *Eagle*'s beginning, rise, and fall is in a sense three stories, all intimately interrelated. It is first of all a story of an institution, a unique and sometimes great American daily newspaper that had a special relationship with one urban community.

Older and established Brooklynites genuinely loved the *Eagle*. This is clear in the letters from former readers and in my conversations with Brooklynites and former writers and executives from the *Eagle*. They remember it well and still long for it as for an old friend. This newspaper and its readership interacted in a very personal way and the readers counted on the *Eagle* to give them a sense of belonging and historical continuity in their community.

Second, this story—though often indirectly—is one of urban social change in one of the world's largest industrial and commercial cities, one that for various reasons has always thought of itself as a small town. Communities, very much like the people who comprise them, long for self-understanding. What Alfred Kazin, who began his life in Brooklyn, has written about America as a nation can also be applied in this instance to Brooklyn as a community.

> As a people, Americans have been absorbed in "making it," in their own success story, in the making of Americans. To be an American is itself a career, as so many Americans, old stock as well as new, have testified. We are a legend to ourselves and though the rest of the world has believed in this legend and has contributed to it, only we have lived it with the absorption that makes it necessary for us constantly to note our progress.[1]

Brooklynites, like other Americans, have been obsessed with "making it," but with a difference. "Making it" has often meant leaving Brooklyn. Those who remained have had to develop a special compensating love for their home town. During most of the nineteenth century, Brooklyn could see and interpret itself as Manhattan's competitor and, in some ways, its moral and cultural superior. It cultivated a quality of life that combined domestic virtues with the American nineteenth century belief in inevitable progress, and it saw its self-confidence unified in the borough's seemingly inexorable expansion. Then, when the city of Brooklyn became a borough of Greater New York, against the *Eagle*'s opposition to consolidation, its identity crisis became more apparent. Throughout the twentieth century dramatic shifts in population—particularly the immigration of lower East Side Jews across the Williamsburg Bridge, the startling rise in the Negro and Puerto Rican population during and after World War II, and the exodus of the more prosperous middle-class—and the rise in the crime rate forced Brooklyn to ask itself again and again what kind of a community it was.

To Betty Smith, author of *A Tree Grows in Brooklyn*, Brooklyn was different because most Brooklynites had been born there, as were their parents and grandparents. They had deep roots and tribal customs. You knew that Brooklyn was different because when the BMT subway rattled across the Williamsburg Bridge you could sense the new mood, the more leisurely human pace, the slower, more rhythmic movement of the car. Yet to Betty Smith, the Brooklyn spirit remained "something indefinable."[2] The *Eagle* could not allow this spirit to remain indefinable. Throughout its history the *Eagle* selected and promoted the images by which Brooklyn could define itself. For 114 years the community which shared in a unique way the American anxiety over "making it" was reminded by the *Eagle* of the beauty of its parks, the wonders of its Bridge, the tranquility of its neighborhoods, the venerability of its churches, the integrity of its institutions, the invincibility of its Dodgers, and the excellence of its *Eagle*. In this sense, then, this book is one more attempt to solve the "riddle of Brooklyn."

Third, this account is the story of individual men who, in their success as journalists, became leading interpreters of the "Brooklyn Spirit." The most significant of them became as personally identified with the *Eagle* as an institution and with Brooklyn as a community as the paper and the city were with each other. Sometimes a great newspaperman can understand, interpret, and articulate the values of a community so well that he personifies the community himself. Brooklyn's journalists, including those who were not born there, shared and lived the Brooklynite's conviction that Brooklyn and its citizens could not be thought of as a national joke, that they had to "make it" in spite of the fact that they lived in the shadow of gilded and fabulous Manhattan.

*   *   *

Inevitably, there have been a number of problems with this study. My decision to concentrate on selected significant issues and personalities that illustrate the *Eagle*'s function as a "community" paper has meant that I've had to give what may appear to be too little attention to national politics, foreign policy, and other stronger *Eagle* features like columnists, comics, and sports. Moreover, the fact that my uncle Frank Schroth was the last publisher, my cousin Frank, Jr. the assistant publisher, my cousin Tom the managing editor, and my father a part-time editorial writer has given me access to important sources, led me to concentrate more on the final years, and raised the question of my objectivity.

I have attempted to maintain a fair and objective attitude in my consultation of American Newspaper Guild sources and my correspondence and interviews with surviving *Eagle* employees and management officials who were critical of the Schroth family. I have become particularly conscious of how personality traits and personal differences can have an adverse effect on labor-management relations. Nevertheless, some bias probably remains. This is a condition which goes with writing about something so close to the writer's personal experience.

This search for the *Eagle* spirit has at least been made more enjoyable by a collection of a young man's memories between 1940 and 1955: watching the Dodgers from the publisher's box in Ebbetts Field; cherishing the baseball signed by all the team—Robinson, Barney, Snider; staring up at the hallowed Walt Whitman portrait outside the publisher's office; criticizing the publisher for the *Eagle*'s sensationalism in 1951 and being told that emphasis on the most important events of the day—the deliberations of the United Nations—does not sell newspapers; and visiting the dead *Eagle* office for the closing auction in April 1955, having been sent to find a horseshoe copy desk for the Fordham *Ram*.

* * *

I thank all those who have helped me in my research: those who have given me their recollections, in letters and interviews; the staffs of the Brooklyn Public Library, the New York Public Library, the New York Historical Society, the Long Island Historical Society, Mr. Arthur Konop of the St. Francis College Archives; and the friends who have encouraged me. However, I would like to give special attention to five men who have been crucial to my writing and academic career or to the completion of this book: Reverend Joseph R. Frese, S.J., of Fordham, who suggested this topic; the late Professor Edward A. Walsh, who encouraged my undergraduate writing at Fordham; Reverend Thurston N. Davis, S.J., editor of *America*, who published my articles on social problems for several years; Thomas N. Schroth, who generously gave me his files and his own share of the *Eagle* spirit; and Professor Robert H. Walker, who welcomed me to The George Washington University and directed my dissertation.

Notes

[1] Alfred Kazin, "The Bridge," *New York Review of Books* (July 15, 1965): 6.

[2] Betty Smith, "Why Brooklyn Is That Way," *New York Times Magazine* (December 12, 1943): 14.

THE *EAGLE* AND BROOKLYN

INTRODUCTION

The *Eagle* in Context: Its Importance and Its Problems

On March 17, 1955, the Brooklyn *Eagle* died. Founded in 1841 as a temporary organ of the Democratic party, it had outgrown its origins within a generation and had become, by the turn of the century, a local daily newspaper of national and even international reputation.

The *Eagle* is usually mentioned only in passing in the standard histories of American journalism, and then it is often remembered for the wrong reasons: because one of its writers—such as Walt Whitman, Richard Adams Locke, H. V. Kaltenborn, Edward Bok, or Winston Burdett—later became famous writing somewhere else; because it was one of the several papers threatened with suspension during the Civil War; or because it was one of the many urban newspapers to die in the midst of a labor dispute at a time when economic problems were bringing a number of metropolitan newspapers to their knees.

The *Eagle* should be remembered for a number of other reasons; it was a unique community newspaper in a unique community. During the Civil War it was the most widely read afternoon newspaper in America; at the peak of its influence under the editorship of St. Clair McKelway its editorials were quoted all over the country and in Europe as well; it won four Pulitzer Prizes and many other awards. Above all, it was a bond of union in one of the world's largest and most diversified urban communities. It was the apostle of what was called the "Brooklyn Spirit." Its primary goal was to reflect the life and promote the welfare of a changing community by both preserving the community's continuity with its past and helping it adapt to threatening times.

The death of the *Eagle* was, in the judgment of a prominent New York journalist and social critic, the first of four central factors in the decline of postwar Brooklyn. Along with the departure of the Dodgers for California, the closing of the Brooklyn Navy Yard, and the immigration of southern Negroes, most of whom settled in Brooklyn rather than Manhattan, the folding of the *Eagle* signified the passing of a community and a particular way of life.[1]

The Impact of the *Eagle* on Those Who Knew It

The *Eagle* seems to have had a mysterious impact on those who worked there and on those Brooklyn citizens who loved it. Interviews with surviving employees and management personnel reveal deeply felt antagonisms between management and labor which time has not healed. This feeling is strongest among those who worked there in the late 1930s. Yet for the most part, correspondence and conversations with those who knew the *Eagle* show a great longing for a revered civic institution. For many its death was traumatic; its loss deprived them of the means of communication that linked otherwise alienated citizens to one another, to their communities, and to their past. They no longer knew who won the grammar school baseball games or when old half-forgotten friends had died.

For James A. Kelly, Brooklyn borough historian, the *Eagle* was the paper that kept Brooklyn from being pushed around by New York. In 1938, when Douglas "Wrong-Way" Corrigan was being brought home in dubious triumph from Ireland for a hero's welcome in New York, it was the *Eagle* that led the fight against Mayor Fiorello H. LaGuardia to make sure that Corrigan, who had taken off from Floyd Bennett Field in Brooklyn, would be welcomed first by Brooklyn on his return.[2] For Helen M. Barton, a commercial artist, the *Eagle* was an important part of her childhood and the beginning of her art career. While still in grammar school Miss Barton made little

sketches for the *Junior Eagle*, edited by "Aunt Jean," and was re-
warded with little gifts, art classes, and tours of the *Eagle* building.
She went on to study at Pratt Institute, was paid for her *Eagle*
drawings, and continued her art career.[3]

Milton J. Slocum, M.D., covered the waterfront from 1924 to
1926, and remembers the *Eagle* office not as a "staid, quiet office of
scholars and specialists," but as a scene from the Chicago drama, *Front
Page*, with the fine voice of debonnaire managing editor Harris Crist
shouting across the city room noises of typewriters, running messen-
gers, telephones, and the clack of teletypes.[4] Harold L. Donson, who
served as reporter, rewrite man, radio editor, feature editor, makeup
editor, and second-string drama, movie, and book critic from 1925 to
1928, also recalls the *Front Page* atmosphere; but he found the office
comparatively staid.[5]

A reader remembers that in 1929 the *Eagle* had arranged to bring in
some reindeer from Greenland as a promotion stunt and that they had
jumped off their barge off Mamaroneck and swum to Hen Island
where they were chased around until lassoed.[6] Mrs. Rogers Flynn,
who was assistant editor of the Sunday Magazine from 1923 to 1925,
writes:

> The *Eagle* had a flavor of its own among big city newspapers;
> it covered the smallest meetings of the Order of the Eastern Star,
> for instance, and Burton Holmes Travelogues at the Academy of
> Music. It also had a respectable front page of international news
> and domestic affairs. I always felt the paper was greatly beloved
> by all true Brooklynites and must have been lamented by many
> when it went out of business.[7]

Stephen L. Mongan, who was with the paper from 1910 to 1917,
recalls that "There was such a thing as 'the *Eagle* Spirit' which caused
us to go to great lengths to help the paper, though why we should be
so loyal considering the poor pay and long hours escapes me"; and a
newsboy during the depression remembers that the newsboys, branch
managers, and head office "screwed" each other on pay and
subscriptions.[8]

In Washington, D.C., George V. Christie, an old *Eagle* alumnus, printed an *Eagle* obituary and circulated it privately among his friends:

> There was a rumbling on the Heights above the River one night last week—a rumbling and a sort of sigh. Could it have been Walt Whitman shifting in the narrow little cell he wore so rebelliously, yet which is a portion of us all? Or could it have been Ernest Poole, whose beautiful, reflective book, "The Harbor," was written in a house above the river, and whose gardens were on the roof of a warehouse four stories up from the street? There were those who were quite certain that the door sagged a little on old Plymouth Church, and the windows looked out a little sadly, and the pulpit from which Henry Ward Beecher thundered in days gone by seemed a bit frail. You see, the Brooklyn Daily *Eagle* was dead, and the shade of its one-time editor, the poet Walt Whitman, was uneasy in his grave.
>
> For 114 years, in good times and bad, the Brooklyn Daily *Eagle* had chronicled the comings and goings of the Great, the near-great, and the little people to whom Brooklyn was a calm and peaceful haven and to whom the paper was as much a part of daily life as the very bread they ate.[9]

Christie went on to reminisce about the *Eagle* in the 1920s, the period when the managing editor was the irascible, domineering, Harris Crist. This had been the era when, in the opinion of many former employees, the paper was at its best. The great bowed windows of the seventh floor newsroom looked out across Columbia Heights and over the mouth of the Hudson River. At one desk sat Eddie Riis, son of the Danish-American journalist and social reformer. At another sat John Alden, descendant of the puritan father, scratching out one of the little poems for the editorial page he wrote every day for thirty years. After World War I, Christie recalled, the *Eagle* was the first newspaper to be delivered by air. Lawrence Sperry flew bundles of fifty out over Long Island and dropped them by parachute into bedsheets on designated potato fields while the local mayor and loyal Boy Scouts stood guard to welcome the "Special

Airplane Edition" and ready to salvage the China silk chute. Quietly, later in the afternoon, more bundles, also marked "Special Airplane Edition," were sent out by train to augment the supply.

The Community Impact

The *Eagle* was important because of its extraordinary influence on the Brooklyn community. Technically, the term "community newspaper" applies to a weekly paper designed to serve the needs of a subsection of the megalopolis. The subsection could be an ethnic enclave in a large city like Chicago or the residential neighborhoods of North Jersey outside New York.[10] It provides news that may be of critical interest to the residents of that section but not important enough to be in the metropolitan dailies. As contemporaries said of St. Clair McKelway's editorship, if a Brooklyn man stumbled on Fulton Street in the morning, he could read about it in the evening in the *Eagle* at his home on Montague Street.[11]

The unique character of the urban community paper comes from the fact that its audience, residing in a specific area, conditions the paper's content and appeal and facilitates its impact. This kind of paper exists and grows because, for most urban families, the place of work of the principal wage earner and his family residence are physically separated. He is a man of two worlds, and his afternoon community paper helps integrate him into the neighborhood where he lives. The content of the community press, therefore, is geared toward the interests and conflicts within the residential community. Furthermore, the community press must maintain local traditions and local identification; it emphasizes the values and interests on which there is a high level of consensus, stressing agreement rather than conflict. It interprets external events in such a way that local residents can put them in a meaningful context, supplies news about local institutions, and gives prestige to local individuals who would be neglected by the ordinary daily press.[12]

The *Eagle* violated the sociologist's definition of the community paper in that it was a daily rather than a weekly publication. Furthermore, although it was proud of its attention to local details during

Brown Bros. photo, Brooklyn Public Library *Eagle* Collection

Lawrence Sperry ready to deliver the *Eagle* edition in Long Island, July 17, 1919.

much of its history, it was not content with being a narrowly Brooklyn paper. This curious blend of appealing to the Brooklynite's provincialism and to his yen to be cosmopolitan was caught by the observant British press lord, Alfred C. Harnsworth, later known as Lord Northcliffe, who had adopted Joseph Pulitzer's techniques for the London *Evening News* and *Daily Mail*. Following his visit to the *Eagle* plant in 1905, he wrote:

> But I never conceived a newspaper office that should be at once a friend of the people; that should be a center of intellectual activity, an information bureau and a government weather bureau; that should be used as a means of instructing hundreds of young people in newspaper making; that should take the pains to amuse and entertain the children of its city through a department especially devoted to them; in short, a paper that had so many and original departments apart from the making of the newspaper itself.
>
> I am aware of no newspaper that has so deeply entered into the life of its readers as the *Eagle*. All this has been done, not at all on the line of cold business—I take it to be a return for the warm sentiment always expressed by Brooklyn people in foreign countries for their paper. The Brooklyn man who enters the Paris office of the *Eagle*—and a very fine department it is, by the way—proceeds to feel homesick at once. He has read the *Eagle* all his life, he has probably planned out his trip abroad in its information bureau, and I should not be surprised to hear that the *Eagle* had insured his life, invested his savings and finally buried him. I did not see those departments, but I was prepared for anything after the first half hour in the *Eagle* building.[13]

Actually, Harnsworth's ironic speculation was close to the truth. There was one occasion in the 1930s when a Brooklynite died in Paris and it was up to Oliver Pilat, the *Eagle* correspondent there in 1933 and 1934, to take charge of funeral arrangements.[14]

The *Eagle* defined its role as a community paper in terms of promotion and service. A quote from the *Eagle*'s official *Newsroom Handbook*, 1919, gives the best description of the paper's self-concept, including its blend of localism and internationalism:

1. The Brooklyn *Eagle* is primarily a home newspaper. It prints all the news, but aims to emphasize what is helpful rather than harmful. It believes in enterprise, but not in sensationalism. As a 3-cent newspaper it must uphold the highest standards of newspaper making. In particular it must always be truthful, accurate and fair.
2. "Brooklyn First" is a cardinal principle of *Eagle* policy. This newspaper is a Brooklyn institution. It is also a public service institution. Whatever helps Brooklyn helps the *Eagle*. The more you know about Brooklyn and about the *Eagle*, the better you will serve both.
3. The *Eagle* ranks as one of the world's greatest newspapers. The world is its province and its interest extends to the interests of humankind everywhere. It is through being liberal and cosmopolitan that you can best do your part in preserving the *Eagle*'s reputation as a broadly representative newspaper.[15]

In its later years the *Eagle* described its community service not so much in terms of its "extracurricular" activities as in its civic betterment campaigns. Edwin B. Wilson, who was with the paper from 1912 till its death in 1955, lists the most important campaigns in his manuscript "History": the *Eagle*'s "ten-point programs" for Brooklyn's development in 1941 and 1951; the 1944-45 series on juvenile delinquency; the contest for the design of the Brooklyn War Memorial, dedicated in 1951; the 1946 *Eagle* histories of the six original county towns; the deepening of the Gowanus Greek Channel; the banning of switch-blade knives; the modernization of the Brooklyn Bridge; the Brooklyn-Battery tunnel; the "Brooklyn Against the World" baseball series that pitted Brooklyn high school all-stars against teams from all over the United States and Canada; and, finally, the climactic series of stories exposing corruption in the police department, pitting New York Mayor William O'Dwyer against his former friend Frank D. Schroth and winning the *Eagle* the Pulitzer Prize.[16] As managing editor Thomas N. Schroth said a year before the *Eagle* died:

> As we roll along with the *Eagle*, one thought dominates our outlook—that the *Eagle* is devoted to the best interests of its community. If Brooklyn is to continue to be a better place in which to live, this will be largely through the efforts of this newspaper.[17]

The Eagle As a Training Ground for Other Papers

The *Eagle* seems to have produced only one man, St. Clair McKelway, who had a national reputation specifically because of his work for the *Eagle*; and only two men who played dominant roles at the *Eagle* for a long while, Thomas Kinsella and Harris Crist, seem to have had colorful personalities and an ability to influence the course of the paper in a creative way. (Herbert Gunnison has been described as extremely influential in the *Eagle*'s history; but he was a manager, not an editor. Edwin B. Wilson was with the *Eagle* in editorial positions for a long while, but he was heavily influenced by Crist and was not considered an innovator.) Therefore, the *Eagle* acquired a "rebound" notoriety, not because of the famous writers on its staff but because of the famous writers—like Walt Whitman—who used to work there. The pattern in the lives of best-known *Eagle* employees, as revealed in Wilson's "History" and in letters and interviews, is very similar: a bright young man comes to New York looking for a career in journalism, makes the rounds on Park Row without success, crosses the Bridge and gets his start at the low-paying *Eagle*, where he stays until a better job comes along. He leaves, but if he "wins success" he in a sense stays forever, incorporated into the *Eagle* myth as a graduate of the *Eagle* school of success.

Don C. Seitz, biographer of Pulitzer and the Bennetts, was an *Eagle* police reporter, Albany correspondent, and city editor. In 1898 Joseph Pulitzer made him business manager of the New York *World*, where he stayed for twenty-five years.

Edward Bok, philanthropist and editor of *The Ladies' Home Journal*
for thirty years, recalls his *Eagle* experiences in his autobiography, *The
Americanization of Edward Bok*. While still in school, he offered the
Eagle a list of the children at a birthday party he had attended and was
given three dollars! Years later, after he learned shorthand, he was
assigned to report on speeches by General Ulysses S. Grant and
President Rutherford B. Hayes at the old Pierrepont Hotel. Hayes
spoke too fast and Bok asked him for a copy so he could beat the other
papers. Hayes liked the boy and took him home in his carriage to A.
A. Low's house on Columbia Heights and invited him back again for a
conversation with Mrs. Hayes. Bok recalled:

> No boy had ever so gracious a listener before: no mother could
> have been more tenderly motherly than the woman who sat
> opposite him and seemed so honestly interested in all that he
> told. Not for a moment during all those two hours was he
> allowed to remember that his host and hostess were the Presi-
> dent of the United States and the first lady of the land! They
> remained friends for years.

On another occasion Bok was sent to cover Rose Coghlan's performance at the Grand Opera House in a play he had already seen. Bok
had another commitment that night, so he faked the review, adding
that the star was better than ever. Unfortunately, Miss Coghlan had
been taken ill that night and there was no show. Young Edward was
rebuked, fired, and, because of his repentance, given another
chance.[18]

Pomeroy Burton came to the *Eagle* as a substitute printer in 1889,
worked his way up through circus reporter to managing editor by
1899, then went on to the New York *World*, Hearst's *American*, and
finally became Sir Pomeroy, director of Lord Northcliffe's chain of
daily newspapers, weeklies, and magazines. William Jay Gaynor
began as an *Eagle* court reporter in the 1870s and later became mayor
of New York. Nunnally Johnson came to the *Eagle* in 1919 and went
on to become a Hollywood screenwriter and producer. Guy Hickok
joined the *Eagle* in 1914 as a waterfront reporter, then became Paris

correspondent, and left in 1935 for a career in radio. Murray Snyder, President Dwight D. Eisenhower's press secretary, had had eight years with the *Eagle* as Flatbush correspondent and political writer. H. V. Kaltenborn joined the *Eagle* in 1902 and stayed over twenty years while the *Eagle*, with considerable courage and foresight, launched him into another career with his radio commentaries. Winston Burdett, Columbia Broadcasting System Rome correspondent, acknowledged in 1955 that he had been part of the Communist cell at the *Eagle* in the 1930s.[19] Finally, Thomas N. Schroth, the last managing editor, went on to become executive editor of *Congressional Quarterly* and *Editorial Research Reports*, and, until he lost in an internal power struggle, founding editor of *National Journal*.[20]

However, the excellence represented by the *Eagle*'s best writers was impossible to maintain. When the paper became financially less secure, news coverage was cut to save money. Editorial quality declined. The *Eagle* began to lose touch with Brooklyn.

With the possible exception of the prizewinning year of 1950, it seems that the *Eagle* was most prestigious when it had the most money, under the Hester family in the first quarter of the twentieth century. When its financial problems became critical during the depression, the paper began a series of economic measures, cutting down on the staff and cutting away many of the features that had given it a fine reputation—the sermon page, the Washington and Paris correspondents, the Long Island special sections—until the 1955 product was rather thin. When asked what was lost when the *Eagle* died, one former columnist replied, "Not much."[21]

Meanwhile, the dramatic increase in Brooklyn's Jewish population in the 1920s, its Negro population in the 1940s, and its Puerto Rican population in the 1950s transformed the old *Eagle*'s Brooklyn more rapidly than the *Eagle* seemed to adapt. At the same time production costs were rising, the unions, particularly the Guild, escalated their wage demands. Moreover, the tight security clause in the Guild contract forced the *Eagle* to keep the oldest and not necessarily the most competent editorial employees, while the brighter younger men moved on to the Manhattan papers. One experienced newspaperman wrote, describing the impact of Guild security on New York journalism: "Today New York journalism is no land of opportunity, but an old man's home. There are no jobs for promising kids from out of town, because the boss can't fire incompetents to make room for them."[22]

In the end, the *Eagle* reflected the ambivalence in its self-conscious relationship with New York. In fact, its tension between its overriding local orientation—its boosterism of Brooklyn—and its necessary attention toward the larger and more complex metropolitan community of New York directly mirrored the tension within the borough of Brooklyn itself. As Harold Coffin Syrett wrote in *The City of Brooklyn 1864-1898*: "The city of Brooklyn, like the borough of today, suffered from an inferiority complex which could have been overcome only by widening the East River to the proportions of an ocean or by the destruction of its elephantine neighbor."[23]

Brooklyn has always described itself as a city of homes and churches, but it has also boasted one of the largest populations and busiest seaports of any city in the world. By inexorable economic necessity Brooklyn was forced to give up its independence as a city and to consolidate with New York in 1898; but the *Eagle*'s Brooklyn continued to yearn for its nineteenth century pre-urban image.

In its own way the *Eagle* suffered the same fate as the city whose pride and self-image it consistently promoted. When the American Newspaper Guild demanded that the *Eagle* meet the same pay scale as the seven Manhattan dailies, the *Eagle* management argued that it could not. The publisher argued that the "provincial and community minded" *Eagle*, although it was already number eight with respect to salaries on the Guild's list of 177 papers in the United States having Guild contracts, could not increase its revenues through increased circulation and advertising. The *Eagle* closed, and the publisher wrote solemnly: "So the Pulitzer Prize-winning paper of Whitman, Van Anden and McKelway has been silenced forever, and Brooklyn, the largest community in America without a voice, will indeed be doomed to be cast in Manhattan's shadow."[24]

The *Eagle*'s main efforts had been to reinforce the community identity of an urban community that was changing so rapidly and so radically that perhaps a sense of community was no longer possible.

George Christie seems to have caught this in the conclusion to his epitaph:

> Now it is all gone and there are a hundred men around these United States who could sit with faces as long as mine and with a little tug behind their breastbones because something real and good and useful has been pushed to death. It does not do to say that time has passed it by and that papers published in Manhattan who established offices and plants in Brooklyn, edged it out, because that isn't true, either. Perhaps if the truth ever really is known, it will develop that there isn't any more Brooklyn, that city of the dramatic societies, and of the trotting races on Ocean Parkway on a Sunday, and thousands of churches, the sleepy Columbia Heights, and Kings Highway winding from one town to another (because Brooklyn is a lot of little towns that grew together), the Brooklyn full of people who lived pleasantly and comfortably and who enjoyed shore dinners at Sheepshead Bay or fishing in the inlet between there and Far Rockaway, or those others who strolled tree-shaded streets or got on the Flatbush Ave. trolley car and went to visit relatives for Sunday dinner. They sat on their front porches and read the paper and visited with neighbors who passed by, and packed themselves off to the Adirondack Mountains in the Northern part of New York State for their vacation. Perhaps that Brooklyn belongs to the past and it may well be that the departure of gentlemen from daily living there brought on the last and fatal illness of a magnificent newspaper property and journalism of the highest order.
>
> Now the raucous and blatant have taken over and people who loved the town in days gone by are a little hesitant to say they lived there because they don't like the word "Bums." And maybe the Brooklyn Daily *Eagle* has served its purpose and now lies down to the pleasant dreams it so richly deserves.[25]

Notes

[1]Pete Hamill, "Brooklyn—the Same Alternative," *New York* 2 (March 1969): 29-33.

[2]Interview with James A. Kelly, St. Francis College, Brooklyn, June 30, 1970.

[3]Letter, Helen M. Barton to Raymond A. Schroth, S.J. (hereafter RAS), February 9, 1970. These letters are selected from over sixty to this author from January to July 1970.

[4]Letter, Milton J. Slocum to RAS, February 10, 1970.

[5]Letter, Harold L. Donson to RAS, February 2, 1970.

[6]Letter, Mrs. William Hillcourt to RAS, February 2, 1970. "It was a great paper!", she concludes.

[7]Letter, Mrs. Rogers Flynn to RAS, February 1, 1970.

[8]Letter, Stephen L. Morgan to RAS, January 26, 1970; Letter, Joe Lasker to RAS, February 1, 1970.

[9]George V. Christie, *The Brooklyn Daily Eagle* (Washington, D.C., 1955).

[10]Jack Lyle, *The News in Megalopolis* (San Francisco: Chandler Publishing Company, 1967), pp. 35-36.

[11]Harold Coffin Syrett, *The City of Brooklyn, 1865-1898* (New York: Columbia University Press, 1944), p. 161.

[12]Morris Janowitz, *The Community Press in an Urban Setting: The Social Elements of Urbanism* (Chicago: The Free Press, 1967), pp. xxi, 2-3, 7, 61, 215.

[13]Reprinted in a guide to the *Eagle* plant, *How a Modern Newspaper is Made: A Story in Word and Picture Concerning the Brooklyn Daily Eagle* (Brooklyn: Eagle Press, undated, after 1911) pp. 38-39.

[14]Interview with Oliver Pilat, June 18, 1970.

[15]*Newsroom Handbook* (Brooklyn: Brooklyn Daily *Eagle*, 1919), p. 4.

[16][Edwin B. Wilson] "The History of the Brooklyn *Eagle*," unpublished MS (1955) in the papers of Thomas N. Schroth (hereafter TNS), pp. 7-16.

[17]Don Malafronte, " 'Brooklyn *Eagle*' Blends Optimism and Economy," *News Workshop* 5, No. 1 (December 1953): 11. Thomas N. Schroth's *The Responsibility of the Newspaper and How It Can Best Serve Its Community*, Remarks in a Panel Discussion at Convention of SNPA, November 21, 1952, White Sulphur Springs, West Virginia (Southern Newspaper Publishers Association, March 14, 1953), discusses the background of the *Eagle*'s campaigns during 1941-1951 in some detail.

[18]Edward Bok, *The Americanization of Edward Bok: The Autobiography of a Dutch Boy Fifty Years After* (New York: Charles Scribner's Sons, 1930), pp. 29, 33, 61.

[19]These examples are suggested by Wilson's "History," pp. 26-41.

[20]Thomas N. Schroth also edited *Congress and the Nation, 1945-1964: A Review of Government and Politics in the Postwar Years* (Washington, D.C.: Congressional Quarterly Service, 1965).

[21]Interview with Al Salerno, November 7, 1969.

[22]Letter, W. L. White to Frank D. Schroth (hereafter FDS), December 7, 1955.

[23]Syrett, p. 11.

[24]FDS Statement, TNS.

[25]Christie, p. 10.

1

THE BEGINNING

Brooklyn in 1841

When twenty-three-year-old Isaac Van Anden lifted the first copy of
the *Brooklyn Eagle and Kings County Democrat* off his hand-operated job
press at 39 Fulton Street on October 26, 1841, Brooklyn was a small
town of 35,000 people. Under Dutch rule from 1636 to 1664, it had
been recognized as a town in 1788, incorporated as a village in 1816,
and finally made a city in 1834. The little city included the Navy
Yard and Fort Greene Park districts, the present downtown Brooklyn, and South Brooklyn. The rest was open country. Brooklyn was
beginning a program of gradual expansion. Between 1855 and 1886
it consolidated with the various country towns of Flatbush, Greenpoint, Bushwick, New Utrecht, New Lots, Gravesend, and Flatlands, and the independent city of Williamsburg, its only economical
rival at the time, until it covered the entire County of Kings.

The city seemed strengthened by its isolation from New York and
it already thrived on its reputation as a place where New Yorkers
could escape the city. In 1823 a Brooklyn real estate man had
advertised lots on Brooklyn Heights:

Situated directly opposite the s-w part of the city, and being the
nearest country retreat, and easiest of access from the centre of
business that now remains unoccupied; the distance not exceed-
ing an average fifteen to twenty-five minutes walk, including
the passage of the river; the ground elevated and perfectly
healthy at all seasons; views of water and landscape both exten-

sive and beautiful; as a place of residence all the advantages of the
country with most of the conveniences of the city. . . . Gentlemen whose business or profession require their daily attendance
in the city, cannot better, or with less expense, secure the health
and comfort of their families, than by uniting in such an
association.[1]

Brooklyn had already developed a strong self-awareness as a city
of homes and churches. It had achieved a community cohesiveness
of spirit and some respectable institutions—churches, private
schools, local press, Lyceum, temperance societies, and musical
associations—that would give a distinguishing quality to the town.
Because of visits from New England religious and educational refor-
mers and because of contacts with the Long Island hinterland, Brooklyn was also intellectually independent of New York.[2] Its psychological and political independence had been declaimed most eloquently in
1833 when Brooklyn community leaders, during a dispute with New
York over harbor jurisdiction, rejected a New York proposal for
corporate union. Their note to New York can be read as Brooklyn's
Declaration of Independence:

> . . . the inhabitants of Brooklyn know and feel the value of
> importance of the rights of freemen, and are accustomed to
> exercise them; . . . they would consider an association with New
> York, under a common government, as virtually implying such
> surrender. Between New York and Brooklyn, there is nothing in
> common, either in object, interest, or feeling—nothing that
> even apparently tends to their connexion, unless it be the waters
> that flow between them. And even those waters, instead of, in
> fact, uniting them, form a barrier between them which, how-
> ever frequently passed, still form and must forever continue to
> form an insurmountable obstacle to their union.[3]

The community itself consisted mainly of a cluster of houses and
shops around the Fulton Street Ferry where businessmen and prominent lawyers embarked daily for New York. Lower Fulton Street itself

was the single busy business thoroughfare, the trade center for the other villages in Kings and Queens counties. The municipal center was at Henry and Cranberry Streets. Sands Street, which in later years would be darkened under an elevated railway, was the one aristocratic residential area.

New gas lights were gradually replacing street lamps. Hand-operated pumps drew water from individual wells. Six stage coach lines connected Brooklyn with the other parts of Long Island. Civic protection was furnished by fifteen volunteer fire companies. Thirty-four teachers taught 2,098 pupils in twelve schools. Neighboring Flatbush was still a garden.[4]

A map in an 1840 guide book, *New York As It Is*, shows a grid pattern about eight blocks wide bordered by Johnson Street on the South and Jackson Street on the East, with the Navy Yard, the poor house, the burying ground, and Fort Greene off to the East.

There were thirty churches in the community which would become known as a "city of churches." It was here in Brooklyn that the famous Henry Ward Beecher would one day attract thousands to a single service in Plymouth Church as he threw fulminations across the East River at Manhattan, the city of sin. There were four banks and one circulating library. There were no theaters.

In the same week the *Eagle* was born, a meeting was held to plan the establishment of a Brooklyn Atheneum; but the completion of the Brooklyn Institute of Arts and Sciences, an imposing three-story Greek-front building on Washington Street, was still three years away. The new marblefaced Brooklyn city hall with its domes and tower on the corner of Fulton, Jerolemon, and Court Streets would not be completed until 1846. Brooklyn's first great fire, which was to start in a furniture store at Fulton and Sands Streets and destroy two hundred homes, three churches, and the post office, was still eight years in the future.

The nation at large was recovering from the panic of 1837. John Tyler of Virginia was president, having succeeded old William Harrison who had died a month after taking office. Western migration was accelerating and the spirit of "Manifest Destiny" which would be encouraged by *Eagle* editorials would soon drive the country into a war of expansion. On the Brooklyn waterfront, the Atlantic Dock Company had recently been incorporated with a capital of one million dollars. Brooklyn's population was mostly Dutch, Yankee, and Irish, but the first mass immigration was bringing Germans and Scandinavians to Brooklyn, then a leading port for clipper ships from Europe, South America, Africa, and the Orient.

The New York Press in 1841

One historian of the American press contends that the American newspaper has gone through three stages of development: it has been an instrument of propaganda, an instrument of personal expression, and, most recently, a business institution.[5]

In more detailed analyses, recent textbooks have put special emphasis on the National period following the Revolution when the new political parties, the Federalists and Anti-Federalists, established their own papers as organs of propaganda—John Fenno's *Gazette of the United States* (1789) and Philip Freneau's *National Gazette* (1791)—and on the recurring periods of what the critics like to call "sensationalism"—in 1620, 1833, the 1890s, and 1920s—when the publishers tapped the spirit and enthusaism of the emerging masses.[6]

Meanwhile, other social and economic changes influenced the character of American journalism. The three million population at the end of the Revolution had expanded to twelve million by 1830. New York, Baltimore, and Philadelphia were now large industrial and commercial cities, with two hundred thousand living in New York. As a result, newspapers multiplied. During the first third of the nineteenth century the number of papers in the country grew from 200 to 1,200, sixty-five of which were dailies. With increased profits from rising circulation and advertising, publishers improved their product with better machinery, faster newsgathering, more shipping news, cultural news and reviews, Washington correspondents, and editorials. It is during this period that the editor-publisher became no longer the printer but the policy director and editorial writer.

In the big cities the aggressive mercantile dailies, the New York

Journal of Commerce (1827) and the *Courier and Enquirer* (1829) with a leading daily circulation of 6,000, dominated journalism. They had been founded not so much to give political news but to provide the mercantile classes with up-to-the-minute news on the arrival of sailing vessels and the offerings of importers; however, they took political stands and gradually developed journalism techniques which became the norm for the American press.

The years between 1830 and 1835 mark a turning point in the history of American journalism. These were the years when the modern newspaper was born, the opening years of the period of the popular penny press (1830 to 1865), the time when newspapers became an instrument for the spread of democracy and the upsetting of traditional class relationships. The growth of large working-class populations in the cities, increased class consciousness on the part of the workers, increased supply of cheap consumer goods brought on by mass production, the demands of workers for economic and political rights, a general increase in literacy with the spread of public schools and colleges, and improved printing technology—all created the cultural climate for the penny press.

According to the creed of the penny paper, the common people should be given a realistic view of social conditions; abuses in the church, the courts, banks, and the stock markets should be exposed. The paper's first duty was to give news, not party support, and local and human interest news was given new importance. In accordance with this news philosophy, papers put less emphasis on the so-called respectable people and more on sensational crime and sex.

When the *Eagle* was founded, Henry J. Raymond's New York *Daily Times*, with its front page crowded with foreign and local news, was still ten years away. However, by 1841 New York had six major daily morning papers and four evening papers, as well as four other smaller dailies. The leaders were the New York *Sun, Herald* and *Tribune*. The *Sun*, founded by Benjamin Day on September 3, 1833, stressed the human side of the news—murder, love, crime, suicide—and by 1839 had reached a daily circulation of 50,000. The *Sun* described its effects on the public: "Already we can perceive a

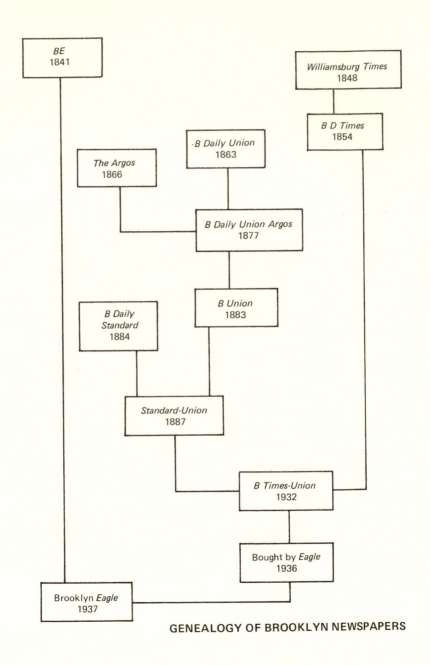

BE
1841

Williamsburg Times
1848

B D Times
1854

·B Daily Union
1863

The Argos
1866

B Daily Union Argos
1877

B Union
1883

B Daily
Standard
1884

Standard-Union
1887

B Times-Union
1932

Bought by Eagle
1936

Brooklyn Eagle
1937

GENEALOGY OF BROOKLYN NEWSPAPERS

change in the mass of the people. They think, talk, and act in concert. They understand their own interest, and feel that they have numbers and strength to pursue it with success."[7]

To rival the *Sun*, the first of the great "personal" journalists (men who sold their papers by selling their personalities to the public), James Gordon Bennett, founded the New York *Herald* on May 6, 1835. Bennett stressed more variety in local coverage, more murders, more candor about Wall Street and more "theatrical chit-chat." As Bennett himself expressed his creed: "I have seen human depravity to the core—I proclaim each morning on 15,000 sheets of thought and intellect the deep guilt that is encrusting our society."[8] Bennett made gathering the news about New York an industry. He introduced more illustrations, hired a Washington correspondent, added more women's news, and recognized the importance of the telegraph in newsgathering. With fifteen years' experience as a journalist he set out to carry the revolution Day began a good deal farther. Directing his paper toward all classes of society, he proclaimed his goal:

> We openly disclaim all steel-traps, all principle, as it is called—all politics. Our only guide shall be good, sound practical, common sense, application to business and bosoms of men engaged in everyday life. We shall support no party—be the organ of no faction or coterie, and care nothing for any election or any candidate from President down to a constable.[9]

Finally, on April 10, 1841, to offset the influence of the more Democratic *Sun* and *Herald*, Horace Greeley, who had failed in 1833 in an attempt to publish the *Morning Post* for two cents, came out with a Whig daily *Tribune* for a penny. It was a paper of great moral and intellectual leadership, dedicated to improving the lot of the poor. "The great, the all-embracing reform of our age," Greeley said a few years later, "is the Social Reform—that which seeks to lift the laboring class, as such—not out of labor, by any means—but out of ignorance, inefficiency, dependence, and want."[10] Greeley proved a cheap paper could be successful without sensational news, kept the literary quality high, and set a high standard for the spirit of reform that the *Eagle* and other papers would try to emulate. Contrary to the penny press philosophy, the *Eagle* was from the beginning a party paper; in time it would emulate the mass circulation papers in that it quickly absorbed the most technological advances—particularly during the 1890s. However, in style it was more a brother to the staid *Tribune* until the Schroth period of the 1940s and 1950s, when Hearstian sensationalism had a belated impact.

The Birth of the Eagle

The *Eagle* was born in the midst of a political crisis,[11] and it is ironic that the paper which lived the longest and eventually absorbed all the other Brooklyn daily papers except the Brooklyn *Citizen* (founded in 1886) was originally conceived as a purely temporary venture. Brooklyn Democrats were attempting to reform and reorganize their party in Kings County following the death of President Harrison so they could make a stronger showing in the coming elections. At a time when newspapers were still primarily party organs, Brooklyn was a Whig city, controlled by wealthy men, in which the Whigs already had two papers: the *Advertiser*, which had been founded in 1799, and Thomas Kirk's *Long Island Star*, which had been founded in 1823 and which was published twice a week.[12] Brooklyn publishers already had a tradition in civic leadership. Kirk had worked to secure Brooklyn's first charter in 1816 and had organized the Sabbath School Union and the first free school, which was conducted in his office. Kirk had sold the *Star* to Colonel Alden Spooner. Spooner, whom Walt Whitman worked for and admired, was a community leader for forty years.

Isaac Van Anden, the founder of the *Eagle*, was a young Poughkeepsie printer, a farmer's son who had moved to Brooklyn with $100 just a year before and had started a small printing plant on the third floor of 39 Fulton Street. He had worked for a few months as business manager for Samuel G. Arnold's Kings County *Advocate* until it was sold to the Whigs. In a series of discussions during the summer of 1841, Van Anden suggested the idea of a new paper to leading Brooklyn lawyer and politician Henry Cruse Murphy. Murphy had at

The First *Eagle* office, Fulton Street, 1841.

first discouraged him, but in a meeting at the law offices of John A. Lott, Murphy, and John Vanderbilt on Front Street, Van Anden convinced the party leader to finance the *Eagle* merely for the duration of the campaign. The paper's name, which was never popular with its early owners, was the suggestion of city court Judge John Greenwood, a former student in Aaron Burr's law offices. The group designated Alfred G. Stephens publisher and Murphy editor, with Murphy handing the job over to the imaginative Richard Adams Locke.

In Locke the *Eagle* managers had hired, if only for a short time, one of the most imaginative—and notorious—figures in the early history of American journalism.[13] Born in England in 1800, a collateral descendant of John Locke, educated at Cambridge, he came to New York in 1832 with his wife and daughter after having failed in two newspaper publishing projects. He got a job at the *Sun* where in August 1835 he composed a fascinating series of four articles allegedly based on the discoveries of British astronomer Sir John Herschel published in the *Supplement to the Edinburgh Journal of Science*, a learned journal which had actually been defunct for some years. By means of "an immense telescope on an entirely new principle" Herschel had spied "man bats" and biped beavers on the lunar surface. In response to the series the *Sun*'s circulation climbed to 19,000, the largest of any daily, and scientists journeyed to New York to see Locke. The *Sun*'s "moon hoax" was successful—until one evening Locke, after a few too many drinks, confessed his joke to a reporter from the rival *Journal of Commerce*.

Leaving the *Sun*, Locke founded his own penny daily, the *New Era*, where he tried out another hoax purportedly based on "The Lost Manuscript of Mungo Park," the memoirs of a long lost Scottish explorer. After his brief stint at the *Eagle*, Locke worked in a New York customs house and died in Staten Island in 1871. We are indebted to Edgar Allan Poe's word sketch in *The Literati* (1850) for a vivid portrait of this extraordinary character:

Like most men of *true* imagination, Mr. Locke is a seemingly paradoxical compound of coolness and excitability. He is about five feet seven inches in height, symmetrically formed; there is an air of distinction about his whole person—an *air noble* of genius. His face is strongly pitted by the small pox and, perhaps from the same cause, there is a marked obliquity in the eyes; a certain calm, clear *luminousness*, however, about these latter amply compensate for the defect, and the forehead is truly beautiful in its intellectuality. I am acquainted with no person possessing so fine a forehead as Mr. Locke.[14]

We might guess that Locke's talents were most needed during the paper's first months. Since Van Anden had previously agreed to withdraw from publishing when the *Advocate* had been sold, he was obliged to remain in the background during the first partisan phase of the *Eagle*'s founding. After the election, when the paper's and the party's success indicated the enterprise should continue, the paper was sold to Van Anden for $1,500 on April 19, 1842, and he assumed full control.

Henry C. Murphy, a lawyer, diplomat, and scholar who was really the *Eagle*'s founder, was also one of the founders of modern Brooklyn. As H. R. Stiles has observed, to write a history of the law firm of Murphy, Vanderbilt, and Lott "would be to write the political history of Brooklyn from 1833 to 1857."[15] It would also be true to say that Murphy's life over the next forty years would typify much of Brooklyn's history and spirit. He combined a scholarly intellect and the practice of public service with a thirst for power and money and a general reputation for uprightness. Murphy graduated from Columbia in 1830 and studied law while writing editorials for the Brooklyn *Advocate*. As a rising politician he had also written for the *United States Magazine and Democratic Review* and the *North American Review*. In 1842, right after starting the *Eagle*, he was elected mayor of Brooklyn at the age of thirty-one. He interrupted his term in a year to go to Congress where he served from 1843 to 1845 and again from 1847 to 1849. At the state constitutional conventions of 1846, 1867, and 1868 he campaigned without success for an advanced program of city

Henry Cruse Murphy (1810-1882), founder of the Brooklyn *Eagle*.

charter, taxation, and government reforms. At the National Democratic Convention of 1852 he lost the presidential nomination to Franklin Pierce by one vote.

President Buchanan appointed Murphy minister to the Netherlands in 1857. Upon his return in 1861 Murphy was easily elected to six successive terms in the State Senate where he introduced the legislation for the Brooklyn Bridge in 1867. After his return from The Hague, Murphy had little chance for national office, and he devoted most of his energies to building up his beloved Brooklyn and to historical scholarship.[16] Because of his interest in the development of Coney Island, he accepted the presidency of the Flatbush and Coney Island Railroad and built the Brighton Beach Hotel at its terminus. Along with a number of *Eagle* proprietors—Van Anden, *Eagle* part-owner and Democratic fundraiser William C. Kingsley, and editor Thomas Kinsella—he labored hard for the construction of the Brooklyn Bridge. The president of the original company, Murphy died on December 1, 1882, just four months before the Bridge's completion.

Murphy was never really a journalist in the professional sense but rather a politician and entrepreneur who started the *Eagle* for pragmatic reasons. However, the *Eagle* was Van Anden's whole life. He was a small, generally reserved and retiring man, faultlessly groomed in neatly tailored suits. His only diversion was his enthusiasm for fine horses. He had a great passion for neatness and on occasion would personally direct the rearrangement of office furniture. Though kind and gentlemanly with his employees, who referred to him as "Mr. Van," he was also strong-willed and demanding, and his associates learned to leave him alone to pace up and down his room when he was losing his temper.[17] He never married, but he made the paper a family enterprise by bringing in his sixteen-year-old nephew William Hester to learn the business from the bottom in 1852. Though an organization Democrat, Van Anden was quick to assert his independence, particularly his independence of Murphy. When Murphy insisted that the *Eagle* publish a hack speech by Long Island Congressman Thomas Cummings as a piece of party propaganda, Van Anden refused; the editorial columns of the *Eagle*, he said, did not belong to the party.[18]

The First Eagle

The *Eagle*, which was first called *The Brooklyn Eagle and Kings County Democrat*, began for a short while as a morning paper. It had four six-column pages, cost two cents, and proclaimed its dedication to the Democratic belief in equal rights in the Jefferson-Jackson tradition.

The statements of purpose in all the mid-nineteenth century newspapers were strongly worded, and the *Eagle*'s was no exception:

Our first and chief privilege concerning it [the *Eagle*] is, that to the best of our judgment, experience, feeling and ability, it shall be strictly Democratic—zealously devoted to the sacred preservation of all the fine old landmarks of the Jeffersonian school, and emulously keeping pace with the advancing intelligence of the age. Opposed to chartered monopolies and special privileges, upon abstract principles as well as practical observations, it will also be watchful of political fanaticisms, crude impractical theories, and reckless disorganization. It will be vigilantly zealous for equal rights both great and small, particular and general. It will contend for everything that is right, and it will submit nothing that is wrong.

The only news stories on the first page were an account of a fire in Georgetown, South Carolina (which had been copied from a letter printed in the Charleston *Patriot*), and a report of a guilty verdict brought against a former Philadelphia officeholder charged with conspiring to defraud the citizens. The rest of page one was mostly ads, medical, legal, and municipal notices, the Long Island railroad and stage coach schedules, and the first installment of popular episodes from Goethe's autobiography about his adventures with his dancing master's daughter. Some of the typical ads were for Sarsasparilla Mend Syrup, the temperance drink, Mrs. Hayes' eye water, the Trust Fire Insurance Company, and Reverend Ward Stafford's proposed Seminary for Young Ladies in South Brooklyn. There was also an account of the 1818 disinterment of General Richard

The Brooklyn *Eagle and Kings County Democrat*,
Tuesday, October 26, 1841.

Montgomery's body, although it is not clear why it was printed. The editorials on page two—"Henry Clay, a National Bank, and a Change of the Constitution" and "Two Primary Objects of Democracy"—had an erudition, scope, dignity, moralistic tone, and touch of sarcasm that were to distinguish *Eagle* editorials for most of the paper's history, Since the whole purpose of the *Eagle* was to promote the Democratic party, the editorials, probably written by Locke or Murphy, were directed to the principal issues of the coming election. The first poked fun at the Whigs who had rejected Clay's candidacy because his support for the bank would make him unpopular, and who had cynically nominated the cleverly noncommital (but pro-bank) Harrison and anti-bank Tyler to capture Democratic votes. Now, not having considered that the wily Harrison was mortal, the Whigs were stuck with Tyler. The second editorial argued for the repeal or amendment of the land distribution bill so that funds derived from the sale of public lands could be allocated to the public universally for the support of education. It also urged the amendment of the bankruptcy law to include banks and other corporations. A final note on the editorial page was a long plea for Democratic party "conciliation, union, harmony."

The editorial page also featured a report on the previous day's meeting of the Brooklyn Common Council, news from Washington of the death of Secretary of State John Forsyth, a piece praising John A. Lott, *Eagle* co-founder, who, along with Mr. Udall, had just been nominated on October 18 by the Kings County Democratic electors for the State Assembly, and a five-month old dispatch describing the British fighting in China. The information in the China dispatch was relayed by A. A. Low, son of alderman and merchant Seth Low. A. A. Low had sailed to China in 1833 for a seven-year stay in the Canton foreign settlement as a partner in Russell and Company. He was the father of Seth Low, who became mayor of Brooklyn and New York.

If there was one outstanding characteristic of the first *Eagle*, it was its frankly partisan tone. The whole issue seemed geared to promote the candidacy of John A. Lott; in fact, it appears that the paper was published on the morning of October 26 so that it could publish the announcement of the general meeting of the party that night to hear reports of the nominating convention the previous week. Of the nine columns of news and editorial content on pages three and four, over half the space was devoted directly or indirectly to Lott. John Vanderbilt, the other law partner and *Eagle* founder, was also vice-president of the Kings County Democratic Convention. Lott explained his views on the issues in a letter to Tammany Hall; he was against special privileges, against the incorporation of banks, and against training state prisoners as mechanics and using them as cheap labor to undercut the regular laboring force. In an anonymous letter, a "mechanic and old democrat" stated that he had known Lott since he was a boy and that the unfavorable letters about him in other Brooklyn papers were not true.

Tucked at the bottom of the editorial page were a few examples of the items for which the *Eagle* was to become famous, the local news squib. A Prospect Hill Irishman, Peter Kearney, broke his leg when he rode his blind horse over an embankment; and Daniel Place, a milkman, broke his leg when he tried to jump off his wagon and caught his feet in the horse's reins.

Notes

[1]Quoted in Charles N. Glaab and A. Theodore Brown, *A History of Urban America* (London: Macmillan Company, 1967), pp. 154-155.

[2]Ralph Foster Weld, *Brooklyn Village 1816-1834* (New York: Columbia University Press, 1938), pp. 258-267.

[3]Long Island *Star*, February 13, 1834, quoted in Weld, p. 52.

[4]*New York As It Is*, containing a general description of the City of New York, list of offices, public institutions, and other useful information: including the Public Offices, etc. of the City of Brooklyn (New York, 1840), pp. 188-191; *Eagle*, October 29, 1941.

[5]John Tebbel, *The Compact History of the American Newspaper* (New York: Hawthorn Books, Inc. 1963), p. 11.

[6]Sidney Kobre, *The Development of American Journalism* (Dubuque: William C. Brown Company, 1969); Edwin Emery, *The Press and America* (Englewood Cliffs, N.J.: Prentice Hall, 1962, latest edition, 1972); Frank

Luther Mott, *American Journalism, A History: 1690-1960* (New York: Macmillan, 1962).

[7]Kobre, p. 227.

[8]The New York *Herald*, July 27, 1836, quoted in Mott, p. 232.

[9]*Herald*, May 6, 1833, quoted in Kobre, p. 233.

[10]*Autobiography of Horace Greeley*, p. 508, quoted in Mott, p. 272.

[11]There are only a few basic facts available on the founding and first years of the *Eagle*. The *Eagle* itself repeated the story of its first days in each anniversary issue, most fully in *The Pictorial History of Brooklyn* issued by the Brooklyn Daily *Eagle* on its Seventy-Fifth Anniversary, October 26, 1916, compiled and edited by Martin H. Weyrauch, p. 17. William E. Robinson's "The History of the Press of Brooklyn and Kings County," in Henry R. Stiles, ed., *The Civil, Political, Professional and Ecclesiastical History and Industrial Record of the County of Kings and the City of Brooklyn, New York, from 1683 to 1884*, 2 vols. (New York: W. W. Munsell and Company, 1884); Stephen M. Ostander, *A History of the City of Brooklyn and Kings County*, 2 vols. (Brooklyn, 1894); and Henry Isham Hazelton, *The Boroughs of Brooklyn and Queens, Counties of Nassau and Suffolk, Long Island, New York 1609-1924*, 6 vols. (New York and Chicago: Lewis Historical Publishing Company, Inc., 1925). The most recent versions, based simply on Stiles and the *Eagle* anniversary histories are Wilson's "History" and Cleveland Rodgers' pamphlet, *Voicing Brooklyn* (Brooklyn: Lincoln Trust, 1955). There is a biography of Henry Cruse Murphy in *Dictionary of American Biography* (hereafter DAB).

[12]The *Advertiser*, Brooklyn's first real newspaper, was originally called the *Courier and New York and Long Island Advertiser*. For a more detailed history of Brooklyn's pre-*Eagle* journalism, with emphasis on Spooner, see Weld, pp. 131-176.

[13]Mott, p. 299 and DAB.

[14]*Literati* (1950) quoted in DAB.

[15]H. R. Stiles in *New York Genealogical and Biographical Record* (January 1883), p. 10, quoted in DAB.

[16]Murphy's chief contributions to American history were translations of works relating to New Netherland: *The Representation of New Netherland* (1849) from the Dutch of Adrian Van der Donck; *Voyages from Holland to America* (1853) from the Dutch of D. P. de Vries; and the journal of Jasker Danken and Peter Sluyter, which Murphy discovered in an Amsterdam bookstore and translated for the first volume of *Memoirs* of the Long Island Historical Society in 1867. DAB.

[17]*Newspaper Comments, Letters, etc., Concerning the Eighty-Fifth Anniversary of the Brooklyn Daily Eagle, October 26, 1926*, scrapbook, TNS.

[18]Stiles, *County of Kings*, p. 1183.

The Brooklyn *Daily Eagle*, Thursday, October 26, 1916.

2

WALT WHITMAN

Young Whitman's Brooklyn

Some people have heard of the Brooklyn *Eagle* only because Walt Whitman once worked there. Yet the *Eagle*, which in its later years was proud to have Whitman's name enhance its own reputation, fired Whitman after less than two years, was antagonistic toward him for years after he left, and felt uncomfortable about the association for an even longer time. Nevertheless, the Whitman *Eagle* years are important for an understanding of the poet, since this was his chief editorship prior to the publication of the first edition of *Leaves of Grass*, and important for understanding the *Eagle*, both because Whitman helped set the *Eagle* tradition of caring for Brooklyn's image and because subsequent generations of *Eagle* managers had to struggle with what the Whitman image meant to them. Furthermore, recent research is showing that Whitman's *Eagle* experience was a high point in a journalistic career that spanned sixty-one years and that would merit the attention of journalism historians even if he had not written *Leaves of Grass*.[1]

Van Anden had replaced Richard Adams Locke with the more conservative and hard working William B. Marsh, a printer and friend of Horace Greeley. Marsh made the *Eagle* an evening paper on December 27, 1841, and gradually built the *Eagle* into the most respected paper in Brooklyn.[2] Marsh died at thirty-three on February 26, 1846, leaving a wife and several children destitute, and on March 3 Whitman published a plea for aid for the Marsh family in the *Star*, where he was working at the time.

A Culver photo from the collection of the New York Public Library

Walt Whitman as he looked when he was editor of the Brooklyn *Daily Eagle*.

Whitman was twenty-seven when he came to the *Eagle*. He was already one of the most experienced journalists in the city—he had edited five newspapers, had helped edit two, and had written for six others—and he was no worse and in some ways better than the other journalists of his day. He had also acquired two reputations, one for bold writing skill and one for laziness, that would mark his journalism career. He had begun as a boy apprentice for the weekly Long Island *Patriot* in 1831, where he made his first appearance in print and where he first met the young writer and politician Henry C. Murphy. It was probably Murphy who recommended Whitman to Van Anden.

At fifteen he contributed to the New York *Mirror*. In 1838, after brief stints as a printer in New York and a teacher on Long Island, he founded his own paper, the weekly *Long Islander* in Huntington. However, young Whitman failed to get his papers out with much regularity and his backers lost faith. In May 1839 he left the *Long Islander* to return to New York and become a part-time contributor to the Long Island *Democrat*. Emory Holloway summarizes the 1836-1841 Long Island period this way:

> Growing out of causes of unrest reform movements and politics, itself perhaps a greater cause of unrest than any other, was Whitman's fermenting literary ambition. It became the stronger because it promised to satisfy his other desires. The political idealist, the dogmatic teacher, the priest of brotherly love, the social reformer, the dreaming poet, and the original artist might conceivably combine in the writer, though the world would have to wait fifteen years to learn just what unique sort of book such a writer would bring forth.[3]

In 1842 Whitman was named editor of the daily New York *Aurora*, which prided itself on its intellectuality, and proclaimed his confidence in his capacity to "make *Aurora* the most readable journal in the republic."[4] The week before, the *Eagle* had noticed the new tone of its New York competitor and remarked: "A marked change for the better has come over this spirited little daily since the accession of Mr. Whitman to the 'vacant chair.' There is, nevertheless, a dash of egotism occasionally."[5] However, editors did not last long in those days; Whitman fought with his employers and left proclaiming, "If you want such stuff in the *Aurora*, write it yourself." One of his bosses is said to have referred to Walt as "the laziest fellow who ever undertook to edit a city paper."[6] It is not clear whether Whitman quit or was fired, but it is probable that his vitriolic editorial attacks on Bishop John Hughes, who wanted public funds for parochial schools, were a factor in his leaving.

For four years he shifted around to various papers, ending up back at the Brooklyn *Evening Star* in 1845 as a reporter and special writer. The *Star*, a Whig paper and Brooklyn's most prosperous publication, was now owned by Edwin Spooner, the less talented son of Colonel Alden Spooner, the father of Brooklyn journalism. In March 1846, when Whitman left to join the *Eagle*, the unhappy Spooner attacked him for his "weakness." Whitman replied in equally abrasive language.[7]

Whitman's two years at the *Eagle* were active and productive ones, contrary to the myth built around a later image of the poet that he had been a lazy dreamer. Since he said in the preface to the first edition of *Leaves of Grass* in 1855 that he had started to turn over the plan of his poems at the age of twenty-eight, he must have been considering them for at least a year of his *Eagle* editorship. In fact, a few of the themes of his mature poetry are evident in his *Eagle* work. Furthermore, as a book reviewer and drama and music critic for the *Eagle*, he began formulating ideas which were to return later in *Democratic Vistas*. These included his call for a native American literature which was not subservient to London and his demand for good American drama, which he felt only New York could provide.[8] Meanwhile, he probably gave more space to literature than any other New York paper. He reprinted tales by Poe, Hawthorne, and Irving, as well as twelve of his own stories.[9]

Whitman saw his contemporaries as a "newspaper ruled" people and he saw his responsibility as editor of the *Eagle* as an occasion to talk to *all* the people of Brooklyn, to educate them. Thus his *Eagle*, like later editions, would have a didactic tone. All that he wrote, meanwhile, would be inspired by the main points of his own philosophy, which was of course imperfectly developed at this time. True to his Jeffersonian principles, his fundamental belief was that the best society was one with the greatest freedom from restrictions imposed by legislative bodies or special interest groups. He wrote on July 26, 1847, that the one rule of government was *"to make no more laws than those useful for preventing a man or a body from infringing on the rights of other men."*

On June 1, 1846, Whitman did what many new editors like to do to stamp their personalities on the publication; he modestly redesigned the *Eagle*, inaugurating a literary column on the first page, giving one to three columns to stories and reviews which were formerly devoted to ads, he printed the paper with new type which was complimented by the *Post*, *Tribune*, and *Star*, and he published his own journalist's manifesto, "Ourselves and the *Eagle*":

> We really feel a desire to talk on many subjects, to *all* the people of Brooklyn; and it ain't their nine-pences we want so much either. There is a curious kind of sympathy (haven't you ever thought of it before?) that arises in the mind of a newspaper conductor with the public he serves. He gets to *love* them. Daily communion creates a sort of brotherhood and sisterhood of the two parties. . . .

The young editor was aware of his potential influence:

> To wield that influence is a great responsibility. There are numerous noble reforms that have yet to be pressed upon the world. People are to be schooled, in opposition to their long established ways of thought.

For the rest of his "creed" Whitman listed the qualities an editor must have: a good quantity of accurate information, fluent style, restraint, and "a sharp eye to discriminate the good from the immense mass of unreal stuff floating on all sides of him."

It is no exaggeration to say that during those years Whitman was the *Eagle* and the *Eagle* was Whitman. There was another reporter for a while and a shorthand reporter for speeches, but for the most part Whitman was the whole staff, and during that time he was very much involved in getting the feel of Brooklyn. Many of his editorials simply recounted Walt's wanderings in the streets. His most consistent grumbles were against dirty streets and the street lamps that did not burn; he even wrote a sarcastic editorial in praise of a lamp that burned all night. In "Autobiography of a Brooklyn Lamp" he projected himself into the character of the lamp as it was fiddled with, lighted, and died.[10] He preached to the young men of Brooklyn, urged them to spend more time outdoors, play more baseball, take more baths, spend less time in bars, and less time gambling and more time with their books.[11]

In a walk down Myrtle Avenue around the area of Fort Greene he saw the poor Irish immigrants, who had fled the current potato famine and for whom he had great sympathy, struggling to keep alive. For some time the *Eagle* had been campaigning for a park in the area. He wrote on August 16, 1847:

> No one with common judgment can fail to see that stretching far and wide the streets here are, in a few years, to be filled with a dense mass of busy human beings. Shall there not be one single spot to relieve the desolating aspect of *all* houses and pavements?

Like the *Eagle* editors a hundred years later he was concerned about juvenile delinquency, and he blamed the police for not cracking down on rowdyism, on "perambulating wretches" who made the night hideous with their vandalism and obscene songs.[12] Brooklyn in that time was only a moderately violent town and Whitman had few local murders to report, but he did keep Brooklynites informed on the killings in "Gomorrah" as he liked to call New York.[13] A very common heading in the *Eagle* during Whitman's tenure was "More Bloody Work," and the usual tale that followed expressed complete revulsion for murder, but insisted nonetheless in letting the honest folks of Booklyn know that brains had been spilled by hoe, shovel, or axe.[14]

At Greenwood Cemetery he mourned over the graves of an eight-

year-old girl, an Indian maiden, and the "mad poet" of Broadway,
McDonald Clarke, who had died in miserable poverty in 1842, his
"startling images" and "jaggedness of style" unappreciated by his
fellow citizens.[15] He visited the public schools, such as PS No. 4 on
Clason Avenue near Flushing Avenue, where he liked the free and
open educational atmosphere. "We think this school an unanswerable
argument in favor of treating youth at school as rational creatures
—treating them gently, and instructing them in such a way that they
understand, and not merely by rote."[16] He wrote a whole series of
editorials against whipping in the school system, and he was a
ferocious opponent of capital punishment. He would review the lives
of the men, women, and teen-aged boys who were executed, show
how much they were society's victims rather than its enemies, and
urged the compassion of Christ.

Whitman's greatest value as a journalist and social historian during
this period was his ability to vividly reproduce the Brooklyn he knew
and loved. This was also one of the *Eagle*'s greatest values throughout
its history. Whitman recorded the changing seasons, the blooming of
lilacs, the moisture of the grass. When he did not know what to write
he would look out his window on Fulton Street, the heart of the city,
and describe the crowds, the snow, or the rain.[17] This long editorial,
"The Foot of Fulton Street," published May 6, 1841, is worth
studying as an example of his style and as an example of an early *Eagle*
attempt to recapture the past—trying to hold onto a Brooklyn that
history was sweeping away:

Of all the busy scenes to be met with in this busy country
—scenes which place it beyond the power of a foreigner to deny
that we are the "tarnalest" nation in the world, for energy and
activity—we have yet observed none that go beyond the foot of
Fulton Street, Brooklyn. We well remember this spot a few
years ago—how much narrower it was then than now, and how
the old Long Island stage houses ranged sleepily on each side,
with the look of portly country farmers, well to do in the world,
but not caring much for appearances. We remember Col.
Downing's huge sign stretching over the side-walk (there was no

law against "obstructions" then,) inscribed with the names of all
the places on Long Island—half of the decent Christian terms
from the Bible, and the other half heathenish words, such as
Quoque, Hopaug, Spenok, and so on. By the by, what has
become of that old sign? Capt. Basil Hall copied it verbatim and
literally in his book on American travels; and if we had on this
island a museum sacred to the relics of our own territory and
people, *that* would be worthy a place by no means the last [*sic*]
conspicuous in the show. We remember old Mr. Langdon, as he
used to sit in his gouty chair, (we don't mean that the *chair* had
the gout,) and what a marvelous piece of mechanism it seemed to
us, wherewith he moved the said chair by turning a little twisted
handle. We remember how the marketmen used to come jogging along (by no means on the locomotive principle of the
present time,) in their canvas-covered wagons painted with
lamp-black, the smell of which made us sick. There was Smith
and Wood's old tavern too, with its snug bar in the corner, and
the queer cast iron stove set in the wall, so as to throw its heat in
two rooms at the same time—and the high wooden press of the
public room, in which the farmers hung their stout homespun
overcoats, their whips, etc., all without fear of theft, for the
world was more honest in those days. Oh, that race of jogging
country-stage men has pretty much passed away! We see one of
them at rare intervals, in a wagon of the old sort, but somehow *he*
has not the old sturdy comfortable look. He has no one to keep
him in countenance: the Long Island Railroad has quelled the
glory of his calling.

But the foot of Fulton Street, now, presents a very different
scene. In the morning, there is one incessant stream of
people—clerks, merchants, and persons employed in New York
on business—tending toward the ferry. This rush commences
soon after six o'clock, and continues till nine—being at its
climax a quarter after seven. It is highly edifying to see the
phrenzy exhibited by certain portions of the younger gentlemen,
a few rods from the landing, when the bell strikes three, the

premonitory of the single stroke which sends the boat off. They rush forward as if for dear life, and woe to the fat woman or unwieldy person of any kind, who stands in their way! How astonishing it is that they do not remember then of another boat, to start right off, in less than five minutes!

Whitman's Day

When he worked at the *Eagle* Whitman reportedly "dressed like a farmer or a workman, with homespun trousers tucked into cowhide boots reaching mainly to the knee, a pea jacket seldom buttoned, a flannel shirt open at the throat, a red kerchief knotted at his neck and the broad brimmed hat recalling the Quaker headgear of his ancestor."[18] He arrived early at the office, received only a few visitors, mostly politicians, wrote his editorials in the morning, and gave them to the printer with instructions that they "follow copy" with his punctuation and spelling. Then, carrying a small cane, he began his afternoon walks, which must have been not mere leisurely strolls but rather observant explorations of his urban environment. When he returned to the Fulton Street office he would read proof, then take the fifteen-year-old printer's devil, William Henry Sutton, known affectionately to Walt as "Hen," down to Gray's Salt Water Swimming Bath at the foot of Fulton Street where he would stay in the water for exactly twenty minutes. Then Hen would work the pump to give Walt his daily shower. Walt was an enthusiast for showers, and wrote several editorials urging Brooklynites to take more baths, arguing that this would make them more amenable to foreign visitors and would generally improve their physical beauty. Brooklyn, he stated, should have several free public baths where the working people could go and clean themselves up. If there were no free ones, they could at least go to Gray's.[19]

Thus refreshed, Walt would take the ferry over to New York where he could ride the Broadway buses, sitting alongside the driver. To Walt, the ferries, as well as the street lamps, took on personality. The ferry functioned like destiny: "Passionless and fixed, at the six stroke the boats came in; and at the three-stroke, succeeded by a

single tap, they depart again, with the steadiness of nature herself."[20]
The Fulton Street Ferry, with its aristocratic seniority, bringing the lawyers and businessmen back and forth from Manhattan, moved on like "iron-willed destiny," while its bustling passengers crammed together, shoving and rushing, vulgarly exemplifying America's "indomitable energy" at its worst. As the ferry approached the dock, the men would leap off when the ship was still five feet from shore, risking the fatal slip that might crush them to death between the ferry and the landing. The Catherine Street and South ferries were more genteel, while the Jackson Street boat was the workingman's ferry, taking home the laborers from the U.S. Navy Yard. On the ferries Walt would occasionally take ten minutes to visit the engine room and feel the engine's throb.

In the late afternoons the editor liked to saunter down to Husted and Kendall's East Brooklyn omnibus. There he could rent a two hour, three mile stage ride on thick, soft, velvet cushions for a sixpence. For another sixpence the driver would take him all the way to his home, and the Brooklyn drivers, he reminded his readers, were friendly and polite, free of the sauciness and impudence and want of civility that marked their counterparts in Manhattan.[21]

Fort Greene

Whitman was one of the first of a long line of *Eagle* directors who saw the identity and spirit of Brooklyn inextricably linked with its conscious contract with the past. Later he would write in a series of articles in the Brooklyn *Standard* between 1861-1862 called "Brooklyniana": "The whole spirit of a floating and changing population like ours is antagonistic to the recording and preserving of what traditions we have of the American Past . . . there will come a time, here in Brooklyn, and all over America, when nothing will be of more interest than authentic reminiscences of the past."[22] His *Eagle* writings stressed the importance of old persons who remembered the city's earlier days and the importance of monuments that served as symbolic links to the community's traditions. A typical symbol which gave Brooklynites this sense of continuity was Fort Greene Park. When a

New York *Tribune* editorial expressed its conditioned sorrow that old Fort Greene would have to be leveled to make way for the "irresistible" progressive forces of trade and commerce in the rapidly urbanizing Brooklyn, Whitman replied that leveling Fort Greene would be just as absurd as New York erasing the Battery, selling the Washington Parade Grounds into building lots, or running blind alleys through Tompkins Square.[23]

Whitman and other Brooklynites also looked to Fort Greene Park and the nearby area around the Navy Yard and Wallabout Bay as a symbolic link with the American Revolution.[24] Over 5,000 American soldiers had been taken prisoners by the British following the battle of Long Island in August 1776 and those who could not be contained in the festering jails on land were incarcerated on the hellish prison ships in Wallabout Bay. Among these were the *Old Jersey* (also known as "The Hell") which held over a thousand men, and *The John*, where American soldiers died of small pox, yellow fever, dysentery, and despair. One of the ships kept hogs on the deck and prisoners would struggle to snatch the bran from the pigs to keep themselves from starving. Each morning, the British would call, "Rebels, bring up your dead!" and the American boys would bury their comrades in the shallow sands of Wallabout Channel. In 1777 several ships had burned and the improvised graveyard became all the more crowded. As the years went by their bones were uncovered by the changing tide. By 1792 a farmer, John Jackson, had collected many of the bones and offered them to the Tammany Society with the hope that, with help from Congress, they could be put in a suitable tomb. By 1808 a tomb was erected on Jackson's land, but by 1846 Jackson's neighborhood changed so much that a movement began under the leadership of Henry C. Murphy to have the martyrs' remains set in a more permanent and imposing site. In Whitman's day the skeletons of soldiers were still visible in the fields by the bay, and children would kick around the skulls while they played.

Meanwhile, the *Eagle* combined its campaign to raise funds for the monument with its campaign to have Brooklyn organize its own independent celebration of the Fourth of July, and it bombarded the Common Council with editorials soliciting money. To enhance the

celebration, Whitman wrote an Ode in honor of the prison ship
martyrs that could be sung to the tune of "The Star Spangled
Banner," and the *Eagle* printed it on July 2, 1846, so the good
Brooklynites could use the *Eagle* as a song sheet when they gathered at
Fort Greene:

> Oh, God of Columbia! Oh, Shield of the Free!
>   More grateful to you than the fanes of old story,
> Must the blood-bedeviled soil, the red battle ground, be
>   Where our forefathers championed America's glory!
> Then how priceless the worth of the sanctified earth
>   We are standing on now. Lo! the slopes of its girth
> Where the martyrs were buried; nor prayers, tears nor stones,
>   Marked their crumbled-in-coffins, their white holy bones![25]

In the July 6 *Eagle* Whitman reported that he was pleased with the
day and the several thousands who attended the fireworks, but he
hated the "diabolical rub-a-dub" music.

Whitman Leaves

Along with Whitman's concern for Brooklyn's more parochial
problems, he was very much a party politician during his *Eagle*
editorship. Van Anden was a party leader, and when he became editor
Whitman was appointed general secretary of the Democratic party in
Brooklyn with the responsibility of organizing political parades and
the annual Fourth of July celebration.[26] Most of Whitman's editorials
had some bearing on what he called the "Democratic Idea" as the
antithesis of the Whig conception of society, with its distrust of the
common people and of the integrity and intelligence of the masses.
He called for more radicalism and more daring experiments to see how
much liberty society could bear. He supported the independent
treasury and free trade. During a strike at the Atlantic Dock and Basin
from March to May, 1846, he supported the Irish workmen's pleas for
higher wages but not their association to "regular" wages.[27] He
attacked the nativist movement. He was for prison reform and against

capital punishment, for temperance but against prohibition. He was against slavery but not an abolitionist.

Although Whitman was a fiercely partisan Democrat, he was also fiercely loyal to his own convictions, and his opposition to the spread of slavery to the new territories brought about his split with the conservative Van Anden and his departure from the *Eagle*. Whitman tells the story briefly: "At the *Eagle* I had one of the pleasantest sits [situations] of my life—a good owner, good pay, and easy work and hours. The troubles in the Democratic Party so broke forth about those times (1848-1849) and I split off with the radicals, which led to rows with the boss and 'the party,' and I lost my place."[28]

Whitman's split with Van Anden did not come into the open until the end of the Mexican War. Whitman had seen the war primarily in terms of his expanding vision of democracy. On May 11, 1846, he wrote, "Let our arms now be carried with a spirit which shall teach the world that, while we are not forward for a quarrel, America knows how to crush, as well as how to expand." A typical war editorial was "The Age":

The United States, most undoubtedly, are the first nation of the earth—in defiance of cockney carpings, and foreign abuse. The pending war with Mexico has drawn out the evidence of this fact; the people *will move*, on the smallest occasion. And there is such superiority in such a nation of freemen, over one which has the mightiest artificial army, as a human life and form, with its own volition, are superior to the most cunning piece of mere machinery. There is no other way. And, for our part, we look on that increase of territory and power—not as a doubter looks—but with the faith which the Christian has in mystery.[29]

However, Whitman wanted limits to the war. When it seemed that the war had been won, when it seemed that enough had been done to avenge our offended honor, he called on all citizens to say firmly that it should go no further. The Wilmot Proviso, introduced in Congress in 1846, to prohibit the extensions of slavery to new territories, won the *Eagle* editor's unflinching support:

If there are any States to be formed out of territory lately annexed, or to be annexed . . . let the Democratic members of Congress (and the Whigs too if they like) plant themselves quietly, without bluster, but fixedly and without compromise on the requirement that *Slavery be prohibited in them forever*. We wish we could have a universal straight-forward setting down of feet on this thing in the Democratic party.[30]

The Democrats had split into two factions, the radical "Barnburners" and the conservative "Hunkers," and Whitman was furious that in spite of his fiery editorials to get out the vote the New York Democrats had been defeated in the 1847 elections. Without specifically identifying himself as a "Barnburner," he blamed the party's defeat on its failure to be radical enough and their temporizing on the Wilmot or "Jefferson" Proviso.

The final split with "Hunker" Van Anden came over a letter which General Lewis Cass wrote criticizing the Proviso on December 24, 1847, to A.O.P. Nicholson of Nashville, Tennessee. It was made public in January 1848. Whitman assailed the Cass argument in a short editorial, "The Late Letter of Senator Cass," on January 3, 1848. Two days later the *Eagle* printed extracts of the Cass letter without comment. We can reasonably speculate that Van Anden had made his editor print the document. A few days later—we cannot be sure of the exact date—Whitman was gone.

The New York *Globe* commented on the changes in the "political conduct" of the *Eagle* and the *Eagle* replied on January 21 that the *Globe* should mind its own business. The same day the *Tribune* reported the rumor that "the Barnburners of Brooklyn are about starting a new daily paper, as, it is said the *Eagle* has returned to its old Hunkerism again, and Walter Whitman, late of the *Eagle*, is to have charge of the new enterprise." The *Eagle* was playing up the anti-Wilmot Proviso Convention in Albany on its editorial page, and it did support Cass for the presidency. On January 23, the Brooklyn *Advertiser*, with which Whitman had been carrying on a rather playful running feud, noted Whitman's departure with cryptic glee:

I, said the sparrow,
With my bow and arrow
I killed cock robin.

After an embarrassed silence of several weeks the *Eagle* replied on February 17, 1848, with clumsy cleverness in "Impromptu Address to the Editor of the *Advertiser*":

It is true, as you say,
We sent Whitman away,
But that is a private affair;
But since you have spoken
Know by this token,
You have no *wit, man*, to spare.

Whitman had gone away to New Orleans for a short stint on a paper there, but he was soon back in Brooklyn. He was elected a delegate to the Barnburner Convention in Buffalo in 1848 where the Free Soil party was formed in a spirit of religious enthusiasm. For a brief while he was editor of the *Freeman*, determined to establish at last a radical paper in Kings County; but when the Barnburners and Hunkers reunited for the State elections he quit, expressing disdain and defiance for his old Hunker enemies.[31]

On July 19, 1849, in response to an *Advertiser* charge that the *Eagle* had fired Whitman for kicking a Democratic politician, the *Eagle* replied with a biting paragraph that reveals an unbecoming bitterness in Van Anden and a lack of appreciation for Whitman's contribution to the *Eagle* as well:

Slow, indolent, heavy, discourteous and without steady principles, he was a clog upon our success, and reluctant as we were to make changes, we still found it absolutely necessary to do so. Mr. W. cried persecution. . . . Mr. W. has no political principles, nor, for that matter, principles of any sort . . . Whoever knows him will laugh at the idea of his kicking any body, much

less a prominent politician. He is too indolent to kick a musketo
[*sic*].

The *Eagle* did not let up on Whitman. When the 1860 edition of the
Leaves of Grass was attacked in the October *Westminster Review*, the
Eagle reprinted the attack and gloated and in 1865, when Whitman
lost his job at the Interior Department because *Leaves of Grass* was
considered evidence that he was "immoral," the *Eagle* seized the
opportunity to hit him again in a July 12 editorial called "Morality in
Washington":

> . . . Most of our readers probably know Whitman by sight; he
> used in his own language to "celebrate himself" so conspicu-
> ously along the streets of Brooklyn. Walt is personally a good-
> hearted fellow, with some ability, but he was bitten with the
> mania of transcendentalism, which broke out in New England
> some years ago, and still flourishes in that region. . . .

The editorial claimed that Whitman "wrote of things no rightminded
person is supposed ever to think of; and used language shocking to
polite ears." It gave him credit for tending the wounded during the
war and added the information that he now had a desk at the Attorney
General's Office "where we suppose they are not so particular about
morals."[32] This defense of morals was probably written by Thomas
Kinsella, editor from 1861 to 1884, an outstanding journalist who
also earned himself a citywide reputation as an adulterer.

This history of Whitman's reputation indicates that the *Eagle* was
founded by a man of limited tolerance. It is reasonable to assume that
Van Anden communicated the "official picture" of Whitman to his
young nephew, William Hester, and that the image of Walt the
loafer was reinforced by oral tradition within the *Eagle* "family."[33] As
time went on, only "Hen" Sutton retained a real memory of Whitman
as an *Eagle* editor, while the rest of the staff projected the Whitman of
Leaves of Grass back into 1846. St. Clair McKelway was not sympa-
thetic to Whitman; Herbert Gunnison, who succeeded Hester as

president of the *Eagle,* was skittish about Whitman and did not want his name associated with the paper. Meanwhile, *Leaves of Grass* was banned in Brooklyn libraries.

The poet's laziness was emphasized at the *Eagle* 1916 Anniversary Pageant at the Academy of Music. *Eagle* editor Arthur M. Howe, speaking at the 1919 Brooklyn Whitman centenary, said of Whitman's *Eagle* work: "He conveys the impression of one who regards his occupation in journalism as something to which he was compelled by circumstance rather than a vocation for which he had any positive affection."[34] Could Howe have read Whitman's *Eagle* editorials, particularly "Ourselves and the *Eagle*," and still have made that statement? In the *Programme* for the eighty-fifth anniversary celebration in 1926, John Alden, who joined the *Eagle* in 1901, wrote a "Folk-lore of the *Eagle* Family" in which the ghost of Isaac Van Anden narrates *Eagle* history. Van Anden says of Whitman, "I liked Walt and he liked me, but it was better to part." He describes Whitman's successor, S. G. Arnold, by saying he "was a worker, and, unlike Whitman, he had no disposition to re-organize the world." The laziness story lasted into the 1930s when publisher Preston Goodfellow thinks he saw it mentioned in minutes of a board meeting, and to the Schroths in the 1940s and 1950s who had an imperfect understanding of Whitman's contribution.

During Whitman's editorship the *Eagle* had prospered. Besides purchasing new type it had moved to larger quarters (a substantial four-story white brick building at 30 Fulton Street) and replaced the Washington hand press, which could print only 250 copies per hour (only 300 or 400 were printed) with a new cylinder press. The paper had won praise from most of its contemporaries.[35]

Whitman's gradual rehabilitation at the *Eagle* began in 1914 when the scholarly city editor Cleveland Rodgers started writing occasional editorials on the *Eagle*'s neglected patron. Under Rodgers' direction the *Eagle* published a special Whitman edition on May 31, 1919, and in 1930 it promoted Whitman for the New York University Hall of Fame by sending copies of a pro-Whitman *Eagle* article to the electors. In retrospect it seems very fitting that an artist who loved

Brooklyn the way Whitman did should be editor of the *Eagle*. It was as a journalist that he learned to walk the city streets with all his senses alive—so he could say in "Song of Myself":

> This is the city and I am one of the citizens,
> Whatever interests the rest interests me, politics,
>   wars, markets, newspapers, schools,
> The mayor and council, banks, tariffs, steamships,
>   factories, stocks, stores, real estate and
>   personal estate.[36]

Notes

[1]Whitman's main activities for the *Eagle* are recounted in Gay Wilson Allen's *The Solitary Singer* (New York: New York University Press, 1955), pp. 73-94. Thomas L. Brasher's *Whitman as Editor of the Brooklyn Daily Eagle* (Detroit: Wayne State University Press, 1970) covers the period in more detail, adding the information that Whitman wrote one series of articles on organized labor and that his religious thought was influenced by Universalism and Unitarianism. Also see Herbert Bergman, "Walt Whitman as a journalist, 1831-January, 1848," *Journalism Quarterly* (*JQ*) 47 (Summer 1971): 195-204; "Whitman on Editing, Newspapers and Journalism," *JQ* (Summer 1971): 345-348; and "Walt Whitman as a Journalist, March, 1848-1892, *JQ* 49 (Autumn 1971):431-437. Bergman's five-volume edition of Whitman's journalism will be published in the New York University Press's definitive edition of *The Collected Writings of Walt Whitman*.

[2]Theodore A. Zunder, "William B. Marsh—The First Editor of the Brooklyn Daily *Eagle*," *American Book Collector* 4 (August 1933): 93-95.

[3]Emory Holloway, ed., *The Uncollected Poetry and Prose of Walt Whitman* (New York, 1921), Introduction, pp. xxxlx-xlix. Hereafter UPP.

[4]*Aurora*, April 9, 1842, quoted in Bergman, "Whitman as a Journalist," *JQ* 47 (Summer 1971): 198.

[5]*Eagle*, March 30, 1842.

[6]Bergman, p. 199.

[7]Cleveland Rodgers and John Black, eds., *The Gathering of Forces: Editorials, Essays, Literary and Dramatic and Other Material Written by Walt Whitman*

as Editor of the Brooklyn Daily Eagle in 1846 and 1847, vol. 2 (New York and London: Putnam, 1920), pp. 7-8. Hereafter GF.

[8]*Eagle*, May 12, 1846. Whitman said the people were responsible for the lack of American literature because they didn't buy American authors; GF, vol. 2, pp. 314-318.

[9]Cleveland Rodgers judged in his *Reminiscences*, pp. 260-265, that Whitman's *Eagle* probably gave more space to literature than any other New York paper. He reprinted Poe's "A Tale of the Rugged Mountains" (October 9-10, 1846); Hawthorne's "Old Esther Dudley" (July 28-29, 1846), and "The Shaker Bridal" (October 8, 1846); and Irving's "The Broken Heart" (October 11, 1847), and "Pelago and the Merchant's Daughter" (October 26, 1847). He reprinted twelve of his own tales in 1846 and one in 1847, but none originally in the *Eagle*. These tales, with the details of their publication, are now collected in *Walt Whitman, The Early Poems and Fiction*, Thomas L. Brasher, ed. (New York: New York University Press, 1963).

[10]*Eagle*, November 23, December 4, 1846; September 7, 1847.

[11]*Eagle*, December 17, 1846.

[12]*Eagle*, August 16, 1847. Today there is a park there, but the neighborhood, all houses and pavements and an elevated line, is desolate. Fort Greene Houses, the largest public housing project in the city, stands between downtown Brooklyn and the half-abandoned Brooklyn Navy Yard. A fifth of the 3,500 apartments are occupied by whites and another fifth are occupied by Puerto Ricans. The neighborhood is poor, violent, and black. Nathan Glazer and Daniel Patrick Moynihan, *Beyond the Melting Pot: The Negroes, Puerto Ricans, Jews, Italians, and Irish in New York City* (Cambridge: M.I.T. Press and Harvard University Press, 1963), p. 24. Personal observation of RAS, July 7, 1970.

[13]Brasher, p. 34.

[14]Ibid., p. 145.

[15]*Eagle*, June 13, 1846.

[16]*Eagle*, March 4, 1847.

[17]*Eagle*, May 3, 1847.

[18]Arthur M. Howe, "Walt Whitman as Editor," Walt Whitman Section, *Eagle*, May 31, 1919, p. 3. Also in Bergman, pp. 202-203. Descriptions of Whitman's day, based partly on recollections of William Henry Sutton, are in *GF*, vol. 1, Introduction, and Bergman, pp. 202-203.

[19]*Eagle*, June 10, 1846.

[20]*Eagle*, August 13, 1847.

[21]*Eagle*, July 13, 1847.

[22]UPP, vol. 2, pp. 222-225.

[23]*Eagle*, July 9, 1846, p. 2. Most of the Battery has been erased; what is left is a monument. Washington Parade Grounds is now Washington Square Park in Greenwich Village. Tompkins Square survives. *AIA Guide to New York City*, Norval White and Elliot Willensky, eds. (New York: The Macmillan Company, 1968).

[24]*Program of the Dedication Ceremonies of the Prison Ship Martyrs' Monument, Fort Greene Park, Brooklyn, New York, Sat., November 14, 1908 and History of Prison Ship Martyrs* (Brooklyn: Society of Old Brooklynites, 1908).

[25]Reprinted in *Early Poems and Fiction*, Thomas L. Brasher, ed. (New York: New York University Press, 1963), pp. 34-35. Whitman published one other poem in the *Eagle*, June 1, 1846, "The Play Ground." It was not until 1908 that the present 195-foot Newport white granite Prison Ship Martyrs' monument was erected at Fort Greene with Hon. William Howard Taft presiding and Thomas Walsh reading a sonorous militant ode of his own, filled with classical allusions. At that ceremony, Whitman and his ode were forgotten.

[26]Stanley J. Idzerda, "Walt Whitman, Politician," *New York History* 54 (April 1956): 173.

[27]*Eagle*, March 26, 1846.

[28]*Specimen Days* in *The Complete Works of Walt Whitman*, 10 vols. (New York and London: G. P. Putnam's and Sons, 1900), V. 34; GF, p. xvii.

[29]*Eagle*, June 23, 1846.

[30]*Eagle*, December 26, 1846.

[31]Idzerda, p. 177; Allen, pp. 90-92.

[32]Allen, pp. 211-212; 345-347.

[33]Rodgers, *Reminiscences* (New York: Oral History Project, Columbia University, 1950), p. 261.

[34]Clara Barras, *Whitman and Burroughs, Comrades* (Boston and New York: Houghton Mifflin, 1931), p. 262, quoted in Brasher.

[35]Bergman, p. 203. Almost ten years later, in 1857, Whitman returned to become editor of the Brooklyn *Daily Times*. The *Times* had been founded as the Williamsburg *Daily Times* on February 28, 1848; and it changed the name when Brooklyn and Williamsburg were consolidated in 1855.

[36]Lines 1075-1077.

3

THE CIVIL WAR

As 1861 began and the newly elected Abraham Lincoln prepared for inauguration, and as the nation and Brooklyn were being drawn week by week into the "irrepressible conflict," the *Eagle*, more prosperous than ever, seemed to have three things on its mind: Henry Ward Beecher's preaching on the war, the opening of the first opera in Brooklyn, and Brooklyn's concept of itself. It was a dignified, six-column, four-page paper printed on a larger page than the Whitman paper, and it sold for two cents. The war would bring dramatic changes in the format. In 1861 page one, except for the literary column, was all ads, page two was editorials and foreign news, page three was war news, ads and gossip, and page four was similar to page one. The conflict would force more and more war news onto the first and last pages, some of it battle reports twenty-four hours old, contradicted by latebreaking reports off the telegraph that afternoon, and all introduced by a string of colorful headlines summing up the stories of the battles. It was the beginning of the period of the *Eagle*'s greatest growth, the years in which Van Anden would boldly claim on his editorial page daily that: "This paper has the highest circulation of any evening paper published in the United States. Its value as an advertising medium is therefore apparent."

Samuel G. Arnold, Whitman's successor, had given the paper some new life. He had reduced the name to *The Brooklyn Daily Eagle* in 1850 and added steam power to the press in 1851, the first engine in a Brooklyn printing office. However, Arnold supported the fiery Henry Ward Beecher's sermons on sending rifles rather than Bibles to "bleeding Kansas," so Van Anden fired him in 1853 and replaced him with Henry McCloskey, who had come to the paper as its first full-time reporter in 1851.[1] Yet as the war drew near, the sharp-tongued McCloskey would bring what Van Anden seemed slow to court—trouble.

Of the over three thousand Northern newspapers, hardly fifty were outright defenders of slavery. Three of these were New York papers: Bennett's *Herald*, which later provided excellent war coverage; the *Day-Book*; and Benjamin Woods' *Daily News*. There was wide diversity of opinion in the other papers on whether the several Southern states which had already seceded should be allowed to leave or compelled to stay. The *Eagle* position, briefly, was that it would like to maintain the union but that the federal government did not have the constitutional right to force the Southern states to remain. Van Anden, a moderate Democrat, had in McCloskey a Breckenridge Southern Democrat whose strong editorials would bring down charges of disloyalty on the *Eagle*. Of the seventeen New York dailies, only five—the *Tribune, Times, Evening Post, Sun*, and *Commercial Advertiser*—were very warm supporters of the administration.[2]

Some of McCloskey's work is worth examining, partly because he communicates some of the flavor of Brooklyn life and partly because his squabbles with Beecher reveal an interesting moral sense and a sharp mind and independent spirit who would rather speak freely than keep a job. For McCloskey's *Eagle*—in a little promotion campaign that probably pleased Walt Whitman—the January 15 opening of the new Academy of Music and the January 22 grand opening of Brooklyn opera, Mercadante's "Il Giuramento," with Mrs. Lincoln and her sons presiding from their box, was further evidence of Brooklyn's superiority to New York. Even the New York *Herald* seemed to agree that Brooklynites supported their opera while New Yorkers did not.[3] This was reassuring; a few weeks before the *Eagle* had complained about Brooklynites who tended to treat their own city like an "overgrown village," and particularly those who set up entertainments in Brooklyn, advertised them in New York papers, and then expected the *Eagle* to give them a free notice.[4]

To prove Brooklyn was no longer an "overgrown village" the *Eagle* printed a positive analysis of the 1860 census. The population had risen from 205,250 in 1855 to 266,674, 150,722 of whom were native U.S. born. The writer regretted that whereas five years before there were 5,000 more females than males, now there were 4,000 less females. The *Eagle*'s explanation: Brooklyn girls were so pretty that outsiders came and married them and took them away. Meanwhile, the Negro population of around 4,000 had also decreased by 1,013 in ten years, and the *Eagle* noted that regret might not be universal that "this interesting class" of the population was going down, and added that there had been six intermarriages, in all of which the woman had been "degraded." Brooklyn now had 30,528 dwellings, an increase of 6,553, and most of these were two-family dwellings, in contrast to the "less healthy" three-family homes in New York. The number of churches had risen from 80 to 140. The Methodists were the largest denomination with 22,500 and Roman Catholics next with 22,050.[5]

Meanwhile, McCloskey was informing Brooklyn minds on the moral issues of slavery and war. When Beecher said the Bible did not countenance slavery, the *Eagle* called him the "Gog and Magog of anti-slavery theology" and attacked him for his generalities and failure to cite chapter and verse.[6] "The sole origin of the present difficulties," said the *Eagle*, "is the meddlesome spirit of a pharisaical and self-righteous element among the Northern people, tracing its origin to New England. It must exalt itself by finding somebody whom it can assail as less holy than itself."[7] It urged that the North "dethrone the negro" from the pedestal he occupied in popular idolatry.[8] On April 13, the day after the firing on Fort Sumter, the *Eagle* wrote powerfully:

> The contest, which in all probability is to carry devastation throughout the land, has commenced. The news from Fort Sumter has inflicted a painful shock on every lover of his country and every friend of popular government. Unless the people shake off the lethargy that seems to paralyze their faculties, and arrest the uplifted hand of fratricidal slaughter, we are destined to rush upon a future of anarchy and ruin, to be succeeded by the creation of an indefinite number of warning and discondent communities, or the erection of a military depotism, the most

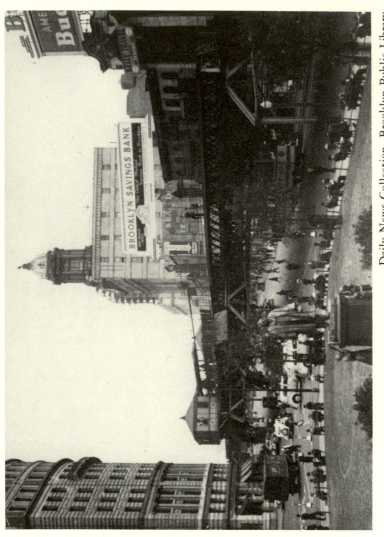

The Henry Ward Beecher statue in Borough Hall Park, the old Fulton Avenue elevated line, and the *Eagle* building in 1930.

rigorous and oppressive that has appeared on the stage of history since the Praetorian guards ruled degenerate Rome, assassinated its chief magistrates, and sold the imperial diadem to the highest bidder.

When Beecher, whom the *Eagle* sarcastically referred to as "that inspired prophet," said, according to a report in the New York *Express*, that he "abhorred peace" and urged soldiers to go to war "with a Christian spirit; not with any angry feeling, but with indignation," the *Eagle* urged him to "act on his own principles and volunteer."[9] However, the fiercest attack on Beecher was to come in July in an editorial headlined "THE GOSPEL ACCORDING TO BEECHER." According to the *Star*, Beecher had argued that since half the human race dies in the cradle and half the remaining half die of old age, sudden death is not to be the most feared. Beecher explained:

> Looking at it in its just view, commend me to a sudden death —death by lightning stroke, by the whistling ball . . . You have much mourning for those who die in battle. A million of men may die on the dung hill and no man mourns, but when life is given to a principle, those who die are crowned ones, those souls have already had resurrection—and men mourn.

The *Eagle* may have been as guilty of racism as most men of its time, but on the issue of war it seemed to sense the moral horror of sending thousands of young men to their deaths more acutely than its contemporaries. It replied that Beecher's doctrine was the antithesis of Christianity:

> Because multitudes "die on the dunghill" therefore it is right that others rend each other and die by mutual slaughter. It was to prevent people from perishing on dunghills that Christianity was introduced into the world. And if multitudes perish on the dunghill it is because its professed ministers devote themselves to stirring up incendiary strife and fratricidal carnage, instead of going into the highways, lanes and alleyes, to rescue the perish-

ing, and teach the world that their mission was not to destroy but to save.[10]

The *Eagle* concluded that if Beecher wanted death "by whistling ball" he knew where he could get it.

Nevertheless, once hostilities had begun the *Eagle* accepted the war, supported the Union, and expanded its operations to increase war coverage. It announced that beginning Tuesday, April 23, with its new 1858 $20,000 four-cylinder Hoe presses, it would publish a daily morning penny *Eagle* with Associated Press news by telegraph and California news by mail. The morning *Eagle* reached a circulation of 20,000 but lasted only till May 6.[11] It could be argued that the *Eagle*'s support of the union was less than spontaneous. The night of Wednesday, April 17 a high-spirited mob of several hundred patriots roamed the Brooklyn streets and visited the *Eagle* offices. "Show your colors!" and "Hang out your flag" they yelled, and tried to break in the door. The only person there was the engineer, and he gladly waved the flag. Jubilant, the mob headed for the other newspapers, the *News, Standard*, and *Star*. The *Eagle* management replied the next day that the *Eagle* had planned to hang out its flag anyway and it would not be intimidated by a mob.[12]

However, the *Eagle* could be intimidated by the government. On August 16, 1861, a New York federal grand jury inquired whether certain newspapers such as the *Daily News, Journal of Commerce*, the *Day Book, Freeman's Journal*, and Brooklyn *Daily and Weekly Eagle* were not guilty of disloyalty and subject for presentment for encouraging the enemy and urging that the North "accede to the demands of the South." The *Eagle* replied defiantly that the government obviously didn't know what it was talking about since there hadn't been a *Weekly Eagle* in seven years! "So far as the principle of free speech and a free press is at stake, we will vindicate and maintain it. It is a right which abolitionists, now in the ascendent, neither gave nor can take away. If this is treason they can make the most of it."[13] They did make something of it. The papers were not indicted, but the postmaster general ordered its New York postmaster not to accept these papers for mailing. On September 7 a notice appeared in which

Henry McCloskey announced he was ending his nine years of *Eagle* service, and the next day another notice reported that the "disabilities" imposed by the postmaster had been removed.

To replace the cashiered McCloskey, Van Anden turned to the young Irish Protestant Thomas Kinsella, who had come to the *Eagle* as a typesetter in 1858. In doing so he elevated the man who was to become one of the central figures in the *Eagle*'s history and one of the most influential journalistic and political leaders of Brooklyn. Born in 1832 in County Wexford in Ireland, Kinsella had served as a printer's apprentice in Cambridge, New York. From there he had gone to Troy, then New Orleans and Vicksburg. After four years in the South he had moved up to Brooklyn and the *Eagle* and a career in Democratic politics to which his editorship was a fine entreé.

Under Kinsella the *Eagle* steered a safe but not timorous course which supported the union but kept Abraham Lincoln subject to criticism. Its major clash with the Administration was brought on by its city editor, Joseph Howard, Jr., a journalist in the Richard Adams Locke tradition. Howard and Albany correspondent Frank Mallison brought on one of the major journalistic crises of the Civil War. In May 1864, with the hope of precipitating a rise in the stock market, they forged, on oiled flimsy paper used by the Associated Press, a presidential proclamation calling for the drafting of 400,000 men. They did this without regard for the fact that from July 13 to 16 a year before, between 50,000 and 70,000 New Yorkers had rioted against the draft. The *Eagle* and most other papers checked the story and refused to publish it, but the *World* and the *Journal of Commerce* were tricked and came out with the story prominently displayed. The federal government, as represented in New York City by General John A. Dix, retaliated by suspending the *World* and the *Journal of Commerce* for two days and jailing the forgers in military prison for three months.[14]

However, the *Eagle* did not let the matter die. To them it was another issue of the federal government's abuse of power. The *Eagle* was strong in its loyalty to the Union, but it did not accept Lincoln's conduct of the war, the high casualties brought on in the pursuit of a complete military victory, or the federal government's decision to

abolish slavery without the consent of the states.[15] Kinsella had been
a delegate to the National Democratic Convention that had nominated George McClellan for President, and the Brooklyn Democrats
were anxious to defeat Lincoln in the 1864 elections, so the *Eagle*
pounded away at the President all during the summer. Lincoln had
told General Dix that his orders superceded State law; Democratic
Governor Horatio Seymour had told his district attorney to ignore
General Dix and Abraham Lincoln. The *Eagle* thought Lincoln was
abusing his power. The long Friday, July 8, 1864, editorial, "The
Difficulty Between the National and State Executives," is a good
example of Kinsella's reasoning and style:

> We challenge the most abject apologists of Mr. Lincoln's con-
> duct, to show that the hands of the government have been
> strengthened by any of the many violations of law committed by
> the present administration. In the case out of which this conflict
> of authority directly arises Mr. Lincoln directed the forcible
> suspension of two newspapers whose only offense was that their
> conductors were imposed upon by a foolish imposter. No
> American, who has not forgotten the teachings of his ancestors,
> could pass by either the *World* or *Journal of Commerce*, while they
> remained in possession of the military authorities, without
> feeling ashamed of himself and his country. Does any man
> pretend that there was anything gained by this foolish display of
> arbitrary authority? The act proved, if anything, that the war in
> which we are engaged could not be carried out except at the
> sacrifice of civil liberty, and it is but a sorry comfort to the
> people to prove to them that to the sacrifices they have already
> made, their civil rights—the dearest of all treasures—must be
> added.

To pave the way for its criticism of Lincoln, the editorial shifts tone
and makes an appeal to the class consciousness of its readership and to
the Brooklynites' pride in the tranquility of their city.

> There is no war in New York; the civil law is, therefore, the

supreme law. Military law has been defined as the absence of all law. What is there in our condition that would justify us of being deprived of the benign protection of the law? Does any man oppose the law in our quiet streets, in our peaceful hamlets, in the villages that slumber in our valleys? If dangerous classes exist among us, they make no show of resistance to any law. Is it becoming in the highest officer of the law to stand in the way of the enforcement of the laws which the most vicious dare not resist? Opposition to the law is not offered to-day by the resident of the slums of our cities; it comes from the White House in Washington. Is it seemly that this should be so? Surely the man who is expected even to-day, to call for 300,000 men to risk their lives for law, should set the example of a religious observance of constituted authority. . . .

The *Eagle*'s reaction to an August 2 meeting of the Brooklyn Republican general committee gives an indication of both the *Eagle*'s influence in Brooklyn and its support of the Union cause. Amid hisses from all over the room, "Boss" Gale proposed that notices of their meetings be posted in the *Eagle* because he had noticed on the ferry that ten times as many people read the *Eagle* as read the *Union*. The *Union* had been founded September 13, 1863, by prominent Republican C. Z. Chittenden in an effort to offset the *Eagle*. He believed that the country's salvation lay in destroying the Southern leaders, disarming everyone below the Mason-Dixon line, and exterminating the slave aristocracy as a political power.[16] According to Gale, the *Eagle* was "as good a Union paper as there is published in the country." The *Eagle* replied with agreement but "no thanks," charging that Gale had refused to give a one-armed veteran a job unless he promised to vote for Lincoln:

Gale is right; the *Eagle* is a strong Union paper. Those who control its columns look to the restoration of the old Union as the first of political blessings. Gale has paid us a compliment; we desire to return it. He says we have done great things for the Union cause; this is true. So has Gale helped by refusing to employ in the Navy Yard a brave soldier, who lost his arm in the service of his country, because he would not pledge his vote for his place. Gale has helped to disgust every man with his hypocritical superiors who affect to be interested in the welfare of the soldiers but still sustain Gale in leaving a war-torn veteran to starve because he believes with three fourths of the people of this city that the interest of the country for which he imperilled his life demands the election of a better man for the Presidency than the salacious joker that now fills the position.[17]

In short, the *Eagle* came through the Civil War with its reputation for loyalty safeguarded, its material prosperity enhanced, and a new editor ready to put his personal stamp on Brooklyn. It also brought its treatment of Henry Ward Beecher more in line with popular sentiment. By March 10, 1869, the *Eagle* was saying of the Plymouth Church preacher: "Our institutions live in him, our thoughts as a nation breathe in him, our muscular Christianity finds in him the most vigorous champion. He is the Hercules of American Protestantism."

Notes

[1]Henry Isham Hazelton, *The Boroughs of Brooklyn and Queens, Counties of Nassau and Suffolk, Long Island, New York, 1609-1924.* 6 vols. (New York-Chicago: Lewis Historical Publishing Company, Inc., 1925), p. 1412.

[2]Allan Nevins, *The Emergence of Lincoln* vol. 2 (New York: Charles Scribner's Sons, 1950), pp. 337-340. Edwin Emery, *The Press and America* (Englewood Cliffs: Prentice Hall, 1962) pp. 231-257.

[3]*Eagle*, January 15, 23, 26, 1861.

[4]*Eagle*, January 8, 1861.

[5]*Eagle*, March 8, 1861.

[6]*Eagle*, January 3, 1861.

[7]*Eagle*, January 11, 1861.

[8]*Eagle*, March 27, 1861.

[9]*Eagle*, April 15, 1861.

[10]*Eagle*, July 30, 1861.
[11]*Eagle*, April 16, 1861.
[12]*Eagle*, April 18, 1861.
[13]*Eagle*, August 18, 1861.
[14]Emery, p. 244.
[15]*Eagle*, August 26, 1864.
[16]Harold Coffin Syrett, *The City of Brooklyn, 1865-1898* (New York: Columbia University Press, 1944), p. 21.
[17]*Eagle*, August 3, 1864.

4

THE AGE

OF KINSELLA

Thomas Kinsella in many ways typified the *Eagle* and the Brooklyn of his day both because he plunged so deeply into Brooklyn political and social life and became a political and journalistic figure of some national importance and because he was a "climber" who personified a rising class of citizens and an expanding city. Seen in the context of the careers of other prominent Irishmen of this era—Henry C. Murphy, "Boss" Hugh McLaughlin, "Boss" John McKane, William J. Gaynor, and Alexander McCue—his career was an example of the rise of the immigrant Irish to wealth and political power through the means of journalism, community activity, and entrepreneurial daring. During Kinsella's tenure at the *Eagle* from 1861 until his death in 1884, he played a part in two of the most significant events in nineteenth century Brooklyn history, the building of the Brooklyn Bridge and the major reform of municipal government.

The *Eagle* office was a hectic place under Kinsella. The four-story whitefaced building with the eagle statue over the front door kept expanding down Front Street in 1872 and 1882 until it filled an entire block with frontage on Fulton, Doughty, and Elizabeth Streets. In 1867, with a new eight-cylinder press, Kinsella enlarged the page size again, then added another eight-cylinder press in 1872, and two Hoe perfecting presses in 1883 which would print on two sides, with folding attachments. Van Anden had also introduced the first newsboys to Brooklyn to make the *Eagle* a paper whose success depended primarily on home delivery. Kinsella greatly increased the staff, and in 1864 made John Stanton, under the pen name of "Corry O'Lanus" one of the first columnists in American journalism. He wrote regular short-sentence "epistles" of humorous commentary. The *Eagle* was staffed by a boisterous, hard-drinking group of self-taught men who saw the newspaper business as a "man's game" and themselves as the heart of Brooklyn's own Bohemia. One summer afternoon they dangled a fellow reporter, a clergyman's son, out the third floor window by his feet and made him yell obscenities to the homecomers from the Fulton Ferry. They were proud of their tricks for getting news, like George Dobson hiding between the ceiling and roof of the tightly guarded Board of Education Building to overhear a secret investigation on the morals of a school principal, and the notorious Joe Howard disguising himself as an acolyte to crash Abraham Lincoln's funeral at Trinity Church.[1] Kinsella's editorial policy also allowed the *Eagle* to indulge in an occasional bit of discreet sensationalism, with illustrations. On October 27, 1864, it printed a drawing of a head severed from a mutilated murder victim so the victim could be identified; then for three columns it detailed where and when the other parts of the body—trunk, pelvis, upper legs, feet, and lower legs—had been found.

Since newspaper ownership was so closely tied to political power in Brooklyn, Kinsella's *Eagle* career was also marked by power struggles within the *Eagle* ownership group. Kinsella supported Andrew Johnson in 1865 and, as a reward, was made postmaster in 1866. From 1868 to 1872 he served on the board of education and used the *Eagle*'s pages to campaign for reforms in the school system. Meanwhile, there were those who felt that the *Eagle* editor, who tried to project the good civic leader and prominent clubmember image expected of members of the "*Eagle* family," needed some reform of his own. While on the board he carried on an affair with the wife of the superintendent of schools. In 1874 he divorced his wife, by whom he had had four daughters, and married Emilie Von Sielem, the divorced wife of poet Thomas W. Field.

Nevertheless, his political fortunes prospered. In 1869 he took a leave of absence to be water commissioner, leaving the editorship to William Wood, and in 1871 he was elected for a term in Congress where he became a supporter of Horace Greeley.[2]

It was around this time that the internal power at the *Eagle* changed hands. In 1870 Van Anden sold the paper to a group of investors headed by Demas Barnes, a congressman who had made a fortune in patent medicines and was editor of the Brooklyn *Argus*, a new paper founded as an independent weekly in 1866, and including Judge Alexander McCue, a close friend of Henry C. Murphy.[3] Van Anden left the company and his nephew William Hester, who had risen from working at the printer's "case" to cashier of the company, left with him. However, Kinsella, who owned stock in the new association, quickly saw that old Brooklynites were slow to accept the idea of the *Eagle* without Van Anden. He sold part of his stock to Hester, and soon Van Anden bought out all Barnes' holdings and had himself elected president of the association. This time Van Anden brought with him another nephew, W. M. Van Anden, who became treasurer of the *Eagle* association. When Van Anden died in 1874 William Hester took his place, and he and Kinsella continued a close collaboration which had begun when Kinsella had started as a printer. In 1882, during another dispute, the two of them briefly bought the *Union* to prove that if they didn't get their way they would quit and run a rival paper.[4]

Meanwhile, Barnes, who had bought into the *Eagle* so he could use its power to make him Mayor of Brooklyn, failed to get the Democratic nomination. He was furious and blamed McCue and Kinsella's powerful friend and *Eagle* part-owner William C. Kingsley, the Democratic fund raiser and contractor. To get revenge on McCue he publicly blamed him for the failure of the Brooklyn Trust Company. McCue sued Barnes for libel and at the end of the trial Barnes was forced to make a public retraction which the *Eagle* headlined: "ON HIS KNEES."[5]

That same year Kinsella started his own Sunday newspaper, the *Sun*, with financial backing from Kingsley. The *Eagle* absorbed the *Sun* in 1877 and the Sunday *Eagle* prospered, overcoming the moral resentment of the time against the "Sunday" press generally known for its sensationalism.[6]

The Eagle and the Bridge

With the *Eagle*, the Dodgers, and the Navy Yard gone, the Brooklyn Bridge remains as Brooklyn's most enduring symbol of common purpose and common historical identity. To a degree that has seldom been appreciated, it was the *Eagle*'s bridge—conceived, promoted, and interpreted by *Eagle* owners and editors. Its first fathers usually saw the projected bridge in terms of Brooklyn's future size. Demas Barnes expected that New York would fill up and that its excess population would spill over the bridge into Brooklyn, making it the largest city in the world. To its philosophical engineer, John Roebling, it was to be one of history's great connecting works, symbolic of the new age like the Atlantic cable, the Suez Canal, and the transcontinental railroad.[7] In spite of Roebling's vision, the bridge began quite unromantically as a business deal, and its construction and financing were marred by negotiations and tragedies that have tarnished the historical reputations of its entrepreneurs; yet it has appropriately gone beyond them into American mythology and into the custody of all its people—its tourists, cyclists, joggers, and afternoon strollers as well as its Joseph Stellas and Hart Cranes.

To Lewis Mumford, in his search for an age that offers us a culture on which we can build, the Brooklyn Bridge was a "stunning act." It was perhaps the most completely satisfying structure of any kind that had appeared in America. With its strong lines and beautiful curves, the bridge proved that "the loss of form was an accident, not an inescapable result of the industrial processes." Thanks to John Roebling's genius, "All that the age had just cause for pride in its advances in science, its skill in handling iron, its personal heroism in the face of dangerous industrial processes, its willingness to attempt the untried and the impossible—came to a head in Brooklyn Bridge."[8]

Cleveland Rodgers, who had been *Eagle* editor from 1931 until 1938 when he left to join the New York City planning board, discussed the bridge in similar terms in his history of New York. "Brooklyn Bridge is a structure of rare grace and beauty. It symbolizes the unity and spirit of daring, as well as the explosive energies, that created New York City. No longer listed as the Eighth Wonder of the World, it still typifies the great community's striving for orderly multiplicity."[9] Yet, as Alan Trachtenberg documents in *Brooklyn Bridge, Fact and Symbol*, these somewhat philosophic considerations, though a profound motivation in the soul of John Roebling, were secondary to the Brooklynite entrepreneurs who carried the project through. As the speeches at the opening ceremonies and that day's special edition of the *Eagle* show, those who had lived through the building of the bridge were most fascinated with the sheer mechanics of it. In the Gilded Age the bridge meant prosperity, and in an age of technological triumph it pointed to the unlimited capabilities of man.

Brooklyn citizens had dreamed of a bridge to New York almost as long as they had been aware of the East River separating the two cities. Jeremiah Johnson, a major general, wealthy farmer, landowner, and mayor of Brooklyn from 1837 to 1840, entered a note in his scrapbook in 1800:

> It has been suggested that a bridge should be constructed from this village across the East River to New York. This idea has been treated as chimerical, from the magnitude of the design; but whoever takes it into their serious consideration, will find more weight in the practicability of the scheme than at first view is imagined.

Johnson's main motive was the same one that would move Brooklyn businessmen to urge consolidation with New York; the bridge would raise land values on the east side of the river.[10] In 1829 the New York *Gazette* reported a proposal for a chain suspension bridge, 2,100 feet from toll station to toll station, arching 160 feet above the East River. Along with raising property values, this would be a monument, it was argued, that would rank New York with London and Westminster, and it could pipe "pure" water from Brooklyn to New York.[11]

In pre-Civil War New York, the solutions to transportation problems were still in the hands of private developers; and the one-tenth of the population of Brooklyn who crossed the river twice a day by ferry were waiting anxiously for the engineer and the capitalists who would combine their resources and unite the cities. The engineer was Colonel Julius W. Adams, who had built a bridge over the Kentucky River for the Lexington and Danville Railroad Company in 1855. At the end of the Civil War Adams had designed an East River Bridge consisting mainly of two elliptical tubes placed side by side and supported by ribbons of steel with three platforms for travelers.[12] Adams took his plans to thirty-four-year-old William C. Kingsley, of the contractors Kingsley and Keeney, in the summer of 1866.

After the bitterly cold winter of 1866, in which the river had been clogged again and again and in which there had been a number of serious accidents—a collision between a tug and a ferry and a fire on a ferry—Kingsley was convinced that the time had come. Kingsley was a self-made man who had worked his way up from Pennsylvania Railroad clerk to the biggest civic-works contractor in Brooklyn. As a lieutenant to Democratic "Boss" Hugh McLaughlin's machine he had earned paving contracts and the privilege of building the water works and Hempstead reservoir. He also built much of Prospect Park and some of Central Park. Now he was regarded as a cultured gentleman with influence in banks and insurance companies and was considered both the chief moneyraiser and brains of the Democratic party.

Kingsley knew he would need "respectable" support, and he naturally turned to Henry C. Murphy, who had returned from The Hague in debt and disappointed in his political career, and was now building a new fortune for himself in real estate. They shared their scheme with Van Anden, Kinsella, Seymour L. Husted, and Judge McCue. According to one account, Murphy was won over to the project at a dramatic meeting on a cold winter night in Murphy's library by Kingsley, McCue, and James S. T. Stranaham, the man behind Brooklyn's new Prospect Park. Murphy took their plans to the legislature, and an act incorporating the New York Bridge Company was passed April 16, 1867, enabling the company to acquire land on either side of the river and to establish laws to govern the bridge upon completion. New York and Brooklyn were authorized to subscribe to bonds and stocks as determined by their common councils, with New York subscribing $1,500,000 and Brooklyn twice that amount. Five

Henry C. Murphy visiting the construction site of the
Brooklyn Bridge in 1878.

hundred thousand dollars was to come from private individuals. Murphy bought 100 shares at $100 a share and Van Anden bought 200, with the construction firm of Kingsley and Keeney picking up 1,600.

Another prominent stockholder was William Marcy Tweed. To make sure the New York Common Council would come through with its support, bridge president Murphy had crossed the river to visit his fellow senator and urge him to influence the Council. Tweed was willing to cooperate for between $55,000 and $65,000, and when Murphy was short on cash he accepted stock instead. In return for an 80 percent reduction in the price of his stock Tweed got Kingsley a 15 percent reduction on all materials he purchased.[13] It may seem harsh to say the Brooklyn Bridge was born with a bribe, but noting the payoff should put some perspective on the moral superiority Brooklyn felt toward New York. The foremost historian of the Brooklyn Bridge evaluates Murphy's behavior in this way:

> Judged by the standards of his day, Henry Cruse Murphy was a politician of exceptional quality, as straight as a string, as the saying went. He was also, plainly, an extremely attractive, accomplished human being. But if the only choice came down to compromising his principles and giving up all hope for a bridge in his lifetime, Murphy apparently was not about to let a squeamish conscience stand in his way.[14]

The next step was to decide on an engineer, since Adams himself had never built a suspension bridge. The leading candidate was John A. Roebling, a Prussian immigrant who had developed a technique in 1841 of spinning wires together to form a wire rope, a cable lighter, smaller, and stronger than hemp. Roebling was also a student of Hegel, who saw America as "the land of the future." He was a prophet of Manifest Destiny, of a great nation linked together by complex nets of railways. In his private papers he wrote: "It is a want of my intellectual nature to bring in harmony all that surrounds me. Every new harmony I discover is to be another messenger of peace, another pledge of my redemption."[15] While stranded one day in 1852 on an

East River ferry surrounded by great chunks of ice, Roebling had determined that the river needed a bridge.

In 1855 he completed his first great bridge, a two-level suspension span over the gorge of the Niagara River just below the Falls. In 1857, he wrote to Abram S. Hewitt proposing a suspension bridge for the East River. He continued his promotion in letters to the New York press until he got some attention in 1864. In April 1869, to consider Roebling and publicize the project, the promoters arranged a six-day railroad tour of Roebling's existing works in Pittsburgh, Cincinnati, and Niagara Falls, bringing along John Roebling and his son Washington, Hugh McLaughlin, seven consultants, three army engineers, Congressman Henry C. Slocum, and Kinsella who wrote long reports on their journey and sent them back to the *Eagle*. Thus *Eagle* readers were hardly surprised to read in June, "ROEBLING PLAN FULLY ENDORSED."[16]

Then tragically, the same day that Demas Barnes was telling his audience at the Atheneum, "Babylon had her hanging gardens, Nineveh her tower, and Rome her Coliseum, let us have this great monument to progress," Roebling accidentally slipped on the deck of the Fulton Ferry and crushed his foot.[17] When he died two weeks later the *Eagle* said, "Henceforth we look on the great project of the Brooklyn Bridge as being baptized by the blood of its distinguished and lamented author."[18] His son Washington, 30, replaced him, but in 1872, like many of his men who had gone down in the caissons, he was stricken with the mysterious "bends"—paralysis, vomiting, deep 'muscular pain, and swollen joints, from coming out of increased atmospheric pressure—and had to spend much of the next ten years in seclusion. He withdrew to his home at 40 Columbia Heights where he watched the progress of his masterpiece with a telescope and continued his personal direction of the work.

The story of the bridge's completion need not be recounted here except to stress that it was a project in which the citizens of New York and Brooklyn and the other newspapers again and again lost faith, often with good reason. The exposure of the Tweed Ring in July 1871 shook confidence in the management of the bridge company. The directors of the company reorganized in June 1872, adding Andrew

Haswell Green, the future apostle of the consolidation of New York and Brooklyn, and Abram S. Hewitt, philanthropist, scholar, congressman, and Henry Adams' example of one of the best men of the age. Due to evidence of mismanagement it was reorganized again in 1874 as a public company, with a new board of twenty trustees including Van Anden and Kinsella, with old Henry C. Murphy back as president and Kingsley on the executive committee. A number of investigators raised questions about Kingsley's role and exorbitant fees he was collecting. In 1876 a long complicated dispute over a wire contract was settled in favor of Brooklyn manufacturer J. Lloyd Haigh rather than Roebling's family company in Trenton, even after Roebling had sold his stock. Kinsella had influenced the decision for Haigh, and it turned out that Hewitt owned the mortgage on Haigh's firm and that the wire was defective.[19] Meanwhile, some of the trustees lost faith in the ailing Roebling. One of them, brash Seth Low, 32, whom the *Eagle* had just helped elect mayor, tracked Roebling down at Newport in 1882 to force him to resign; he refused. At the end of that year, on December 1, Henry Murphy died at 72 after a brief bout with pneumonia. It was the end of an era in Brooklyn's history—just five months away from the opening of the new age for which Murphy had labored.

Kinsella vs. McLaughlin

Meanwhile, in the last few years, Kinsella began to show a few more signs of independence from the Democratic machine. It is clear in retrospect that he and the *Eagle* were too silent about the corruption involved in building the bridge and too close to the project financially to maintain journalistic independence. His support for the Haigh-Hewitt faction among the trustees was possibly motivated by their support for Samuel Tilden for President and the editor's own higher ambitions. However, Kinsella now turned his attentions to the reform of the Brooklyn party and the removal of the well known boss Hugh McLaughlin from control. McLaughlin was the prototype of the nineteenth century urban boss, the first political manipulator to be called "Boss." The youngest of ten children of Irish immigrants,

Gardner Leo photo, Brooklyn Public Library

Hugh McLaughlin, nineteenth century Brooklyn Democratic party boss.

McLaughlin had worked on the docks and managed a fish market. He rose through the party ranks as a volunteer fireman and lieutenant of Henry C. Murphy. In 1855 McLaughlin was made master foreman in the Brooklyn Navy Yard, where he was extremely popular with his Irish fellow workmen. McLaughlin, who had no grand political ambitions beyond Brooklyn, was content to leave New York to the Tweed Ring. He was satisfied to control Kings County Democracy. Inarticulate, uneducated, a poor speaker, never a vicious fighter, McLaughlin remained throughout his life a simple man, temperate, Catholic, and devout. However, he was careful to surround himself with able men, like William C. Kingsley, his liaison to the Murphy Wing of the party, and the wealthy Alexander McCue, who later became Solicitor of the Treasury and Assistant Treasurer of the United States under Grover Cleveland.

The origins of Kinsella's feud with McLaughlin are unclear. Kinsella had invited McLaughlin on the famous Roebling tour. He had often been the boss' right-hand man at state conventions and he was chairman of the party's gatherings at Rochester in 1872, but as the elections of 1880 approached it seemed that either Kinsella's dislike of Brooklyn one-man party rule or, as some said, some remark McLaughlin had made about a Coney Island prizefight in which Kinsella had an interest, moved Kinsella to take on McLaughlin in the editorials of the *Eagle*. When the boss was elected delegate to the Democratic National Convention the *Eagle* called him: ". . . An armless man in a row boat in the middle of the Atlantic Ocean would not be any more hopelessly at sea than the 'Boss' would be at Cincinnati as the representative of the Democratic party of the State of New York."[20] As the presidential campaign went on Kinsella was angry at McLaughlin's failure to support the Democratic presidential candidate, General Winfield S. Hancock, whom Kinsella had been instrumental in nominating at Chicago. The *Eagle* worked for the defeat of the local Democratic machine. A third party was even suggested but it failed to materialize. As the election approached, the *Eagle* commented that two of the Democratic nominees were satisfactory, but that ". . . Of the remaining names on the ticket, comment is hardly necessary. They will, doubtless, be looked upon with great

favor by the admirers of barnacles and parasites."[21] Kinsella organized a Hancock and English Campaign Club, also known as the
"Jefferson Hall Democracy," to work for the national ticket without
endorsing the local candidates, and, partly as a result of *Eagle* pressure, the Democrats won only two offices in the city and county that
year.

Kinsella continued his campaign against McLaughlin rule, advis-
ing the boss and his "henchmen" to disband. McLaughlin was "an
exploded humbug" and his friends were a "pack of gibbering imbe-
ciles, not worth the pains to hoist them out of the Democratic
leadership."[22] Meanwhile, the New York *Herald* declared that "Mr.
McLaughlin (had) no more moral or political right to rule Brooklyn
than any tramp in the street."[23] McLaughlin had neither the literacy
nor the urbanity to make an intelligent public response. Perhaps
recalling Kinsella's marital problems, McLaughlin called the editor a
"man whom I have branded as unfit to be associated with by decent
people who respect their families."[24]

Finally, the *Eagle* had to reform the Democratic party by asserting
its own independence again and backing the handsome young Republican lawyer Seth Low in the Brooklyn mayoralty election of 1881.
Low won by 4,000 votes. In Syrett's judgment:

> The election of 1881 marked Brooklyn's emergence from the
> stone age of municipal government. The boss had been routed.
> The best available man had been elected mayor. A system of
> responsible home rule was about to go into effect. In short, all
> signs pointed to the dawn of a new era. For once the signs were
> right.[25]

Low was reelected in 1883 and went on to become President of
Columbia University and Mayor of New York.

This beginning of good government in Brooklyn, considered one of
the outstanding developments in municipal history, is partly attributable to Kinsella. As Syrett sums up:

> Despite the dubious appearance of his official record, Thomas

Kinsella was a real power in Brooklyn and on most occasions a power on the side of good government. He was shrewd, keen, belligerent, and tough. Under his editorship, the *Eagle* may have been wrong, but it was never dull and it never pussyfooted. Nor did he ever permit it to become a machine organ. He made many mistakes which some enemies attributed to unscrupulousness or hypocrisy, but the *Union* at the time of his death conceded that his greatest faults were "those of the expansive, robust and undisciplined type of man, not of the narrow, timid and calculating."[26]

The Bridge and Brooklyn

On May 24, 1883, the *Eagle* building, not far from the foot of the bridge, was decorated with a giant gas jet representation of an eagle. A special edition of the paper for the opening ceremonies broke all circulation records, selling over 250,000 copies. The *Eagle* published a complete history of the project, four large etchings made from new photographs of the structure, and one whole left-hand column of headlines running all the way down the page:

UNITED

Brooklyn and New York by
the Great Bridge
The Story of its Origin
and Erection

A month before the opening Henry George had written in *Frank Leslie's Illustrated Newspaper*:

We have brought machinery to the pitch of perfection that, fifty years ago could not have been imagined; but in the presence of political corruption, we seem as helpless as idiots. The East River Bridge is a crowning triumph of mechanical skill, but to get it built a leading citizen of Brooklyn had to carry to New York sixty thousand dollars in a carpet bag to bribe a New York

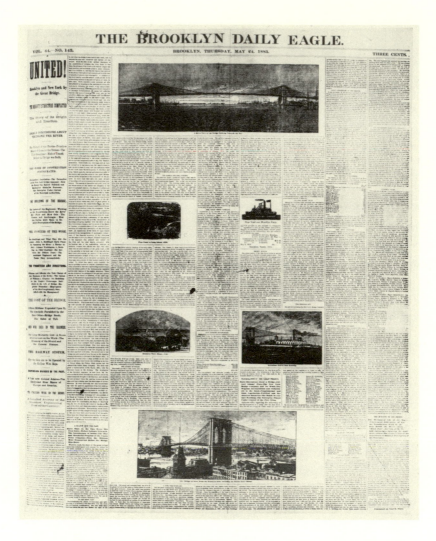

The Brooklyn *Daily Eagle*, Thursday, May 24, 1883. The opening of the Brooklyn Bridge.

alderman. The human soul that thought out the great bridge is prisoned in a crazed and broken body that lies bed-fast, and could only watch it grow by peering through a telescope. Nevertheless, the weight of the immense mass is estimated and adjusted for each inch. But the skill of the engineer could not prevent condemned wire from being smuggled into the cable.[27]

The *Eagle* had none of Henry George's ambivalence toward the triumph. In eight crammed pages of very small type it presented the whole history of the construction, glossing over the charges of political corruption in which its stockholder and first editor had been involved with a vague reference to accusations of corruption. It called the bridge "A completed monument to human ingenuity, mechanical genius and engineering skill." It added that the *"Eagle* has believed in the project throughout and championed it in the face of assaults of almost every description."[28] The *Eagle* historian speculated that man had dreamed of bridging the East River ever since the "aborigines" used to paddle their canoes across in 1642 from the same spot where the Fulton Ferry now made its crossing. He expressed his resentment that the legislature had granted a ferry monopoly to New York since the beginning of the nineteenth century.

The Brooklyn Bridge special issue was an excellent amalgam of the elements that made the *Eagle* an outstanding and unusual paper: the glorification of Brooklyn and its achievements with the emphasis on local history, the assertion of Brooklyn independence with occasional criticisms of its neighbor, and the special features that gave it a cosmopolitan tone. The history of the construction included a long interview with the aging Colonel Adams. There were detailed descriptions of the lives and deaths of the twenty men who had been killed in the thirteen years of labor, some horribly crushed by falling stone blocks, some crippled by caisson disease.

Alongside columns and columns of statistics on the bridge was a long letter from a Scotsman who had just visited New York, a letter from Paris correspondent Emma Bullet informing the Brooklyn society ladies on the bonnets and ornamental birds their Paris counterparts were wearing that year, and a light piece on the current "crazes" or popular notions of the day. Girls were wearing bangles and ornamental tarantulas on their bosoms, and if they were particularly fond of a young man they would sew his initials on a band of silk and he would wear it in his hat. The Scotsman's letter about New York could be read as another cannon shot in the *Eagle*'s war against consolidation, or as a description of New York today:

> It is the dirtiest city I have ever been in. Its streets are ill-paved-ill-kept—its street traffic as badly regulated as it is possible for it to be, or rather, apparently not regulated at all; its liquor saloons are a disgrace to a civilized community; its police system is bad; its tenement house system an abomination . . . everything a large city ought not to be.

From the beginning of the project very little had been said about the bridge's long-range effects on the urban environment on either side of the river. The *Eagle*, for one, did not seem to have considered the possibility that in sponsoring the bridge it was also forging a link with New York that would eventually destroy "old" Brooklyn. The collection of neighborhoods that also saw itself as one of the world's greatest industrial cities would inevitably die. At the same time, the Brooklyn Bridge threatened the relevance of the *Eagle* as a unique community paper. Speakers at the opening ceremonies for the bridge said very little about its importance to the solution or creation of urban problems; rather, they depicted it as the American version of man's triumph over nature, as proof of his courage, enterprise, skill, faith, and endurance.[29]

For the next eight years *Eagle* editors and employees watched the towers of the bridge from their offices, and some came to consider themselves the spiritual custodians of its traditions. The *Eagle* published special issues on the bridge's anniversaries and fought for its modernization in its ten-point plans from 1941 to 1955.

On May 26, 1923, one of the *Eagle*'s most scholarly and talented writers, Martin H. Weyraugh, published his own poem, "The Bridge Speaks," in which the edifice argues nostalgically against its own modernization. It is possible that Hart Crane, who had moved to

Brooklyn Heights to work on his poem, "The Bridge"—and would move into Washington Roebling's old room at 110 Columbia Heights the next year—read these lines:

> I think we ought to have
> At least one personality
> In this City of Wild Motion
> That stands for the solid
> The poised,
> The quiet
> Things of Life.

As the implicit task of the speakers on the Brooklyn Bridge's opening day had been to instill the bridge in the historical and spiritual consciousness of the people of the cities, it became the newspaper's task to nourish this presence and the city's sense of historical continuity by constantly reminding Brooklyn's humblest citizens of the bridge's traditions. The *Eagle* headlined its Brooklyn Bridge Fiftieth Anniversary issue of May 24, 1933, "Brooklyn Bridge Born of Necessity" and gave most prominent display to an old Currier and Ives print. It ran a retrospective feature story on Professor Robert Emmet Odlum and Steve Brodie, two men who both "took a chance" by jumping off the bridge. The first "chance" ended in an ugly death in 1885; the second "jumper" opened a bar and nourished a dubious fame.

Throughout most of its life the *Eagle* had made a point of publishing letters from elderly Brooklynites in which they reminisced about their youth, recalling old buildings, favorite street corners, forgotten neighborhood characters, and, above all, emphasizing the fringe participation of the humblest citizen in great events. Thus, readers of the May 29, 1933, *Eagle* would learn, from the fading recollection of their neighbors, that Dr. George H. Burns, the first veterinarian to graduate from an American school, was the first man to ride a horse across the bridge, and the late Henry Fleer had been the first man to drive a car across the bridge, having set out the day before to be at the head of the line. Mrs. Lena McDicken had lost her hat and had her dress torn off in the 1883 Memorial Day bridge tragedy when, for some unknown reason, the crossers on that day had thought the bridge was falling, had panicked and killed twelve in the stampede. Mrs. R. T. Nathan had set out to attend the opening ceremonies but changed her mind and went to a concert in Fort Greene Park. P. T. Barnum had wanted his elephant, "Jumbo" to cross the bridge before anyone else.

This 1933 issue also emphasized the *Eagle*'s concern for city planning. It reminded its readers of the campaign it had fostered almost from the turn of the century—the plan for a civic center from Borough Hall to the Brooklyn Bridge of "architectural beauty and magnificence in keeping with Brooklyn's greatness." The *Eagle* boosted the particular plan of architect Harvey Wiley Corbett which involved changing the name of Washington Street to Gunnison Plaza for Herbert Gunnison, the late publisher of the *Eagle*. The *Eagle* lost; the plaza was named for Brooklyn clergyman S. Parkes Cadman. Again the *Eagle* indulged its "futurism," asking the business and civic leaders to predict Brooklyn's next fifty years, with virtually all of them painting vistas of infinite possibilities with headlines like "Anything Possible . . ." and "No Limit to Possibilities. . . ." Only the letter of Mrs. William P. Earle, Sr., suggested that the promise of Brooklyn's future was conditioned by its willingness to institute sweeping social reforms in better housing, a guaranteed minimum living standard to the poor along with improved health and educational standards, a control of the congested environment which is threatening the young. She implied that there might be as much illusion as reality in the borough's vision of the bridge:

At night from the high towers of Brooklyn Heights, when the day's work is done, and the beautiful arch of the Brooklyn Bridge carries its string of lights, then the bridge is indeed a rainbow and it seems certain that the bag of gold must be at its end.

Alfred Kazin wrote of the bridge in 1965:

And because it is so beautiful in its power, complex but un-adorned, it has become the symbol of the American longing to wrest beauty out of a purely industrial environment, to find in the skills of our native capitalism and the hardness of our cities some hint of a more humane order, even of the spiritual fruition that the churchless individual might yet find in this country; so dreamed the transcendentalists in the nineteenth century and many a liberal and utopian mind in the twentieth.[30]

By then, largely as a result of the *Eagle*'s campaigns for the remodeling of the bridge and the rejuvenation of the downtown business district, and the construction of the Civic Center, the bridge had become the gateway to Brooklyn and Long Island in a new way. The Brooklyn entrepreneurs and *Eagle* editors who first promoted the bridge had not been primarily concerned with wresting beauty out of an industrial environment, nor with bringing a sign of humane order to the hardness of the city. They were moved rather by that spirit of the age and the community that dictated that bold men must seize oppor-tunities to use technological progress for personal and community profit. The later editors of the *Eagle* had more time to see the bridge in its larger context. As the city changed and declined the bridge became its most authentic symbol of its former greatness and, as the en-tranceway to the proposed Civic Center, its promise of Brooklyn's eventual rebirth.

Notes

[1]John Alden, "Folklore," in the Program for the Seventy-Fifth Anniver-sary of the Brooklyn Daily *Eagle*, October 26, 1916, pp. 24-28; Hamilton Ormsbee, "Twenty years in the *Eagle*'s Service," *Eagle*, October 26, 1911. Wilson's "History," pp. 19-22, summarizes the history of the *Eagle*'s buildings, as do the various anniversary issues. The new equipment is described and depicted in the commemorative volume, *The Eagle and Brooklyn*, Henry W. B. Howard, ed. (Brooklyn: Brooklyn *Eagle* Press, 1893), pp. 101ff.

[2]For biographical material on Kinsella, see DAB; Harold Coffin Syrett,

The City of Brooklyn 1865-1898 (New York: Columbia University Press, 1944), *passim*; and David McCollough, *The Great Bridge* (New York: Simon and Shuster, 1972).

[3]The *Argus* became a daily in 1873 and amalgamated with the *Union* in 1877, becoming simply the *Union* in 1883.

[4]*Col. William Hester, 1835-1921. The Story of His Career As Told By the Contemporary Press with Resolutions of Organizations and Tributes From Friends* (Brooklyn: Brooklyn *Daily Eagle*, 1921), pp. 7-10.

[5]*Eagle*, June 3-6, 1874.

[6]Ralph Foster Weld, *Brooklyn in America* (New York: Columbia University Press, 1950), pp. 124-125.

[7]McCollough, p. 27.

[8]Lewis Mumford, *The Brown Decades* (New York, 1931), pp. 96-106.

[9]Cleveland Rodgers and Rebecca Rankin, *New York: The World's Capital City* (New York: Harpers, 1948), p. 3.

[10]In Alan Trachtenberg, *Brooklyn Bridge, Fact and Symbol* (New York: Oxford University Press, 1965), p. 26.

[11]*Engineering News* 10 (May 26, 1883): 241; Trachtenberg, p. 38.

[12]*Eagle*, May 24, 1883.

[13]Syrett, pp. 147-148; McCollough, pp. 117-137.

[14]McCollough, p. 137.

[15]Trachtenberg, p. 57.

[16]*Eagle*, June 25, 1869.

[17]*Eagle*, July 22, 1869; McCollough, p. 90.

[18]*Eagle*, July 22, 1869.

[19]McCollough, pp. 393-396, and 444.

[20]*Eagle*, April 20, 1880; Syrett, p. 98.

[21]*Eagle*, October 21, 1880.

[22]*Eagle*, November 17, 1880.

[23]*Herald*, February 18, 1881.

[24]*Union-Argus*, February 17, 1881; Syrett, pp. 99-101.

[25]Syrett, p. 106.

[26]Ibid., p. 95.

[27]*Frank Leslie's Illustrated Newspaper*, April 14, 1883.

[28]*Eagle*, May 24, 1883.

[29]*Opening Ceremonies of the New York and Brooklyn Bridge; May 24, 1883* (Brooklyn: *Eagle* Press, 1883).

[30]Alfred Kazin, "The Bridge," *New York Review of Books* (July 15, 1965), p. 6.

5

ST. CLAIR McKELWAY AND THE AGE OF CONFIDENCE

The last decade of the nineteenth century has been called the watershed of American history. It was a "restless decade," which saw the gradual disappearance of the old America and the emergence of the new.[1] These years saw the passing of the frontier, the arrival of more than three and a half million immigrants, and the migration of a great part of the rural population to the cities. The Industrial Revolution definitively transformed America from an agrarian to an urban society and brought with it a complex modern urban civilization, with all its problems of overcrowding, poverty, and industrial strife.

These were years of urban governmental reform, inspired at least in part by the emergence of the Social Gospel movement. They were years of rising nationalism and national self-confidence. They were also years of spiritual and intellectual confusion, agony, and despair. In the judgment of Henry Adams, the American people "were wandering in a wilderness much more sandy than the Hebrews had ever trodden about Sinai; they had neither serpents nor golden calves to worship. They had lost the sense of worship. . . ."[2] And a labor journalist wrote in 1894:

91

Do we hear cries of distress from a million idle people? The wail of hunger, from men, women, and children? The groans of anguish from the multitudes who suffer in many a great city? Do we see hordes of men, mingled with women, looking for work by which they may earn their daily bread? . . . Do we see Grover Cleveland ordering his generals to whet their swords for blood?[3]

Or, as Ignatius Donnelly wrote in the Populist party platform of 1892: "From the same prolific womb of governmental injustice we breed the two great classes—tramps and millionaires."[4]

America was, therefore, a largely divided nation, caught up in its faith in progress, yet still half-conscious of its poverty. For the Brooklyn *Eagle*, however, this was the great gilded age of confidence, beginning with the opening of its magnificent new building in 1891 and continuing for a few years after the celebration of its seventy-fifth anniversary in 1916. The *Eagle* itself, like the Brooklyn Bridge, became a symbol of its age and of its community; but, seen against the backdrop of its own time, the clear image of prosperity, stability, and upper-class respectability projected to turn-of-the-century Brooklynites now seems narrow and unreal.

In contrast to a larger metropolitan culture torn by philosophical, class, ethnic, and religious factions, the *Eagle*'s Brooklyn remained stable, homogeneous, business-oriented, and Protestant. In its special issues and brief biographies of prominent citizens the *Eagle* promoted the image of a particular type of successful man, the professional man who promoted and personified long-established Brooklyn institutions, owned an imposing private home, belonged to the Crescent Club and the Riding and Driving Club, invested in real estate, and saw Brooklyn as the heart and capital of Long Island, if not the center of the universe. Between 1890 and 1920 the *Eagle* reached the height of its influence, won the praise of Joseph Pulitzer and Sir Pomeroy Burton, entered so fully into the life of the community with its various promotional schemes, and began to celebrate its own greatness. At the same time the *Eagle* began to lose touch with history. In a period of unprecedented demographic change, the *Eagle* remained overly devoted to Brooklyn's oldest families; in a period of labor upheaval, the *Eagle's* policy was that of Grover Cleveland. Its editors were slow to appreciate the extent to which Brooklyn was becoming a heterogeneous community, how the Brooklyn Bridge had irrevocably linked Brooklyn both economically and politically to New York, how old suburban nineteenth century Brooklyn was passing away. In its vision of Brooklyn's future it promoted a dream that was both grandiose and unrealistic in that it failed to realize Brooklyn's economic and political dependency on Manhattan and failed to foresee that the economic development of Long Island would result not from its Brooklyn "parentage" but from its transportation links with New York. Finally, in the 1916 Anniversary Pageant, the self-conscious *Eagle* showed that it was little by little losing touch with its own history by idealizing itself in a series of episodes depicting its publisher as the fulfillment of the gospel of success, as the individualistic self-made man.

American journalism had undergone another revolution by the time the *Eagle* entered its fiftieth year in 1891. It had entered its own Gilded Age. As a result of the expanding population, daily newspapers had increased from 387 to 2,326 and national daily circulation rose from 3.5 million to 15 million. Advertising revenue expanded four times, topping $95,000,000 by the end of the century.[5] While both New York and Brooklyn had made staggering progress in industrial expansion, mass transportation, and communications, New York was more than ever a city of contradictions, reminding one visitor of "a lady in ball costume, with diamonds in her ears, and her toes out of her boots," while Brooklyn retained its rustic isolation.[6]

At the same time, New York was forging more links with its neighbors. New elevated lines reached both northward and southward to Brooklyn. The Washington Bridge over the Harlem River was finished in 1889 and the Williamsburg Bridge, linking the lower East Side with Brooklyn, was to begin construction in 1896.

Henry Raymond, James Gordon Bennett, and Horace Greeley had been dead almost twenty years; Raymond died in 1869 and Greeley in 1872. The new leaders in journalism were now attuned to an age of quick wealth, westward movement, and fantastic mechanical improvements such as the new Hoe presses, and they were forming the distinguishing character of their institutions so solidly that they would endure well into the twentieth century. Urban social changes forced changes in journalistic techniques. City staffs expanded for more local coverage, the city editor became more important, and the managing editor directed overall news operations. It was the age of the reporter, with the more aggressive papers sending correspondents to Washington, Paris, and even Africa. This was the age when newspaper work became romantic—a "game" played by fast-living and often hard-drinking individualists. For the most part, the editor was a dramatic or flamboyant personality, while the publisher remained an invisible business manager, selling a commodity—news and advertising space. Finally, to advertise the stability of their enterprises, the Gilded Age publishers built imposing buildings as symbols of themselves and of their age.

Charles A. Dana revitalized the New York *Sun* in 1868, stressing the humor and pathos of the news and working for humanitarian reform. He established the *Evening Sun* in 1887 with the outstanding reporters Richard Harding Davis and Jacob A. Riis on his staff. Riis' son, Eddie, made his way to the *Eagle*. James Gordon Bennett, Jr., put the *Herald* through some difficult and exciting years as he attempted to direct his late father's paper from Paris, where he had fled to escape a scandal; in 1877 he had fought a duel with his fiancee's brother, who had accused him of insulting her while drunk. In 1883 Whitelaw Reid gained control of the *Tribune* and redirected it to appeal to the wealthy and educated. In 1895 the thirty-two-year-old William Randolph Hearst would come from San Francisco to buy the New York *Journal* and introduce a new level of successful sensationalism, and Adolph Ochs would take over the *Times* in 1896 and modernize that floundering paper.

Joseph Pulitzer was at the heart of the Gilded Age newspaper revolution and his influence on the *Eagle* was profound. He had left Hungary in 1864, "recruited" by an agent to serve in the Union Army. As owner of the St. Louis *Post-Dispatch* he had made his paper the "people's champion" with his campaigns against civic corruption. He bought the New York *World* from Jay Gould for $346,000, declaring, May 11, 1883:

There is room in this great and growing city for a journal that is not only cheap but bright, not only bright but large; not only large but truly Democratic—dedicated to the cause of the people rather than that of the purse potentates—devoted more to the news of the New than the Old World—that will expose all fraud and sham, fight all public evils and abuses.

The *World* called itself a "public service newspaper." It emphasized the pathetic, the sentimental, the sexual, and the sensational. It featured more illustrations, more extensive sports coverage, disaster coverage, and crusades in the public interest. It campaigned against the New York Central Railroad, against tolls on the Brooklyn Bridge, and, in 1885, for a pedestal on which Bartholdi's Statue of Liberty could stand. To celebrate his success, Pulitzer erected in 1890 the largest building in New York, topped it with a gilded dome, and published a special supplement of the *World* when it opened on December 10, 1890.

The *Eagle* had watched the growth of its New York counterpart. The conservative Van Anden and Hester families would not imitate the *World*'s sensationalism but called the *Eagle* a "public service" newspaper, and under the management of Harris Crist in the 1920s and during the ownership of Frank D. Schroth in the 1940s and 1950s the *Eagle* sponsored a long series of similar exposés and campaigns. The *Eagle* would never be as daring as the *World* in selecting the targets for its campaigns—it had its own sacred cows—nor did it try to catch the attention of the lower classes.[7]

In its fifty-first year, on the eve of moving into its magnificent new quarters at the corner of Washington and Johnson Streets, the *Eagle* was a prosperous, handsome, and dignified paper. *Ayer's Directory* does not have the *Eagle*'s circulation for 1891, but in 1898 it was 35,000 daily, 45,000 Sunday. This is approximately half the circulation of the *New York Times* and *Tribune* and 13,000 more than the *Brooklyn Citizen*, its closest rival. The daily paper had nine columns and was four to six pages long. The first page was still mostly ads, although each year more and more space was given to news. Page two consisted of editorials and news, page three was filled with classified ads and legal notices, and the last page had late news and feature stories such as "CUT TO PIECES" about the head and arms of a human being dropping from the train at the Twenty-Fifth Street Station.[8] The Sunday edition had seven columns and was twenty pages long. Each week there was a "BATCH OF LOCAL POEMS," two columns of verse from "Brooklyn Pens Which Are Tipped with the Divine Afflatus," two columns of news from New York City, two columns by "Rambler" on walks through Brooklyn, and feature stories on Brooklyn groups such as the Loyola Men's Club or "SWARTHY SONS OF ITALY, Thousands of Them Finding Homes in This City" with sketches of the "cream" of Brooklyn Italian society.[9] The Monday paper featured a very popular sermon page which in later years was mailed around the world. The most prominent Brooklyn clergyman, S. Parkes Cadman, called the *Eagle*'s sermon page "the most potent religious influence in America."[10]

In 1893 the *Eagle* published a giant book, *The Eagle and Brooklyn*, commemorating its move from its old physical plant on lower Fulton Street. The new plant housed three improved presses that would print, cut, and deliver four to twelve page papers at the rate of 24,000 per hour or twenty-four pages at 12,000 per hour. The new *Eagle* building, inspired by Pulitzer's, was a celebration of the spirit of a new Brooklyn and one of the best plants in the world.[11] The commemorative publication is a clue to the *Eagle*'s image of Brooklyn and to Brooklyn's vision of itself as the turn of the century approached. Its theme is that the history of Brooklyn and the history of the *Eagle* are so interconnected that it is impossible to think of one without the other. To the *Eagle* editors, Brooklyn was its past, its "prominent men," its institutions, and particularly its private clubs. These books set the pattern and provided the basic material for the many future *Eagle* special anniversary issues and the *Eagle*'s 1946 pamphlets on the history of Brooklyn's six original towns.

This history of Brooklyn, beginning with the first arrival of the Dutch, concentrated on pictures of old landmarks, old homes, river crossings, street scenes, and, finally, industrial growth. Every "leading citizen" merited a solemn portrait and at least a half-page biography, but all the biographies seem virtually interchangeable; each subject was a beloved family man, active in civic projects, and a member of several clubs. In fact, except for a few who were designated "men of their times"—probably because they did not fit in any other established category—the men were mostly departmentalized according to their private clubs.

St. Clair McKelway

The editorial genius of the *Eagle* during this period of its greatest influence was St. Clair McKelway.[12] Born of a Glasgow father and a Dublin mother in Columbia, Missouri, McKelway came east in 1853 where he settled in New Jersey and was educated by his grandfather in Trenton. He began his writing career at seventeen when he sent an article on Confederate sympathizers in Trenton to Horace Greeley's *Tribune*. After leaving the New Jersey State Normal School he studied law first in Trenton and then in New York under Judge Samuel Blatchford. He was admitted to the bar in 1866. McKelway wrote for the Trenton *Gazette*, the Trenton *True American*, the Trenton *Monitor*, and the New York *Tribune*, and in 1868 was the Washington correspondent for the New York *World* and Brooklyn *Eagle*. From 1870 to 1878 he did editorials for the *Eagle*, and in 1878 he went to Albany to edit the Albany *Argus*, where he became a friend and supporter of Grover Cleveland. He returned to the *Eagle* in 1884 and replaced Andrew McLean as editor in 1886. McLean, who replaced Kinsella when he died in 1884, was a thirty-six-year-old Scotsman who had worked his way to America in 1863 and had served on a monitor in the Navy till the end of the Civil War. An anti-machine Democrat like his predecessor, he rose through the ranks at the paper as a city editor and managing editor. He had a reputation as a brilliantly intellectual editorial writer.

McKelway was one of the last of a special group of four editors called the "personal journalists" which included Henry Watterson of the Louisville *Courier-Journal*, Samuel Bowles of the Springfield *Republican*, and Charles A. Dana of the *Sun*. They wrote the editorials themselves, shaped the policy, and shared in the ownership of the papers they edited. The *Eagle*, therefore, was an extension of his

St. Clair McKelway, the most influential *Eagle* editor and one of the last
nineteenth century "personal journalists."

personality. A popular after-dinner speaker, an outstanding rhetori-
cian with a long-sentence style that has been compared to Macaulay's,
a gigantic, bearded, forbidding figure, and a highly opinionated
individual, he is alleged to have once barked, "What's the use of
running a newspaper according to the rule? The fun of having a
newspaper is to run it just the way you please."[13]

To McKelway, journalism was a vocation to be served "as loyally,
bravely, unselfishly, intelligently, and honestly as church or state,
army or navy, university or a sovereign."[14] He was, in the words of
Oswald Garrison Villard, "a field marshall of the pen, he believed in
that strategy which deals the mightiest possible frontal blows at the
chosen point of attack." He once described a spokesman of a delega-
tion who called on President Harrison: "Clad in the frock coat of
statesmanship, he placed the right hand of oratory in the bosom of
spontaneity."[15]

Yet if McKelway was a great individual, he would not be considered socially enlightened or even liberal by today's standards or by
his truly progressive contemporaries. In a Labor Day editorial in 1901
he lamented that "Tender hearted old women in trousers are still
telling us that the laborer does not get his proper share of the fruits of
his toil," and suggested the true objects of Labor Day praise should be
J. P. Morgan, J. D. Rockefeller, and Nicholas Romanoff.[16] In an
extremely long and occasionally witty editorial, McKelway, who was
active in the education of Southern Negroes, defended the right of
President Theodore Roosevelt to have Booker T. Washington to
dinner at the White House but in another editorial he suggested that
the rise in lynching had been caused by the fact that "negroes," who
should go to Tuskagee, were reverting to savagery.[17]

Nevertheless, the combined influence of the new building and the
brilliant editor were said to have "civilized the *Eagle* staff." The new
more professional atmosphere also killed some of the "old spirit." In
the "old" *Eagle* men wrote their stories with pencils; now there were
enough typewriters to go around. Now everyone had his own desk and
phone, and reporters could interview by phone rather than hustle
around the city. In the "old" *Eagle* there were a number of men who
needed spelling lessons—especially on local trick words like Jorale-

mon Street—and a few heavy drinkers who would fake reports on sermons they slept through the day before. Now life was more businesslike and more competitive.[18]

Political Reform

In the tradition of Kinsella, who once referred to his political enemies as a "rogues gallery," McKelway once wrote of Brooklyn Mayor Daniel Whitney in 1887:

> The Mayoralty of Brooklyn is occupied, not filled, by an honest mass of trembling jelly. Its powers are exercised by a mixed confederacy of knaves, incapables and trimmers. The idea that the official incumbent is any other than a titular sense Mayor makes car horses laugh and citizens blush. Brooklyn owes its salvation from the grave evils to the Providence which has taken mercy on its own conditions.[19]

As Kinsella had his McLaughlin, so McKelway had his John V. McKane. McKane was the absolute ruler of Gravesend, population 8,000, which included a stretch of Coney Island where he established a building monopoly, constructing half the hotels and two-thirds of all the buildings in the area. Starting as constable in 1867, he became commissioner of common lands and town supervisor and had himself made chief of police. McKane, who did not smoke, drink, or gamble and who served as superintendent of the Methodist Sunday School, kept the veneer of a respectable Brooklynite while Coney Island, under his regime, became wide open for gambling, drunkenness, and prostitution. By 1893 he had become the favorite target of the crusading *Eagle* and *New York Times*.

McKane was also independent of the Kings County Democratic party, delivering his neighborhood to Cleveland in one national election and to Harrison in the next. When he refused to support the young Gravesend attorney William J. Gaynor, who was running with Republican and reform backing for State Supreme Court, Gaynor sent representatives to copy the town's election list, which everyone knew

McKane was padding.[20] McKane threw them in jail. When a group of merchants, lawyers, ministers, and doctors, armed with an injunction, returned on election day morning, McKane met them with a mob, told them "injunctions don't go here," and began battering them to the ground. The *Eagle* ran the story off the press that afternoon, crying "This is Civil War. It is successful rebellion. It is treason triumphant."

The Republicans carried the election overwhelmingly and an enraged citizenry, spurred on by the *Eagle*, organized to indict McKane and send him to Sing Sing. At a packed rally on a stormy night at the Brooklyn Academy of Music, McKelway, the principal speaker, said:

> For a city to demand in mass meeting the punishment of criminals is an unusual and startling proceeding. If it occurred on the Cherokee strip or in one of the silver mining towns, it would not be a surprise. . . . In Gravesend, where every natural prospect pleases, only man is vile. Politics and partisanship I cast aside until honesty is established, the purity of government assured, and the punishment of crime be made certain.[21]

Within two weeks of his indictment McKane was found guilty and sentenced to six years at Sing Sing. Interestingly, McKane's biography in *The Eagle and Brooklyn*, published when he was in jail, never mentioned his corruption; it praised his family life and love of the poor. Of McKane's contemporary, Hugh McLaughlin, *The Eagle and Brooklyn* said: "Despite the warring of factions, petty local discussion, national and state party differences, he maintains his place—a trusted leader; the structure of whose reputation and position is based upon the belief of both opponents and allies that 'his word is as good as his bond.' "[22]

The Eagle and Brooklyn's Future

Perhaps no issue during the age of McKelway engaged the *Eagle* more than the future of Brooklyn. *The Eagle and Brooklyn*, along with regular McKelway editorials, interpreted the Gilded Age as one of inevitable progress, and Brooklyn's sudden leap in industrial wealth and population was seen as a mere foreshadowing of its inevitable expansion. Paradoxically, Brooklyn's growth was accompanied by its political absorption when it was consolidated into Greater New York at the end of 1897. The *Eagle* fought consolidation tooth and nail but, seduced a bit by the imperialism of the time, it did not compromise its dream of a Brooklyn that would one day reach from the Brooklyn Bridge to Montauk Point.

In a December 20, 1891, editorial "Brooklyn of the Future," the editor answered the question of whether New Utrecht should be annexed affirmatively, assuring the readers that New Utrecht suffered from a few petty evils that would disappear as soon as the town joined Brooklyn:

> While Brooklyn already has large responsibilities to bear its citizens are eager to welcome every accession which enhances her dignity and increases the area of her territory. When New Utrecht, Flatbush, Flatlands and Gravesend are embraced on one side, and Long Island City, Jamaica, Newtown and the intervening settlements are taken in on the other, a fair beginning toward the upbuilding of the Brooklyn of the future will be made. Where the end will be cannot now exact definition from the wildest exercise of prophecy or speculation. Later generations need never be surprised to find a Brooklyn stretching far away into the new rural regions of salubrious and spacious Long Island. Who can deny that one day the confines of this town will be limited only by the shore line of the historic island on which it stands?[23]

This vision, of course, raises a number of questions. In what sense is Long Island an entity? The *Eagle*'s idea of Long Island did not acknowledge how much this area is open to non-Brooklyn influences, such as the Bronx, Connecticut, and the rest of New England. It did not foresee the bridges that would cross the East River up to Throgs Neck, relating Queens and Nassau to New York rather than to Brooklyn.

Actually, within seven years, another chain of events, founded on a different and perhaps more realistic philosophy of what Brooklyn was, was to move Brooklyn's future not toward the country but toward the metropolis.

Consolidation

Perhaps the turning point in the history of Brooklyn and the *Eagle* was what many Brooklynites have come to call "the great mistake," the consolidation of the borough into Greater New York in 1898. The consolidation was accomplished through the combined forces of Republican politicians, who were anxious to broaden their power base to offset the Democratic power of Tammany Hall, and the business interests who foresaw the economic benefits of belonging to the larger city. It was fought resolutely by the *Eagle*, an institution that depended on Brooklyn's often nostalgic sense of solidarity for its own prosperity. This psychological remoteness of Brooklyn gave the *Eagle* a unique strength; it was the chronicler of that mysterious person whom the New York *Tribune* described in a condescending editorial in 1892, "The Brooklyn Man."

> . . . Brooklyn men, as we see them about the town in the daytime, seem peaceable and quiet. When they get off this end of the Bridge in the morning there may be a slightly confused air about them, but this is apt to be seen in anyone when he arrives in a great city like New York. The Brooklyn man does not have that hunted look seen on the face of the dwellers in the suburban villages which comes from the ever gnawing fear that he is going to miss his train, for the Bridge stands always ready for the Brooklyn man's retreat at any moment. But when he mounts the Bridge at half-past five o'clock in the afternoon to return home, there is an air of resolution, with perhaps a touch of gameness, about him which convinces us that the Brooklyn man must be an entirely different sort of person at night in Brooklyn. Whether this comes from the night or from being in Brooklyn we cannot

say, since it is never possible to catch a Brooklyn man in town
after seven p.m. Anyhow, we believe that at home after sun-
down the Brooklyn man is a sly dog.[24]

The most spectacular change in Brooklyn leading up to consolidation was the astounding jump in population. Brooklyn was a village
of 3,000 when Henry Murphy was born in 1810. By the end of the
Civil War the population had risen to 300,000, and grew by another
100,000 in the next five years. When Murphy died in 1882, Brooklyn was a metropolis of more than half a million. By 1890 the
population had risen to 806,343, with 261,700 citizens of foreign
birth. By the turn of the century, when Brooklyn included all of
Kings County, the figure had risen to 1,166,582.

The population rise was accomplished by a building boom in every
section of the city. The *Tribune* painted a vivid picture of the new
bustling city hall district in 1893:

> Fulton Street is entirely transformed. . . . Hotels, newspaper
> offices, theatres, business stores, and other places have grown up
> as if by magic and in a night, possessing all the advantages of
> space, of comfort, and of convenience, very little if at all inferior
> to similar places on the New York side of the river. It is an
> endless succession of wonders which greets the eye.[25]

The neighborhoods were also changing as a result of shifts in the
population. Many more private homes went up; more were terra cotta
and yellow brick, fewer were brownstones. New businesses, banks,
and real estate and insurance companies moved into the Heights,
driving some of the older families to the newly fashionable Park
Slope. Remote Greenpoint was taking on a more urban character,
with only South Brooklyn retaining its rustic air.

Along with new homes, Brooklyn gained new parks. The *Eagle*
editorials had attacked the city commission for neglecting small
parks, and it had opposed the building of Prospect Park, but it had
proud words when it was completed: "When our Park is regarded in

connection with the great boulevard running to the sea, it is beyond all question the finest pleasure ground on the Continent.[26]

By the end of the century Brooklyn was the fourth largest industrial city in the United States. With its long shoreline and superior warehouse facilities, the Brooklyn waterfront could handle four times as much shipping as New York. With its 10,583 factories employing 109,292 workers, however, the city was not free from social and industrial unrest. In the Knights of Labor strike against the trolley companies in 1895, there were frequent armed clashes between militia and strikers, wires were torn down, and cars were derailed. Soldiers used bayonets against the crowds and one man was shot. The entire press, except the Brooklyn *Citizen*, was pro-management.[27]

The great increase in public transportation facilities that had accompanied the opening of the East River Bridge in 1883 was also a mixed blessing. The elevated lines were ugly and could cast once bright neighborhoods into shadow. By 1892 Brooklyn had reached its saturation point on street railroads. It was estimated in 1895 that since their adoption the trolleys had killed an average of one person a week. Public irritation with the elevated lines shows up in this bit of verse the *Eagle* printed in the February 22, 1891, issue:

> Blinded visions, ruined dresses
> Broken heads and thoughts of—well,
> Are among the mad distresses
> Wrought upon the Brooklyn "L".
>
> But we must have rapid transit
> In this time at any cost.
> Take a walk—but if you chance it
> Count yourself among the lost.

The movement to destroy the autonomy of Brooklyn—and the end of the *Eagle* as well—can be traced back to 1833. The village of Brooklyn applied for a municipal charter that year and the New York State Legislature refused the petition because of the opposition of some New Yorkers who felt that the two communities would inevitably be joined together and that to encourage Brooklyn then was to postpone the creation of the larger city. Brooklyn got its charter in 1834, but only against New York protest.[28]

The antagonism engendered during the debates in the State Legislature over Brooklyn's incorporation kept growing. One of the irritants was that New York kept Brooklyn in a subservient position with regard to its rights to use the East River for commercial purposes. New York City claimed that on the basis of the Cornbury and Dongan charters it had first rights to establish and maintain ferry service, with exclusive authority over the East River to the low water mark on the Brooklyn side. In 1842, as a way of breaking New York's monopoly, Brooklynites, urged on by *Eagle* editorials, agitated for the State Legislature to establish an independent board of commissioners to regulate river traffic, landing places, and wharves. The *Eagle* also contended that the New York corporation operating the ferries had no right to run them at a profit but should put the money back into improved facilities or lower fares. When the New York councilmen advertised in 1844 for bids to operate the ferries, the *Eagle* cried that Long Island was now "entirely at the mercy of the mammoth city which lies opposite to us, the narrow views and selfish interests of whose up-town landholders induce them to throw every obstacle which they can in the way of our growth."[29]

Brooklyn citizens held a series of mass meetings and sent Judge John Greenwood, the original namer of the *Eagle*, to Albany to lobby for the independent commission, resolving that:

> The act of residing in the city of Brooklyn, instead of the city of New York, violates no one of the Ten Commandments, and is innocent in law and in morals; and is not, therefore, a crime which the municipal authorities of the city of New York should be allowed to visit with a fine and penalty.[30]

The Legislature did establish the commission, but the dispute continued for ten years over who had the right to establish new ferries and whether or not Brooklyn's boundary line extended to the middle of the East River. Meanwhile, Brooklynites and New Yorkers were each offering proposals for both tunnels and bridges to link the cities, although the Long Island *Star* warned, "New Yorkers are extremely anxious to take us into their embrace. We are old and strong enough to look out for ourselves, and so long as we can keep well regulated and expeditious ferries we are satisfied."[31]

Talk of union was revived when Brooklyn annexed Williamsburg in 1854. In 1857 Henry C. Murphy conjectured, "It requires no spirit of prophecy to foretell the union of New York and Brooklyn at no distant day. The river which divides them will soon cease to be a line of separation, and bestrode by a colossus of commerce, will prove a link which will bind them together."[32] What Murphy was predicting for Brooklyn was to be the pattern for all the great American cities. Cities like Chicago, Boston, and Philadelphia were growing by annexing their contiguous areas which had been made dependent on them by improved transportation.

The consolidation drive picked up impressive momentum in 1870 when it gained a leader, Andrew Haswell Green. He was a full-time reformer and a member of the New York Park Board who came to be known as the "Father of Greater New York." Green issued a voluminous report containing a comprehensive program of public works in which he argued that since public improvements require administration of the entire metropolitan district the surrounding territory of New York should be put under one administration. This, he said, would improve the maintenance of the water and sewage systems, better regulate the navigation of adjacent waters, and facilitate the bridging of the intervening rivers. Furthermore, he noted, many people worked in New York without contributing to the cost of governing it. Other proponents of the union argued that consolidation would improve the government of both cities, lower taxes, enhance realty values, and accelerate urban growth.

The completion of the Brooklyn Bridge intensified the struggle and, to a great extent, marked its turning point. However, the *Eagle*, which had published a daily column on the bridge to encourage its completion, and had gloried in the opening of the bridge, was unwilling to live with its consequences. "We are getting on in years;

are 'too set in our ways' to think of changing. We might have thought of matrimony once, but now it is utterly out of the question."[33] When the New York Chamber of Commerce argued for consolidation in its annual report in 1888, the *Eagle* replied in its tired voice, "We have our own little imperfections to contend with and find the struggle sufficiently arduous without incurring the extra labor, expense, and anxiety which annexation would involve."[34]

The *Eagle*'s stand had some support from its rival, the *Standard-Union*, who editorialized April 18, 1889, that Brooklynites ". . . will hold to their independence and take care of themselves . . . will not allow themselves to be overwhelmed by the horde of plub-ugly politicians that control New York, as they would be if consolidation took place."[35] However, the next year Green sent the Legislature a long memo arguing the inevitability of consolidation:

> It is not a question of policy or of plans but of progress of the law
> of evolution, no less natural . . . than the meeting of the waters
> which, fed by inexhaustible streams first find lodgments in
> separate places among various depressions of the surface, but
> rising higher with the growing volume surmount the barriers of
> division and became one.[36]

On May 8, 1890, Governor David B. Hill signed the bill creating a commission "to inquire into the expediency of consolidating the various municipalities in the state of New York occupying the several islands in the harbor of New York." The commission, with Green himself as president, unanimously favored what had been called the inevitable union, and they drew up a bill which was forwarded to the legislature but delayed in committee. For the next four years pro- and anti-consolidation forces slowly mounted their propaganda drives. New Yorkers were motivated most of all by the pride they expected would come from being citizens of the greatest city in the world, while the Brooklyn consolidationists, many of whom were large landholders and real estate dealers, argued the economic blessings of union. One example is the 1891 pamphlet by Brooklyn lawyer Edward C. Graves, *How Taxes in Brooklyn Can Be Reduced One-Half*.

Brooklyn's taxes were high, he claimed, because it was primarily a residential area, while the great taxpaying properties, such as railroad lines and steamship companies, were in New York. The following year the Friends of Greater New York, numbering anywhere between 25,000 and 41,000, organized into a Consolidation League and began publishing more pamphlets and holding more public meetings in an attempt to build up enthusiasm in a campaign marked more by apathy than by strong feelings. Their summary statement with their twelve reasons for union was printed up on a card in English and German and circulated widely in the fall of 1894:

1. A reduction of one-half in our tax rate.
2. Increase of capital for investment and lower interest on mortgage.
3. Better and cheaper homes in our great vacant spaces.
4. Increase of employment for labor and increased wages.
5. Increase of prestige for all commercial and financial institutions.
6. A healthy stimulus to all branches of business.
7. Increased social prestige and civic pride in the Greater New York.
8. A comprehensive system of public improvements, such as bridges, tunnels, water works, parks, roadways, and means of rapid transit.
9. A new charter and better safeguards for good government.
10. New life and vigor resulting from harmony. . . .
11. Leadership of American cities for Greater New York.
12. Finally the honor and dignity of the first city of the world.[37]

The *Eagle* remained the only paper unalterably opposed to consolidation on any terms. Like the consolidationists, the *Eagle* saw Brooklyn's wealth as tied to the value of its real estate, but it was convinced land values could be increased without political union. The editorial, "Brooklyn and the Future," October 5, 1897, explained how the paper had mailed *Eagles* to 7,000 rich men encouraging them to buy property in Brooklyn. According to the *Eagle*, the "twelve reasons" were "twelve frauds" and should secure the defeat of consolidation, not its adoption. Every day the *Eagle* ran a leader on its editorial page:

> Brooklyn is a city of homes and churches.
> New York is a city of Tammany Hall and crime government.
> Rents are twice as cheap in Brooklyn as in New York and
>   homes are to be bought for a quarter of the money.
>   The price of rule here is barely more than a third
>   of what it is in New York.
> Government here is by public opinion and for the public
>   interest. If tied to New York, Brooklyn would be
>   a Tammany suburb, to be kicked, looted and bossed
>   as such.
> Vote against consolidation now and let the speculators
>   wait till a better time, when New York will offer
>   something like fair terms.

As the purely advisory 1894 plebiscite which Green had requested approached, the main anti-consolidation argument remained sentimental; Old Brooklyn deserved devotion and loyalty. Nostalgia lost, but by a hair. The vote in the proposed area of Greater New York showed a 44,188 majority for consolidation, with New York City voting 96,938 for and 59,959 against. Brooklyn voted 64,744 in favor with 64,467 against—a margin of 277 votes. There was some surprising support for union in the older wards.[38]

In 1895 Senator Lexow introduced a bill to permit the Green commission to draw up a Greater New York charter. By now Brooklynites were divided into three factions: the League of Loyal Citizens and the *Eagle* opposed consolidation in any form, the Consolidation League and the *Citizen* favored union under any circumstances, and Mayor Charles A. Schieren and the *Union* recognized their city's absorption into New York as inevitable but wanted to work out the details first. The *Eagle* had counted on powerful Republican politician Thomas C. Platt holding out against the "inevitable," but Platt cracked when he saw his opportunity to pull a power coup by reviving the legislative commission system in Greater New York with Republicans in key positions. He switched to the consolidationists and wrote an angry letter to Governor Levi P. Morton in January 1896 threatening that if the governor did not abandon his "dishwater" position on Greater New York, Platt would not help Morton become President of the United States.

In May 1896, the Governor signed the Legislature's Greater New York bill creating the charter commission and setting the date for establishing the unified city as of January 1, 1898. The commission worked hard all that summer and sent their final charter to the Legislature on February 19, 1897, giving Brooklyn very good terms, providing that taxes and valuations would be equalized for the entire territory of the proposed city. Brooklynites were overjoyed, while New York taxpayers cried in anguish. New York Mayor William L. Strong, although he had voted for the charter and was a commissioner, opposed it as Mayor, not because of the tax issue but because he was dissatisfied with its failure to provide a single legislative governing chamber, a single police commissioner, and a Mayor with unrestricted power of removal. The Governor signed the bill and independent Brooklyn was gone.

The *Eagle* prepared Brooklyn for its passing with funereal editorials, assuring Brooklynites old Brooklyn would not change and reaffirming Brooklyn's moral superiority to New York.[39] Nevertheless, the *Eagle* assumed the responsibility of celebrating consolidation with a special issue of the paper, a beautiful seventy-three page *Consolidation Number*, January 1, 1898, crammed with small print on glossy paper in a magazine format. *Eagle* historians detailed the history of the consolidation movement but, much like the mammoth *Eagle and Brooklyn* which had been published five years before, the whole editorial thrust of the issue seemed to be to boost the civic pride of a community entering a period of self-doubt. Much of the editorial content was centered on Brooklyn's glorious past—histories of the settlements of the old county towns, biographies of famous Brooklyn politicians, histories of the various clubs, the glories of Brooklyn real estate, the old-time theater, the waterfront, the bridge, and the cemeteries and churches. There were biographies of judges and lawyers and leaders in medicine and a list of the city's twenty-five mayors from George Hall through the "brilliant" Henry C. Murphy and "magnificent" Seth Low to Frederick W. Wurster. A gigantic fold-out illustrated map of Brooklyn was an artist's attempt to capture the city at its best and last.

On New Year's Eve Mayor Wurster and five of his predecessors held open house in the City Hall. In a spirit of forced gaiety, they held a meeting in the common council chamber to hear St. Clair McKelway deliver the principal "hail and farewell" oration. It was long. The editor began with a few light-hearted remarks, then went on to remind the borough how it had been free from judicial and police corruption, riots against the poor, and the corrupt mayors. The New York City charter, he said, had been inspired by Brooklyn. His last words were a call to the borough to retain its individuality: "And, therefore, not farewell to Brooklyn, for borough it may be, Brooklyn it is. Brooklyn it remains, and Brooklynites we are."[40]

As the City Hall clock struck midnight the American flag was lowered and reappeared in a few seconds, joined by the municipal ensigns of the two cities that had just become one.

The "Brooklyn Spirit"

Having lost its own war against New York, the *Eagle* turned its attention to Brooklyn's role in America's war against Spain. So that its readers, particularly the children, could join at least vicariously in the conflict, the *Eagle* published a giant colored naval warfare map with tiny ship models. The youngsters could cut out the models, place them on the map, and follow the ship movements and naval battles as the *Eagle* reported them.

In its January 1, 1899, *Peace Number*, the *Eagle* published a magazine-sized complete history of the Spanish-American War, with the same wealth of detail, careful research, and excellent illustrations that distinguished its special editions on the Brooklyn Bridge and Consolidation. Just as the *Eagle* had zealously recorded Brooklyn's contribution to the war, so did it make every effort to report the *Eagle*'s role. The paper was particularly proud of its own tents set up in the Long Island training camps, Camp Black on Hempstead Plains, where "men went forth lusty of limb and hefty of heart," and Camp Wikoff on Montauk, where they returned "shattered in spirit and broken of body." During the war, coverage of the camps stressed their homelike atmosphere and the presence of the *Eagle* tent. On May 6, 1898, an *Eagle* correspondent wrote:

> Yesterday afternoon the new tent of the *Eagle*'s headquarters at Camp Black flung its big banners to the breeze, welcoming the Brooklyn soldiers and their visitors to the cozy interior. It is not only the largest and most comfortable tent in camp, but commands a fine view of the white, cone-shaped canvas homes of the boys which stretch in a bright line for over a mile and a half on Hempstead Plains . . . the tent is white and occupies a considerable area in comparison to those surrounding it . . . yesterday the interior was decidedly picturesque and looked like the stage setting of a war drama. Four cots were ranged along the back, the sleeping quarters of the *Eagle* correspondents . . . Big swaying lamps will be put in in a short time, so that the officers who may wish to glance at the war news, may come in at night and take advantage of the files, where not only the *Eagle*, but the weeklies may be had. . . . Just as soon as the visitor steps from the train and looks toward newspaper row, the big red banners and the large, white square tent attract his attention.

In its history of the war the *Eagle* praised its own relief work at Camp Wikoff: "No institution was so widespread in its endeavors and certainly no work was received with more appreciation than that of the *Eagle*." With its two large tents the *Eagle* had provided a place where troops would be welcome and had given them material with which to write letters, 60,000 sheets of the "most tasteful" *Eagle* stationery. In the *Eagle* tent the boys wrote three hundred letters a day—one fourth of the total letters leaving the camp—granting the *Eagle*, of course, considerable free advertising. The tents were also information bureaus and centers where lost family members could be reunited with one another. The *Eagle* tent staffs distributed gifts sent to the troops and also sent around stenographers to write letters home for sick soldiers—on *Eagle* stationery.

As the *Eagle* went on to its seventieth year, it returned again to the themes it had developed earlier under McKelway's influence—the definition of the "Brooklyn Spirit," the rebuilding of the city on a grander scale, and the extension of Brooklyn into Long Island. By staying with these themes the *Eagle* could reassure Brooklynites that their community had not changed radically and that it still had a great destiny.

By its seventieth anniversary in 1911, the *Eagle* had only partly accepted the fact of consolidation. It had not yet incorporated the joining of Manhattan and Brooklyn into the overall interpretation of Brooklyn history which had inspired *The Eagle and Brooklyn*; Brooklyn's history was one of inexorable growth and expansion. Since the *Eagle*'s founding the borough's population had risen from 36,233 to 1,634,351, the number of churches had increased from thirty to 339, church membership had gone from 10,000 to 590,890, and now there were 164 schools rather than twelve. There was every reason to believe that this growth pattern would continue. Therefore, the city had grown in population and industrial might and would continue to do so, but it must and would retain its unique residential and religious character in spite of what rapid growth and industrialization were doing to other cities.

The October 26, 1911, special anniversary issue followed the standard anniversary issue format which the *Eagle* retained with only minor variations until it died. Special features praised real estate as the basis for Brooklyn's prosperity, the borough's fine school system, and the many clubs which fostered the neighborhood spirit in the big borough. There were biographical sketches of famous Americans of the Brooklyn bench and bar, representative women, leaders in church and charity work over the past seventy years, famous pulpit orators, and famous artists and musicians of Brooklyn, letters from famous men—such as Oscar Strauss—who read the *Eagle*; and, in a typical *Eagle* gesture of granting fame to the otherwise unknown, little notes on the hidden lives of elderly Brooklynites who had read the *Eagle* for fifty years or more.

This complacent pride in Brooklyn's present economic and social well-being gave the *Eagle* and its constituency a fundamental optimism with regard to the borough's future. In this spirit of confidence that so much of America shared prior to the First World War, the editors asked the "experts" what the next seventy years would bring. They forecast very few problems for Brooklyn. While New York would be overcome by dirt and grime, Suffolk County, 500,000 acres of gleaming fruit and vegetable gardens, would be an extension of Brooklyn, while in Far Rockaway and Port Washington 2,000,000 people would live without congestion. Joseph Caccavajo, an expert on the growth of cities, told the anniversary *Eagle* that in 1950 Brooklyn's population would exceed 7,000,000 and Queens would have 6,000,000. Montauk Point would be a mighty harbor linking Brooklyn to Europe and a harbor was to be built in Jamaica Bay at a cost of $100,000,000. Subways and trolleys were to crisscross Long Island like a spider web joining together a pleasantly balanced landscape of factories, workingmen's villages, bustling cities, and great estates with all roads leading back to Brooklyn, the great shopping center and mother city of it all.

The *Eagle* made its own attempt to define the elusive "Brooklyn Spirit." The spirit had its origins, the *Eagle* said, in the New England conscience and energy which had been softened by Dutch thrift and Dutch love of the comforts of home. This spirit manifested itself in the Brooklyn home and church, the "May Walk," and the pioneer movements for home rule and municipal government. "The Brooklyn that was, the Brooklyn that is, and the Brooklyn that is to be, have one increasing purpose, and one pervasive and persistent spirit. The purpose is home-building. In consolidation there was no merging with Manhattan . . . Rather than concede that Brooklyn was being swallowed up by Manhattan, the *Eagle* maintained that if any swallowing is to be done, Brooklyn is to be the swallower." The *Eagle* foresaw that with the proposed tunnel from 39th Street to Staten Island, Brooklyn would eventually be able to annex Richmond; Richmond people would not spend the extra half hour to go to New York to shop when they could get the same things cheaper in Brooklyn.

Yet there were "newcomers" in Brooklyn. Although the newcomers were not identified, there were heavy influxes of Jews and Italians at this time. The Williamsburg Bridge opened in 1903, and Jews poured across from New York's lower East Side. Williamsburg changed overnight from a fashionable resort, with hotels catering to such sportsmen as Commodore Vanderbilt and Jim Fisk, to an immigrant district. Old brownstones were broken up into multiple dwellings. At that time Brooklyn had nearly 400,000 Jews to Manhattan's 600,000; within twenty years Brooklyn's Jewish population was to approach a million. The Italian immigration continued till the First World War.[41] What would be their effect on the "spirit"? From the *Eagle*'s point of view the newcomer was obliged to adapt himself to the *Eagle*'s Brooklyn:

> It behooves every man who becomes a resident of this borough to do his share in maintaining and perpetuating the intangible atmosphere that has made Brooklyn different from any other community. If the newcomer, and, in these days his name is legion, will join his neighborhood civic association, become a member of the Brooklyn Institute, enter freely into the activities of whatever church of his faith is nearest to him, play tennis or golf in Prospect or Forest Park, and become a genuine old fashioned Brooklynite, he and his family will soon realize that there is no narrowness, and no exclusiveness about the Brooklyn spirit and that whoever seeks to make a quiet, decent, comfortable home here is assured of an honest Brooklyn welcome.[42]

As the newcomers claimed the old neighborhoods, the wealthier older inhabitants looked toward Long Island. Today it would be generally accepted that the suburbs have grown at the expense of the cities and that in its expansion Long Island, for example, had drained the best population, the financial resources, the very life out of its mother city, Brooklyn. Half a century ago, however, Brooklyn city planners did not foresee the development of Long Island as a threat. Long Island was the land of promise, the promise of a greater Brooklyn. Just as the original city of Brooklyn had grown by annexing its neighbors, they expected that the borough of Brooklyn would continue its own imperialism until it overshadowed its old enemy the isle of Manhattan in population, wealth, and power.

Forward, Long Island

In April 1912 the *Eagle* published a series of supplements on city planning called the *Development Series*, devoted to Brooklyn's participation in the "City Beautiful" movement, the new Brooklyn city plan, and the effects of city planning on the future of Brooklyn and Long Island.

Ironically, the *Eagle*'s promotion of Long Island real estate seems in the very long run to have had one of the same effects as its promotion of the Brooklyn Bridge—the end of the *Eagle*. Both events introduced such drastic changes into Brooklyn's culture that the old Brooklyn which the *Eagle* had dedicated itself to serving and preserving could no longer exist. As soon as the bridge had opened, horsedrawn delivery wagons loaded with Manhattan newspapers clattered across to give the *Eagle* competition and, more important, to get Brooklynites used to thinking like New Yorkers. The more the *Eagle* promoted Long Island the more it encouraged the exodus of its middle class and the loss of its own readership.

The creation of Brooklyn's city planning committee, which later became the Brooklyn Committee on City Plan, can be traced back to May 1909 and the opening of the city planning exhibition in the Twenty-Second Regiment Armory in Manhattan. Inspired by the exhibition, the *Eagle* and other Brooklyn citizens urged the mayor to establish an official city planning commission along the lines of the Municipal Art Commission, the city's art board. There was little official response, so Brooklyn's urban revitalization was left to individual initiative. Reverend Dr. Newell Dwight Hillis, the pastor of Beecher's old Plymouth Church, sailed to Europe in the summer of 1911 and toured London, Paris, Berlin, and Vienna to study the marvelous transformation that had taken place in these cities. He returned to tell his fellow citizens that Brooklyn had fallen behind the rest of the world in its architectural development. From his pulpit and

Brooklyn Public Library *Eagle* Collection

The *Eagle* float in the Queensboro Bridge Celebration, June 16, 1909.

in public forums he criticized Brooklyn's lack of planning, and he published an outline of his own suggestions for urban reform. Prominent citizens—engineers, businessmen, fellow clergymen, and lawyers—wrote letters to the *Eagle* in Hillis' support. Borough President Alfred E. Steers responded to the letters by calling a conference of interested citizens and the "Brooklyn Beautiful" movement was born.[43]

After two months of meetings the conference formed the Brooklyn Committee on City Plan and invited Daniel H. Burnham to visit Brooklyn. Burnham, president of the United States Fine Arts Commission, had been the Director of Works of the World's Columbian Exposition in 1893, and since that time he and his colleagues had become the giants of the City Beautiful movement. Under their inspiration, the centers of a number of American cities—Chicago, Washington, Cleveland, and Duluth—were being reconstructed with malls, wide thoroughfares, government buildings, clubs, banks, and libraries on a Roman Renaissance scale. Was the new Brooklyn to model itself on Renaissance Rome?

Burnham arrived the morning of December 16, 1911, and spent a rainy morning with prominent citizens touring the borough in an automobile, pausing for a formal luncheon at the Hamilton Club where about 180 representative citizens had gathered to hear his suggestions. He told them that Brooklyn had a splendid opportunity for city planning and that they should "start right." At the end of the luncheon the permanent planning committee was proposed and by January 30, 1912, the Brooklyn Committee on City Planning held its first formal meeting in the Montague Street Arts Building. Frederic B. Pratt was elected president of the development movement and Herbert F. Gunnison, *Eagle* Business Manager, was appointed to the Executive Committee. Others present and working for the plan included Colonel William Hester, his son William V. Hester, *Eagle* Secretary and Treasurer Andrew McLean, and Don C. Seitz.

The group chose Burnham's associate, Edward H. Bennett, to plan the future Brooklyn. Bennett had worked with Burnham in redesigning Chicago and San Francisco but he was coming to Brooklyn at a time when the vision of the "City Beautiful" inspired by the world's

Columbian Exposition was beginning to fade and the economic demands of the business interests were putting the "City Practical" in its place. The real possibility of planners remaking cities had dimmed. As Christopher Tunnard wrote in *The Modern American City*, American society was not ready to accept the constraints that planning might put on individual initiative. "It was . . . during the period 1910 to 1930 that the seeds of the City Practical were sown. Its wretched harvest was reaped in the 1930s in the era of Robert Moses, while the present generation is left gazing at the stubble, wondering what to do next."[44]

Some Brooklyn leaders were slow to accept the idea that an outsider could come in and redesign their home. On April 11, 1912, the Brooklyn Engineers Club invited the Committee on City Plan to listen to their objections. The city planning movement must go slowly, the speakers said. Brooklyn could not accomplish in a few years what European cities had taken centuries to do. Furthermore, the new plan should not be based on the ideas of an outside specialist who would map it out in a few days or weeks; it should be accomplished under the supervision of a man familiar with the history and character of Brooklyn and its civic needs. Richard Schermerhorn, Jr., read a paper insisting that a "City Practical" must come before a "City Beautiful" and that the subdivision of streets, parks, and open spaces were of first importance.[45]

The Schermerhorn address reflected some of the Brooklyn community's anxiety about social change and introduced themes which returned in later *Eagle* editorials and programs. The Brooklyn City Beautiful-City Practical movement was the germ of the *Eagle* Ten-Point Program of thirty years hence for the revitalization of a shaken urban community. Although Brooklyn had been joined to New York, it never ceased looking for something, some tangible project, that would restore its separate spiritual identity. In the minds of the "prominent citizens" and in the columns of the *Eagle*, the grand old Brooklyn might be reborn in the Plan—to put it boldly, in the construction of grand new thoroughfares and public buildings—and the dissipated spiritual enthusiasm of the people might be rekindled by striving together for this common goal.

The linotype room at the *Eagle* in 1904.

The *Eagle* city room in 1905.

Brooklyn Public Library *Eagle* Collection

The advertising and information desk at the *Eagle* in 1914.

Brooklyn Public Library *Eagle* Collection

Delivering the *Eagle* by horse wagon and truck.   Brooklyn Public Library *Eagle* Collection

Brooklyn Public Library *Eagle* Collection

In its many community service projects, the *Eagle* gave awards and trophies
for practically everything—bowling, swimming, sailing, music . . . and
spelling. Pictured here is "Winner of the Brooklyn *Eagle* Spelling Contest,
January 1914."

Schermerhorn's address, which the *Eagle* reported in great detail on April 12, 1912, urged both caution and modesty in the planning. He urged that first priority be given to the complex street system, to connect adequately the many small villages and towns which had been drawn together during the city's expansion, then the bridges, the gateways, to the city, and then the executive center and public buildings. He warned against too ambitious dreams and the imposition of ideas from non-Brooklynites who did not know the pulse of the city. The *Eagle* editorial response to the criticisms from the Engineer's Club was to support Bennett on the grounds that Burnham had recommended him and to endorse the suggestion that Bennett have a Brooklyn engineer as his associate.

The *Eagle Development Series* appeared in four sections: Brooklyn planning, waterfront and industrial, Long Island planning, and outdoor life. The attractive blending of grandiose futuristic drawings, brief biographies of leading businessmen, their dreams for the borough's future, and advertising stressed one theme: Brooklyn was a community of virtually unlimited natural and human resources, destined to take on a new face, a new physical grandeur that would reflect the spiritual quality of the community's life and character.

Edward H. Bennett's own proposals gave priority to the building up and beautification of central points in the city's circulatory system and the establishment of monuments or parks at the junctions of Atlantic, Flatbush, and Fourth Avenues, Broadway, Graham, and Flushing Avenues, and Fulton Street and Flatbush Avenue. Brooklyn Heights should remain the most attractive residential area. He did not share the insistence of some men that the Brooklyn Bridge terminal should be transformed into a magnificent plaza, nor was he as anxious as others for a great boardwalk at Coney Island; he didn't like the clattering noise. However, he did want a road along the waterfront and he looked forward to the day when airships would cross the Atlantic and need an airport to land at in Brooklyn.

The *Eagle* also proposed constructing a one hundred and twenty mile Central Island Boulevard running from the terminus of Eastern Parkway all the way out across the flat lands of Long Island to the tip of Montauk Point where the "waves of old ocean roll in with tremendous force and beat upon the crag on which the lighthouse is situated." This road would reopen Long Island to dairy farming and milk trucks could hurry in fresh milk and cream to the children of Brooklyn. Two other boulevards would run out to the Point along the North and South shores of the Island, and Peconic Bay would become an international port, the Gateway to America.

The articles on business conditions pointed out that the completions of the Panama Canal and New York State Barge Canals would bring new capital to the port of Brooklyn, the completion of the new Interborough subway would link Brooklyn with both Manhattan and the Bronx, and the new BRT lines to Manhattan would boost real estate values considerably. Most Brooklynites still lived in the two-story houses with basement apartments and paid rents of forty dollars a month. A great manufacturing center was springing up along Atlantic Avenue and more jobs were available in the growing waterfront sections. A new eighth ward market was projected for the warehouse area near Gowanus Bay, and Bennett suggested that the roofs of the warehouses could be transformed into playgrounds where, said the *Eagle*, "cool breezes from harbor and bay could make the children comfortable on the hottest days. It would equal in health-giving ozone a water trip to Coney Island or the Rockaways."[46]

Finally, the *Development Series* made it clear to what extent the *Eagle* considered itself a Long Island newspaper and how much the *Eagle* was geared to the wealthy upper classes. The *Series* tended to reinforce their ideas of the good life through its extensive coverage of their yachting, cricket, golf, mansions, and palatial bungalows. Not one illustration in the 120 pages indicated that any part of Brooklyn was anything but beautiful.

Notes

[1] Henry Steele Commager, *The American Mind* (New York: Bantam, 1950), pp. 42-55; Harold V. Faulkner, *Politics, Reform and Expansions* (New York: Harper and Row, 1959), pp. 1-22.

[2] *The Education of Henry Adams* (Boston: Houghton Mifflin, 1961), p. 328.

[3]John Swinton, *Striking for Life: Or Labor's Side of the Labor Question* (Philadelphia: A. R. Keller Company, 1894), p. 297, quoted in Almont Lindsey, *The Pullman Strike* (Chicago: University of Chicago Press, 1942), p. 1.

[4]*Living Ideas in America*, Henry Steele Commager, ed. (New York: Harper and Row, 1964), p. 459.

[5]Sidney Kobre, *Development of American Journalism* (Dubuque: Wm. C. Brown Company, 1969), pp. 349-350.

[6]J. F. Muirhead, *The Land of Contrasts* (New York, 1898), p. 193, quoted in Arthur M. Schlesinger, *The Rise of the City, 1878-1898* (New York: Macmillan, 1933), p. 85.

[7]H. V. Kaltenborn's *Reminiscences* (Oral History Project: Columbia University, 1955) and interviews with Al Salerno, November 6, 1969, and Oliver Pilat, June 18, 1970.

[8]*Eagle*, January 2, 1891.

[9]*Eagle*, December 20, 1891.

[10]Charles Grant Miller, "The Making of Better Citizens in Brooklyn," *Editor and Publisher* (February 12, 1921): 14.

[11]One factor in the decline of newsprint during the 1870s was the advent of mechanical wood pulp. Previously, the only satisfactory newsprint paper had been made with rags, though there had been experimentation with star, bark, and wood. In 1869 the *Eagle* was reportedly printed on paper made from straw pulp. On June 22, 1870, the New York *World* announced that it was printed on paper made from 40 percent wood pulp and 60 percent rag. The *Eagle* followed the *World* and experimented with wood pulp (July 22, 1871). James M. Lee, *The Daily Newspaper in America* (New York: Macmillan, 1937), p. 102; Frank Luther Mott, *American Journalism: A History, 1690-1960* (New York: Macmillan Company, 1962), p. 402.

[12]The sources for McKelway's life are the repeated *Eagle* brief biographies which stress how the *Eagle* executives have risen from humble origins to positions of eminence; "St. Clair McKelway," a series of brief commemorative essays in *Proceedings of the Fifty First Convention of the State of New York* (1915); and DAB. I have also interviewed his former secretary, James Henle.

[13]Clipping in *Eagle* file in Brooklyn Public Library, n.d.

[14]*Outlook* 110 (July 28, 1915): 697.

[15]*Proceedings*, p. 37.

[16]*Eagle*, September 2, 1901.

[17]*Eagle*, September 2, October 20, 1901.

[18]Ornsbie, *Eagle*, October 26, 1911.

[19]*Eagle*, June 27, 1887.

[20]See Mortimer Smith's *William J. Gaynor: Mayor of New York* (Chicago: Henry Regney Company, 1951), pp. 23-25; also Louis Heaton Pink, *Gaynor: The Tammany Mayor Who Swallowed the Tiger* (New York: The International Press, 1931), pp. 69-79, and Harold Coffin Syrett, *The City of Brooklyn, 1865-1898* (New York: Columbia University Press, 1944), pp. 222-224.

[21]Pink, p. 78.

[22]Henry W. B. Howard, editor, *The Eagle and Brooklyn* (Brooklyn Eagle Press, 1893), p. 446.

[23]*Eagle*, December 20, 1891.

[24]*Tribune*, January 7, 1892.

[25]*Tribune*, May 7, 1893.

[26]*Eagle*, October 1, 1874. Kinsella had argued ten years before that for half of Brooklyn's population, New York's Central Park was closer than the proposed Prospect Park. "We believe it is the duty of the civic authorities not to suffer the Prospect Park scheme to go any further. We have, in Bath, Coney Island, and Sheepshead Bay very delightful places of public resort. All of them are, or very soon will be, easily accessible to the poorest class of our people. At those places the attraction of the country, with the benefits of sea bathing, are combined. For the wealthier classes, who desire to display their handsome equipages, the boulevards will afford an opportunity. Brooklyn cannot hope to compete with New York in gigantic parks. . . ." *Eagle*, January 15, 1864.

[27]Syrett, pp. 233-245.

[28]Ralph Foster Weld, *Brooklyn Village* (New York: Columbia University Press, 1938), pp. 39-53.

[29]*Eagle*, May 7, 1844; Jacob Judd, "A Tale of Two Cities: Brooklyn and New York, 1834-1855," *The Journal of Long Island History* 3 (Spring 1963): 23.

[30]In Judd, p. 25; *Eagle*, February 25, 1845.

[31]*Star*, January 2, 1850; Judd, p. 31.

[32]John Foord, *The Life and Public Services of Andrew Haswell Green* (New York, 1913), p. 178, in Syrett, p. 246.

[33]*Eagle*, June 5, 1884.

[34]*Eagle*, May 1, 1888.

[35]Syrett, p. 248.

[36]Foord, pp. 192-309, in Syrett, pp. 248-249.

[37]Syrett, p. 254.

[38]*Brooklyn's Relationship to the City of New York*, Princeton Surveys (Brooklyn: Brooklyn *Eagle*, 1942), pp. 5-6; Syrett, pp. 256-257.

[39]*Eagle*, October 19, 1897.

[40]*Consolidation Number*, pp. 68-71.

[41]*AIA Guide*, p. 318; Weld, *Brooklyn*, p. 110.

[42]*Eagle*, October 26, 1911.

[43]*Eagle, Development Series*, April 12, 1912.

[44]Christopher Tunnard, *The Modern American City* (Princeton: Van Nostrand, 1968), p. 67.

[45]*Eagle*, April 12, 1912.

[46]*Eagle, Development Series*, April 12, 1912.

6

TRIUMPHALISM:
THE *EAGLE*
AT SEVENTY-FIVE

St. Clair McKelway died in 1915. Up to the end, he remained a strong personality independent of publisher Hester. In 1912 he leaned a bit toward Taft and was later faithful to Woodrow Wilson who, according to Cleveland Rodgers, would have named McKelway ambassador to the Court of St. James if the President and the editor had not quarreled.[1] In the last years, his powers had begun to decline and his style was out of harmony with his time, but he remained active till the end, making no concessions to the mob, still writing grand sentences to an age of moviegoers that, as Villard said, wanted its language like it wanted its food, direct and plain.[2] Brooklyn was a little more conscious of itself as a changing community. Writing in the fashionable society weekly *Brooklyn Life*, Samuel B. Moore described, not without a note of sadness, how the city had passed from a homogeneous to a heterogeneous community.[3] Largely as a result of consolidation, real estate values had gone from $445,288,844 in 1890 to $8,049,859,914 in 1912, but Moore lamented that the days of two- and three-story houses when everyone knew his neighbors and when people lived in their houses for a long time were gone: "Nobody knows who lives next door and nobody is in the least concerned." Many of the old residences had been converted into flats or into two- or three-family houses. The old frame dwellings with green shutters and close-cropped lawns had been replaced by towering apartment houses with ugly fire escapes. The suburbs had grown and the old landmarks were disappearing.

The *Eagle*'s reputation was, in many respects, at its peak. Lord Northcliffe, following his 1905 visit to the *Eagle* plant, had dictated a statement to his hosts:

> The Brooklyn *Eagle* is the only non-metropolitan newspaper —and I use the phrase to distinguish it from the Manhattan dailies—that is known in England and France. Its editorial opinions have a wide circulation in both countries. In fact, in Paris you are known as Sir Brooklyn Eagle, as I presume you have seen. Its opinions are frequently quoted there, which is a rare thing in the case of an American paper.
>
> Your paper has a simply amazing hold on Brooklyn itself. I do not speak of it from a business standpoint, but I mean a hold on the minds and hearts of Brooklyn people, such as I have never seen anywhere else. In this respect it is unique, to my mind. The paper has an importance in foreign countries suggestive that it is the organ of a whole metropolis and not a part of it. I do not understand why it is not called the New York *Eagle* or simply the *Eagle*. Its editorial opinions are quoted all over the world, and its editor, Mr. McKelway, is a man who is known to newspaper men wherever our language is spoken.[4]

Joseph Pulitzer, the greatest journalist of his time, wrote to the *Eagle* just before he set out on his last voyage in 1911:

> This is what I sincerely feel about the Brooklyn *Eagle*:
> In the first essentials of any newspaper to be respected and be respectable—Integrity, Independence and Intellect—I consider it among the foremost newspapers of the Nation—and there are very few indeed I would call foremost.
> *Secondly*—As a newspaper emphasizing the word "News," it is absolutely unique, because I do not know of any journal in New York City or in the whole country using such lavish liberality in space and printing the local news of Brooklyn with such impar-

tiality, non-partisanship and broad variety.

Thirdly—On the editorial page, I find it courageous, non-partisan, able and free to attack abuses in both parties. My ideal. In specially difficult situations which test courage, character and capacity, I find the *Eagle* rises to the importance of the occasion and brings out great latent strength in reflecting the moral sense and public opinion of the community, which it largely creates.[5]

There was also a turning point in the institution's history as the passing of McKelway and the aging of Colonel William Hester, in reality two men of the nineteenth-century *Eagle*, allowed for the emergence of new personalities. Two important new figures, Secretary and Treasurer William V. Hester and the brilliant Business Manager Herbert F. Gunnison remained for the most part in the background.

Hester, the only son of Colonel Hester, had come to the *Eagle* as a clerk in the business department in 1881. He was a member of the Brooklyn, Hamilton, Nassau County, Metropolitan, Brooklyn Riding and Driving, Brooklyn Civic, and Piping Rock Clubs and many other charitable and social organizations. Gunnison came to the paper in 1882 as a reporter. After three years as an Albany correspondent, he became editor of the *Eagle* Almanac which was published from 1896 to 1929. He was a graduate of St. Lawrence University, where his brother became president, and kept an active association with that school. He was one of the founders of the American Newspaper Publishers Association and was one of those most responsible for the *Eagle*'s various business enterprises, such as the Eagle Warehouse and Storage Company and the *Eagle* travel bureaus and world tours.

The *Eagle*'s public face was presented by McKelway's successor, Arthur M. Howe, who had been helping McKelway with editorials since 1902, and the irascible and electrifying managing editor Harris M. Crist.[6] Crist, who joined the *Eagle* as an office boy in the Washington bureau in 1893 and had built his reputation as a political reporter at the Conference of Peace Commissioners of Russia and Japan at Portsmouth, New Hampshire, in 1905, seems to have been the dominating personality at the *Eagle* until his retirement in 1935.

Scottish Highlanders marching past the Paris office of the *Eagle* in the Great
Allied Parade of August 1916.

As one man said, he was the *Eagle*'s "soul." Crist was remembered for his immaculate attire, his pince-nez glasses, his magnificent white hair, and ruddy complexion, but he was not remembered for his good disposition. As one *Eagle* veteran recalls, Crist did not like anybody. He reserved a special rough manner for job applicants, particularly those who had gone to journalism schools. Perhaps indifferent to the fact that Pulitzer had once made McKelway a Columbia Journalism School trustee, Crist told a young graduate in 1926 to "Go over to Manhattan and get a job . . . any kind of job . . . and when you forget all that you learned at Columbia, come back and see me."[7] Meanwhile, Crist maintained a reputation as a crusader, although the targets of his crusades were more likely to be minor figures than the real power structure of Brooklyn. Like Kinsella and McKelway he was anti-machine and anti-corruption, but some of his contemporaries recall that his vision and his righteous anger were limited by other factors: he was a member of the Brooklyn Club, a Republican, and a Protestant. I. Kaufman, who was at the *Eagle* from 1919 to 1922 and 1925 to 1955, said Crist told him a Negro would not be qualified to be an *Eagle* reporter because he couldn't cover the Brooklyn Junior League Ball. Crist also told Kaufman that there were no Jewish names on the Society page because there were no prominent Jews in Brooklyn. Oliver Pilat, who was there from 1936 to 1937, confirms that the old *Eagle* was anti-Semitic. He also said that the way to get a job under Crist was to get to Crist himself and "show audacity."[8]

Kaltenborn and Rodgers

Meanwhile, two important young men just beginning careers at the *Eagle* were Hans Von Kaltenborn and Cleveland Rodgers. Kaltenborn, more than anyone else, became the *Eagle*'s public personality, so much so that he himself came to believe that the *Eagle* was famous because he had gotten his start there. Young Kaltenborn had met McKelway's son in Paris in 1900 and had applied for an *Eagle* job, which he did not accept, on the strength of that friendship.[9] Rather than work full-time he learned typing and stenography and did night assignments at eight dollars a week keeping track of prices on the New York Stock Exchange. Although the *Eagle* did not usually pay for poetry, Kaltenborn got five dollars for his imitation of Southey's "Cataract of Lodore," inspired by his impressions of the crowds at the Brooklyn Bridge:

> From the buildings that rise till they reach to the skies
> From twentieth floors and department stores,
> They start, run and stop before a bright window,
> Then suddenly starting again are departing.[10]

In 1903 he won an increase to twelve dollars a week, but unlike most newsmen of his day he was convinced he needed formal education. He left the *Eagle* for Harvard in 1905, then traveled through Europe and the West Indies as tutor to Vincent Astor for a year after graduation. Returning to the *Eagle* in 1910, he got a job as drama critic at forty dollars a week. In one review he panned *Trail of the Lonesome Pine* and was infuriated when the producers lifted a few favorable lines out of context and printed them as part of the promotion. Kaltenborn reprinted his critical comments and the theater operators retaliated by dropping their *Eagle* advertising. Hester, who thought plays should be reported and not evaluated, gave Kaltenborn very little support.[11] Eventually he rose to editorial writer, assistant managing editor, and associate editor. He recalled the *Eagle* as the "proud aristocrat" among New York papers, a big city paper run along small town lines, trying to balance local, New York City, and national news and giving international news the least space of all.

> . . . I did feel at that time that there were too many sacred cows around the place. Certain things you couldn't say because Colonel Hester was interested in certain corporations, and we were told to be careful. Colonel Hester was the president of the firm and he had diverse financial interests. He might also have a particular interest in this or that person. Once in a while it concerned someone in the theater or music world. There were always a few sacred cows kicking around. We had to be on the look out for them, and I didn't like it.[12]

After a brief stint in Paris in 1914, he was brought back to the Brooklyn office where he conducted current events lectures and war talks to crowds as large as five hundred. In 1915 he began the famous *Eagle* tours, conceived by Gunnison as a promotion stunt to attract resort advertising, that from 1915 to 1925 would send adventurous bands of wealthy Brooklynites to Alaska, Hawaii, the Grand Canyon, Brazil, and the Old World.

The *Eagle* made good money on the tours. The profit for the 1925 European trip was $15,000, of which Kaltenborn demanded and got $5,000. The history of one tour, 1920, is an attempt to relate Brooklynites to a larger, sometimes mysterious world and return them unscathed and unchanged to their homes. The history also exemplifies many of the characteristics that have always distinguished the *Eagle*: its attention to individuals and their daily activities whether the activities themselves are noteworthy or not, unflagging optimism, the tendency to interpret as many events as possible according to their relationship to Brooklyn, the practice of memorializing *Eagle* events with plaques and songs, and the love of flattering statistics. In thirty days the 119 tourists and thirteen officials, including two physicians, a geologist and librarian, a barber, and a maid, covered 8,098 miles, visited six national parks and monuments and forty-three cities, and suffered no accidents or illnesses and nary a rainy day.

The tourists, most of them heavyset, prosperous looking, middle-aged citizens who seldom removed their topcoats or loosened their ties, called themselves "Eaglets" and seem to have survived a month on the railroad train singing original song parodies and joking with one another with hardly an interruption in their sustained joy —except perhaps for Mrs. Florence Gunnison of 1123 Albermarle Road, Brooklyn, who was saved from the fangs of a rattlesnake while exploring the remnants of the old Indian Village in the Arizona Casa Grande National Monument.

Throughout the trip they chanted the *Eagle* cheer:

> Eaglets, Eaglets, Eaglets, we!
> Out on a jolly jamboree!

E. von der Lancken sketch, 1928, Brooklyn Public Library *Eagle* Collection

H. V. Kaltenborn, one of the *Eagle*'s most famous alumni.

Are we happy? Well, I guess
Brooklyn, Brooklyn, Yes, Yes, Yes![13]

Cleveland Rodgers had come to the *Eagle* in 1906 after spending his youth as a printer wandering through Southern cities from Greenville, South Carolina to Palm Beach, Florida.[14] He had always wanted to be a playwright, and when he arrived in New York he was led on by the Schuberts to write two plays, *The Legal Frolic* and *The Legend of the Hills*. Ironically, they are both about labor-management conflict and were written to resolve his own anti-union feelings stemming from a fight during a strike in his youth. *The Legend of the Hills* ends with workers and employers getting together to save themselves from anarchy. Rodgers was to leave the *Eagle* in sadness during the first strike of the New York Newspaper Guild.

Rodgers remembered old McKelway sitting on a high stool in the composing room rewriting editorials in the galleys and inviting people at random to lunch with him at the old Clarendon Hotel, where he would have the waiter bring him crunched crackers and milk and send the crackers back if they were not crunched enough. Rodgers had also lunched with Howe, who ate bear meat stuffed with chestnuts and drank several kinds of wine. Rodgers, like Kaltenborn, had been allowed to try drama criticism, but, along with Alexander Woolcott of the *Times*, he had been banned from Schubert theaters for unfavorable reviews. As a result, the *Eagle* lost much of its Manhattan theater advertising for many years.

Colonel Hester

These were young men, and the *Eagle*, on the eve of its seventy-fifth birthday, did not yet belong to them. It belonged to old Colonel Hester, whose life was about to be immortalized in the *Eagle*'s anniversary pageant.[15]

William Hester grew up in Poughkeepsie and was educated at Rhinebeck Academy. In 1852 at sixteen, he came down the Hudson on the old steamboat *Rip Van Winkle* with his uncle Isaac to launch his career in the world. Sensitive to the charge of nepotism, he worked as a typesetter until he was promoted to the front office as clerk in 1857. He set type once again in 1881 when the news came in that Garfield had been shot and he and foreman William Sutton were the only men in the office at the time. Hester succeeded his uncle as president when Van Anden died in 1875 and remained in power until his own death in 1921. Hester's contemporaries describe him as a strong though not domineering, broad-minded, pragmatic, tolerant, decisive, and conservative gentleman whose two rules of life, in the estimation of one of his staff, were "No business deal is a good business deal unless both sides profit" and "Kindliness is of supreme importance."

Hester visited McKelway almost daily to formulate policy, often in long and frank discussions in which McKelway would match his eloquence with the publisher's sometimes superior logic and sound judgment. Although Hester was more a businessman than a writer, he had published a twenty-two page domestic comedy about journalism, *That Husband of Mine*, in 1878. He was not a politician, but the Democrats had persuaded him to run for Congress in 1882 in the third Congressional district in a hopeless race to cut down the Republican majority. The Colonel ran well and lost by only 2,500 votes. Like the other men of his class he joined clubs—the Nassau Country Club, Crescent Athletic Club, Riding and Driving Club, Metropolitan Club, and Brooklyn Club. He directed several of the borough's financial institutions and promoted the development of Coney Island and the Brighton Beach Hotel. In the winter he lived at 158 Remsen Street, within walking distance of Borough Hall and the *Eagle* office, and in summer he roamed Europe with friends or cruised to Buzzards Bay or the Thousand Islands in his sailing yacht. The Hester tours were not the wanderings of a wealthy Brooklynite but a means of expanding his own and Brooklyn's view of the world.

He was, in many ways, the embodiment of that legendary American hero described in Irwin G. Wyllie's *The Self-Made Man in America*:

> He has been active in every field from politics to the arts, but nowhere has he been more active, or more acclaimed, than in business. To most Americans he is the office boy who has become the head of a great concern, making millions in the

process. He represents our most cherished conceptions of success, and particularly our belief that any man can achieve fortune through the practice of industry, frugality, and sobriety.[16]

The Eagle Pageant

As the *Eagle* got ready to congratulate itself on its seventy-fifth anniversary, the Reverend Maurice Ambrose Levy of the Greene Avenue Baptist Church made newspaper morals the subject of his address, "Have the Newspapers Bungled the Gospel?" The moral tone of newspapers, he said with specific reference to the *Eagle*, was high. "There is good copy in the things of the Kingdom," he said. "There is no paper of which this is more true than the Brooklyn Daily *Eagle*. It has long given generous space to religious thought and life and the Monday edition, as developed by Colonel F. P. Sellers, has carried the evangel from the pulpits of Brooklyn into every state and many a far-away country." The Monday sermon page, which published over 15,000 words a week—mostly Protestant—was another of Hester's innovations. Levy concluded with his own version of the "newspaper gospel" and a series of quotes that showed, to his satisfaction, that religion was identical with true morality. "The square life is the summing up of Christianity. The keynote is character set forth as the saving principle. A man must save himself, work out his own salvation. That seems to be the gospel according to the press —salvation by a good life."[17] Thus assured that God was on their side, the Hesters decided to celebrate the *Eagle*'s birthday as if it itself were an historical event of major proportions. The event was to be commemorated by a staff-written and staff-acted pageant at the Brooklyn Academy of Music and by a special 180-page issue of the *Eagle* including a one hundred page book, *Pictorial History of Brooklyn*, a twenty-four page Historic Feature Section containing the nostalgic reminiscences of old Brooklynites, a twenty-four page Anniversary Feature section filled with the predictions of eminent men on what life would be like in 1991, and twenty-four pages of regular news and eight pages of special news.[18]

The common Brooklynite's personal recollections and the forecasts

Colonel William Hester (1915?), publisher when the *Eagle* reached the peak of its influence.

The Hester family's Glen Cove, Long Island, home.

of its eminent citizens provide a fascinating glimpse into at least a few 1916 minds. The first man to cross the Brooklyn Bridge recalled his triumph in detail, but the most interesting recollections are thirty-five letters describing the crossing of the East River on the ice in the days before the bridge was built. Several of them are from people who remember meeting Henry Ward Beecher on the ice, usually striding across with a group. In 1867 one man rescued two women who were slipping in and found out later they were Mrs. Henry Ward Beecher and Harriet Beecher Stowe. Mrs. Ellen J. DeFollett, 78, wrote from the Bronx that she remembered crossing the river once forty-one years ago. She still read the Sunday *Eagle* because it was "clean and instructing," and she wished she were back in Brooklyn.

A great deal of space was devoted to the eminent citizens' view of the future. Nearly all the predictions were extremely optimistic. Dr. Newell Dwight Hillis predicted that tomorrow would bring Christian unity, with all the denominations "marching as a solid army." Dr. Alma Webster Powell, focusing on women's fashions, prophesied the "full bloomer, the loose washable blouse and embroidered bolero with a long coat. There will be no fat women." Rabbi Nathan Kraus said religion would solve the world's social problems. Chauncey M. Depew said the population would exceed 200,000,000 and be more American, and that the power of the executive branch of the government would grow. Henry Bruere said he was no prophet but would express his hopes for New York: "The people of the city will be kindly, neighborly, united in civic patriotism, and fused by long acquaintance, intermarriage, and common experience into a great united community." As he said, he was no prophet.[19]

Over three thousand friends and employees of the *Eagle* crowded into the Academy on the night of October 26. Sitting up front were the venerable Colonel William V. Hester himself, president, still in charge after sixty-four years of service, and eighty-six-year-old William H. Sutton with his white beard and full head of white hair and a faraway look in his eyes. The *Eagle* pageant is worth a brief analysis and description because, considered along with the copious History and collections of reminiscences, it reveals a venerable and powerful institution on the brink of deceptive self-indulgence. Henry Steele Commager has written in *The American Mind* that Americans have a quantitative cast to their thinking and that when an American asks what a man is worth he means material worth—hence the American's (and the Brooklynite's) passion for population statistics, railroad mileage and production records and his toleration of giant corporations.[20] *Eagle* histories of Brooklyn and of itself were crammed with flattering statistics. Yet the *Eagle* did not overtly measure its success in terms of quantity alone; perhaps one of the more remarkable elements of the old *Eagle*'s self-consciousness was its attempt to combine material success and "spiritual" values, although the intangible values were both vague and conventional. It just happened that its many public service activities—children's clubs, welfare clubs, library, travel guides, and card files on the whereabouts of 60,000 Brooklyn and Long Island service men—were also good business. The *Eagle*'s own prosperity, personified in the lives of its managers, could therefore be interpreted as verification of the Protestant ethics of hard work and self-help.[21]

The pageant, produced and directed by Martin H. Weyraugh, presented, in five episodes, the key moments in the *Eagle*'s history.[22] Young Weyraugh, who had been with the *Eagle* since graduating from Union College in 1908, had also edited the *Eagle*'s *Pictorial History of Brooklyn* and had written the Historical Pageant of Brooklyn, performed the year before at the Twenty-Third Regiment Armory with a cast of 2,000 before an audience of 20,000. The *Eagle* pageant was on a slightly smaller scale.

The pageant was the old institution's attempt to present its own image to itself in dramatic form. It was a way of publicly reinforcing those concepts and values which the institution deemed most important to its survival and to its prosperity. The authors of the various episodes selected moments in the *Eagle*'s history that would appeal to the audience's desire for reassurance and continuity. With this in mind, two of the acts were built around two of the oldest employees present.

The saga depicted the consistent triumph of truth, integrity, and the independent spirit. It assured the audience in the Academy of

Music that the *Eagle* had not sacrificed its integrity to gain its wealth. As the story unfolds, the *Eagle* is founded and taken over by a bold young Van Anden who immediately asserts his independence from the Brooklyn Democratic bosses who had sponsored the venture. Walt Whitman loafs about the office soliloquizing:

> I loaf and invite my soul;
> I lean and loaf at my ease, observing a space
>   of summer grass.

Meanwhile, young "Hen" Sutton hustles about his job, declaring that he'll work his way to the top. Many old employees remember the *Eagle* for its hard work and little pay; it must have been pleasing to the 1916 management to see the venerable Sutton held up as an example of industry, even though he never got to be "boss." The firing of Whitman is not portrayed, but the pageant does pretend that Van Anden recognized the poet's hidden genius. Since Whitman did not fit the Hester-*Eagle* success story pattern, it was necessary for the pageant to portray him as manifesting evidence of his later genius while he was *Eagle* editor, although there was little evidence of this having been the case. Young William Hester comes to work for his uncle but insists on starting at the bottom. The firing of Henry McCloskey is portrayed as Van Anden, threatened by a mob, asserts the *Eagle*'s loyalty to the Union and replaces him with Kinsella lest the *Eagle* be banned from the mails.

One famous scene from the *Eagle* mythology shows the encounter between Thomas Kinsella and Henry Ward Beecher. According to the pageant episode, based on the recollections of *Eagle* columnist William C. Hudson, who was *Eagle* city editor in 1872, Beecher visited Kinsella in his office just as Hudson was preparing a news story based on Theodore Tilton's accusations of adultery and the reports in the November 2 *Woodhull and Chaflin's Weekly*. Kinsella accepts Beecher's personal assurance that he is innocent of all charges, promises him he will not publish them until the case has come to court, and orders Hudson to tear up his article.[23] It's a good story, reinforcing the *Eagle*'s image as the defender of Brooklyn institutions under attack, but it doesn't quite square with the record.

The actual adultery trial began January 11, 1875, and lasted till July 2, 1875; but the *Eagle* headlines read "THE BEECHER-TILTON SCANDAL, Warrant Issued for the Arrest of Woodhull and Chaffin" on November 2, 1872. For the next three years the *Eagle* mentioned the scandal continually and on July 17, 1874, published Theodore Tilton's biography of Mrs. Woodhull, a move which prompted young William J. Gaynor, then a reporter for Demas Barnes' *Argus*, to request a warrant for Tilton's arrest for libel.[24] Meanwhile, the *Eagle* constantly reaffirmed its belief in Beecher and praised his dignified silence and his decision to have a church committee investigate.[25]

Seeing Itself as Others Saw It?

How did the *Eagle*'s conception of itself in a changing community compare with the outlooks of other papers on the *Eagle* and on Brooklyn? In his essay on the *Eagle*'s special character in the anniversary *Eagle*, Arthur M. Howe did not hesitate to describe it as a "class paper."[26] For one thing, the *Eagle* and the New York *Post* were the only New York papers to dare to charge the high price of three cents for an issue, thereby attracting, thought Howe, a class of highly intelligent and prosperous readers. He was proud of the paper's editorial conservatism, meaning that it saw sensationalism only when sensation was there. Under his editorship, the *Eagle* saw itself as aware of the changes in Brooklyn, and it saw the necessity to plan for architectural growth as had been emphasized in the *Eagle*'s plan for the growth of Long Island five years before. However, the *Eagle* insisted that the changes in Brooklyn were only superficial and not revolutionary. It brushed aside the claim that Brooklyn had lost its distinctive qualities with the infusion of "new elements":

The old qualities of citizenship that gave Brooklyn its distinction as a city of churches and homes, that put a premium on

education, cultivation, thrift, and clean living, are still alive and
influential here, although they are manifested in new ways and
under altered conditions. . . .

Howe underlined the theme of community and newspaper identity
that later editors up to the last one would repeat again and again:

Newspapers and communities grow side by side. They are in the
truest sense interdependent. The newspaper advertises the
community. The community sustains, stimulates, and
strengthens the newspaper.

Yet, Howe's analysis of who constituted the "community" indicated
that he and the *Eagle* may have defined the term too narrowly. He was
trying to answer the charge of the cynics that newspapers are published primarily to make money and he perhaps ended up identifying
his newspaper too much with the monied class:

A newspaper to survive and prosper as the *Eagle* has for seventy-
five years must identify itself with movements and with men
commanding the confidence of the community. It is sometimes
the duty of a newspaper to initiate and lead such movements. It
is sometimes its privilege to discover and support such men.
These things the *Eagle* has done, making its policies, and
purposes those that appeal to the highest class of citizenship, and
securing in turn from that class a moral support upon which rests
a material prosperity uninterrupted from the day of the birth to
that of the Diamond Jubilee.

The *Eagle*'s anniversary was noticed by papers and national leaders
all over America.[27] President Woodrow Wilson's July 12th letter of
congratulations is cold, terse, and impersonal: "It interests me very
much to learn that the *Eagle* is about to celebrate the seventy-fifth
anniversary of its establishment." On July 8, his Vice-President,
Thomas R. Marshall, wrote a longer and more philosophical—also
more confused—note, urging that the "spirit of liberty . . . be kept

awake and vigilant by ceaseless agitation." He confesses: "I do not speak from special knowledge of the 'Brooklyn *Eagle*' but it must in the main have sought honestly to serve its day and generation and still to be so seeking, or it would not have survived this three-quarters of a century." The editorials of congratulations often contained moments of insight and gave a fair idea of what the paper's national reputation really was. On September 6, the Brooklyn *Times* praised the *Eagle* for its campaigns for civic improvements, its clean contents, and its taboo on sensationalism. The Amityville, New York *Record* of September 15 mixed wit with its praise:

Almost the only friend of Brooklyn, the *Eagle* is a powerful one. Without the *Eagle* to stand up for it Brooklyn would inevitably become a part of New York City.

Occasionally one may shudder a little over the Brooklynishness of the *Eagle*. "Brooklyn Man Injured in Illinois Railroad Wreck. Prominent Heights Resident Who Married Park Slope Girl at Pretty October Wedding Last Year, Suffers Painful Sprain in Wrist When Pullman Leaves Tracks. Sixty-One Others Killed in Wreck." Such a headline may not be cosmopolitan, but it is strictly local, and students of newspapers say that the local paper is the success of the future among newspapers.

The *Record*'s quip is reminiscent of H. V. Kaltenborn's remark years later that the toughest assignment for the Brooklyn *Eagle* reporter was to get a pageful of Brooklyn names at the Emerald Ball in the old Waldorf Hotel on the site of the Empire State Building. (*Eagle*, July 19, 1953).

In lengthy and thoughtful editorials, two of the *Eagle*'s main competitors, the *Standard Union* and the *Citizen*, reflected on the *Eagle*'s past and its role as a community paper. Both seemed especially sensitive to the *Eagle*'s perhaps rather enlarged conception of itself and of their own places as younger brothers who may, perhaps, be aware of aspects of the community life that the *Eagle* may have missed. The *Union* began:

Any institution which wraps itself in the American flag for a week and occupies the Academy of Music for a night may fairly be judged to have laid aside, for the time at least, that shrinking modesty of which it never claimed monopoly and is entitled, at least, to real and unreasonable publicity.

The *Union* then went on to discuss the broader implications of the *Eagle*'s anniversary. It was already worried by a trend toward newspaper mergers and it predicted that the era in which new New York dailies could be founded had passed. "Modern communities, particularly modern cities, can no more live without their newspapers than without their Government," the *Union* lamented, and quoted with sadness a recent New York visitor to Boston who said that none of the Boston papers was worthy of respect. In a paragraph that seemed to prophesy the decline of the New York dailies in 1955, the *Union* said it was also worried about the recent trend of some papers to neglect news for:

. . . specialities, departments, syndicates and all specious and devious vagaries and variants of those who for one reason or another, chiefly their own political or pecuniary profit, infest newspaper offices and sometimes hypnotize managers; all lead more or less directly to the same end, a scattering and disintegration of forces, lowering of vitality, and sincerity, a sort of general structural weakness and mental and business flabbiness, sure precursor of decay and dissolution.

The day after the celebration the *Eagle* published a self-congratulating editorial in which it argued that the 700 men who were employed by the *Eagle* represented 700 families from all over the Brooklyn community and that "All the currents of Brooklyn flow through this office as those of neighborhood feeling flow through a public school.[28] The *Eagle* attitude can be contrasted with that of the Brooklyn *Citizen*, the Democratic paper edited by Andrew McLean, who had edited the *Eagle*. On October 29, the *Citizen* celebrated its own thirtieth anniversary with a more critical and more realistic evaluation of what was happening in Brooklyn. First of all, the *Citizen* viewed social change without sentimentality or nostalgia:

> In those older days Brooklyn, as our readers will remember, was not only a separate city, but was distinctly known as the City of Churches. It was rather as the domestic suburb of New York than as a community having sources of wealth and employment within itself, that it was deemed worthy of attention by the country at large. It was part of the good fortune of the *Citizen* to be here in time to assist in the development of the new conditions, and to help in effecting the union with New York which has had the double effect of making secure the position of the metropolis at the head of American cities, and bringing to Brooklyn the volume of population and diversity of manufacturing and other industries which have already raised it to equality with Manhattan and must shortly lift it to the first place in the list of boroughs.

The *Citizen* went on to indicate what the special editions of the *Eagle* did not refer to, that the most significant change in Brooklyn was in the character of its population as a whole. Up to the present, said the *Citizen*, there were really only three numerically important elements in the city, specifically, the native American, the Irish, and the German. The others, even the Dutch, were quite negligible from the political point of view. Now Brooklyn had more Italians than Germans and more Hebrews than either if not both combined. Furthermore, says the *Citizen*:

> . . . the opening of the new bridges and tunnels has brought Brooklyn into such intimate relations with Manhattan that the impress of the latter has practically effaced, in at least four-fifths of the community, the earlier picture. In other words, old Brooklyn survives to-day as a memory, but men who imagine that it has not passed away are the victims of their own pleasant dreams.

* * *

This, as far as I can ascertain, was a moment of realization at which the *Eagle* never arrived.

Notes

[1]*Reminiscences*, p. 110.

[2]*Proceedings*, p. 39.

[3]Samuel B. Moore, "Brooklyn—Past and Present," *Brooklyn Life* 51 (May 25, 1915): 35-70.

[4]*How a Modern Newspaper is Made*, p. 38.

[5]Ibid., p. 37.

[6]There are brief biographical sketches of Hester, Gunnison, Howe, and Crist in Martin H. Weyraugh, ed., *Pictorial History of Brooklyn* (Brooklyn Eagle Press, 1916) p. 47. The evaluation of Crist's influence is based on correspondence and conversations with people who knew him, particularly James Henle, who was McKelway's secretary from 1912 to 1915, and Edwin B. Wilson, who was at the *Eagle* from 1912 to 1955.

[7]Letter, Albert W. Quinn to RAS, January 26, 1970.

[8]Interview with I. Kaufman, June 15, 1970; interview with Oliver Pilat, June 18, 1970.

[9]This summary is based on Kaltenborn's *Fifty Fabulous Years* and on his *Oral History Reminiscences* described in the Preface of this essay. Kaltenborn's enormous MSS are at the State Historical Society of Wisconsin at Madison. Boxes 1-55, 205 and 213-214 are reported to contain some mention of the *Eagle* in correspondence and manuscript articles. There are two doctoral dissertations on Kaltenborn: Giraud Chester, "The Radio Commentaries of H. V. Kaltenborn: A Case Study in Persuasion" (University of Wisconsin, 1947) and David Gillis Clark, "The Dean of Commentators: A Biography of H. V. Kaltenborn" (University of Wisconsin, 1965). Besides the Ph.D. dissertations of Chester and Clark, another is in process: David H. Culbert, "Tantalus' Dilemma: Public Opinion, Six Radio Commentators, and Foreign Affairs, 1935-1941" in American History at Northeastern University. Letter, David A. Culbert to RAS, January 28, 1970.

[10]Kaltenborn, *Reminiscences*, p. 22.

[11]Kaltenborn, *Fifty Fabulous Years*, p. 69.

[12]Kaltenborn, *Reminiscences*, p. 52.

[13]Edwin B. Wilson, *The Story of the Eagle's 1920 Tour* (Brooklyn: *Eagle* Press, 1920).

[14]This brief biography is based on Rodgers' *Oral History Reminiscences*.

[15]The fullest source of information on Colonel Hester is *Colonel William Hester 1835-1921* (Brooklyn: Eagle Press, 1921), a sixty-four page memorial booklet printed at his death. It contains a reprint of Hester's own recollections, first printed in the *Eagle* on October 26, 1901, editorials from many papers on his death on June 9, 1921, speeches from the funeral service, and recollections of his friends.

[16]Irwin G. Wyllie, *The Self-Made Man in America* (New York: The Free Press, 1954), p. 6.

[17]*Eagle*, October 23, 1916.

[18]*Advertising News*, November 3, gave one of the few negative press comments on the *Eagle* anniversary splurge. In their view, these mammoth editions were a waste of valuable white paper and a tremendous drain on the advertising community, which is compelled to buy expensive space as a forced birthday gift to the publication. They predicted the readers would stow away these precious 180 pages of expensive type and love them without reading them: "The habit of special and specially large editions ought to be discouraged. It is not an admirable habit, on the whole, though not a vicious one. It has its admirable phases. It nurses a mild sort of egotism. It gives opportunity to estimate anew the motives of the publisher, and recall his great services to the city. It serves to test the embellishing qualities of the features for the staff, and the ex- and former staffs. It may be a sort of safety valve for the relief of the workers who are notoriously underemployed. It puts bunches of advertisers' money into more active circulation. But it is, on the whole, scarcely worth preservation."

"Conceding the habit, this special edition of the *Eagle* is really a remarkable performance. One hundred and eighty pages in one daily paper: Whew! That is going some, and some more!" (Clipping in TNS).

[19]*Eagle*, October 26, 1916.

[20]Henry Steele Commager, *The American Mind* (New Haven: Yale University Press), p. 7.

[21]In 1906 the *Eagle* Press published *The Autobiography of Emma Bullet*, their Paris correspondent, as an inspirational self-help tract. Miss Bullet encouraged young women who would achieve fame and success to "paddle their own canoes."

[22]The script for the Pageant is in the evening's Anniversary Program,

which along with photographs of the players and newspaper clippings of the occasion, is preserved in the scrapbook, *Newspaper Comments Concerning the Seventy-Fifth Anniversary of the Brooklyn Daily Eagle, October 26, 1916*, TNS.

[23] William C. Hudson, "Incident in Beecher's Life," reprinted in *Between the Lines, Random Recollections* (Brooklyn: *Eagle* Library No. 177, 1913), p. 32.

[24] Pink, *Gaynor*, pp. 22-27.

[25] *Eagle*, July 11, 1874.

[26] Arthur M. Howe, "Years of Great Achievement," in Weyraugh, *Pictorial History*, pp. 45-47.

[27] All these editorials and the originals of the letters cited are in the unpaginated scrapbook *Newspaper Commentary*, 1916, TNS.

[28] *Eagle*, October 27, 1916.

7

DECLINE

A writer from *Editor and Publisher* visited the *Eagle* plant in 1921 to do a feature article on the *Eagle*'s renowned physical plant, its presses, and its financial success; but he discovered something more:

> As the human soul is greater than the body and its shell, is not the spirit of a newspaper of more importance than its physical plant and its routine methods?
>
> About the Brooklyn *Eagle* there shines steadily the light of a great soul.[1]

The friendly visitor did not say exactly what the "soul" was, but the gist of his article was that the *Eagle* spirit was the Hester-Gunnison conviction that community service and good business were the same thing. Ironically, the *Editor and Publisher* praise appeared in the year of Colonel Hester's death.

When Colonel Hester died in 1921 he was succeeded by his son, William V. Hester, who served as President until his own death in 1924, when he was succeeded by Herbert F. Gunnison. Under Herbert F. Gunnison, Raymond M. Gunnison was Vice-President and William V. Hester, Jr., the grandson of Colonel Hester, was Secretary. The *Eagle* had been in good financial condition (in 1922 it made a $400,000 net profit on a gross of nearly $4,000,000[2]), but Mrs. Hester had been advised that too much of the family money was tied up in *Eagle* stock. She sold and Gunnison became the largest stockholder, but when men outside the *Eagle* began buying into the corporation the *Eagle* men reorganized and a group of seven got control of the common stock and began building the paper up for sale, making large profits during the boom but not putting the money back into the paper.[3]

Frank E. Gannett of Rochester, head of an expanding newspaper chain, bought the *Eagle* in 1929 and paid too much for it. He had also just bought the Hartford *Times*, the Rochester *Democrat and Chronicle*, the Albany *Knickerbocker-Press*, the Albany *Evening News*, and the Ogdenburg *Republican Journal*, all for incredibly high prices in a get-rich-quick era.[4] To do so he borrowed from the International Power and Paper Company, a subsidiary of the power trusts, which had been buying shares in newspapers all over the country. A Senate investigation that year revealed that four-fifths of American newspapers had cooperated in one way or another in the power trusts' propaganda war to prevent federal control of water power resources, either by accepting "good will" advertising or by publishing packaged articles and editorials that favored power interests. It was disclosed that International Power and Paper Company had interest in the *Eagle* totaling $1,954,500 in notes and four hundred shares of common stock.[5]

Gannett later explained to Rodgers, who was ghostwriting the publisher's autobiography, that he had been naive in accepting the trust's money; he thought they had merely wanted the paper's newsprint contract. Gannett's other papers, he said, had criticized the power trusts and the *Eagle* would not be compromised. Nevertheless, Gannett was subjected to heavy criticism, even in the *Eagle* in columns by H. V. Kaltenborn. Gannett returned the $2,700,000 loan to IPC within forty-eight hours of the federal exposure, but he had to borrow from banks to do it. With the 1929 crash, Gannett could not repay the notes he had given to common stockholders. The crisis was made worse by the Gannett Company's expansion program—a new *Eagle* building and new presses. As Crist exclaimed when he found out what was happening to his paper, "My God! There isn't a dollar in the till, and they have bought new presses."[6]

When the former owners, the Gunnison-Hester group, realized what was happening, they mustered up enough cash to buy the *Eagle* back and put in M. Preston Goodfellow as publisher in 1932.

Goodfellow, who had begun his career at the Brooklyn *Times* after studying journalism at New York University, had come to the *Eagle* business staff after service in World War I. Villard wrote of the transaction in 1944:

> It was understood at the time that in reselling the *Eagle* he [Gannett] lost two million dollars. He was undoubtedly wise in taking that loss, for that historic old paper, which once exercised such a commanding influence in Brooklyn, has since gone downhill.[7]

The Influential Rodgers

The young men who cavorted in the skits in the 1916 pageant were now running the paper. Kaltenborn, having retired from his world tours, was becoming a radio personality through the *Eagle*'s sponsorship.

In 1921 he gave an experimental "miracle of radio" broadcast over WJZ to the Brooklyn Chamber of Commerce. In 1923, in his role as an *Eagle* editor, he gave weekly extemporaneous news analyses over WEAF, but his controversial comments made him the "Wandering Voice of Radio" as he was driven from station to station until WOR stood firm in 1925.

The outset of World War I found Rodgers in Copenhagen where the *Eagle* cabled him to report on the German army. He took over the war desk when he returned to Brooklyn, and he ended up writing military analysis not because of his expertise but simply because there was no one else around to do it.

When Arthur Millidge Howe retired in 1931, Rodgers took over as editor. He was a remarkable man, like so many outstanding newspapermen of his day, self-educated as a dramatist, foreign affairs expert, and finally as a city planner. However, he is perhaps best understood through his relationships, as he recorded them in his *Reminiscences*, with other prominent men: Walt Whitman, Franklin D. Roosevelt, and Robert Moses.

As the local "rehabilitator" of Walt Whitman, he saw the *Eagle*,

Cleveland Rodgers, city planner and *Eagle* editor in the 1930s.

like himself, as still being moved by the spirit of Whitman. He looked back on the first *Eagle* as part of the surge of democracy that put Andrew Jackson in the White House, and he saw contemporary Brooklyn as a showcase of modern democracy. To Rodgers, Whitman's prose was the quintessence of liberalism, "as virile, sweeping, and impressive as any similar expressions appearing that time or since."[8] This same liberalism, he thought, was the essence of the *Eagle*. The owners had been Republicans, but the editors had been Democrats; the owners had "never" interfered with editorial policy, and on great issues, such as the Sacco-Vanzetti case, the *Eagle* had taken the "liberal" stand.

Rodgers' relationship to Roosevelt is a good example of how his own political vision and the *Eagle*'s influence grew at the same time. Rodgers had flirted with anarchism and socialism during his early years in Brooklyn, and on writing assignments he had interviewed and been favorably impressed by Elizabeth Gurley Flynn, Bill Haywood, and John Reed. In state politics Rodgers reserved his first admiration for Al Smith. When Roosevelt as governor had appointed twelve new judges when he had privately admitted to Harris M. Crist that only three were needed, Rodgers saw Roosevelt as the expedient politician who compromised ideals too easily, and later he saw Roosevelt's attempt to pack the Supreme Court as a sacrifice of the President's liberalism. However, Rodgers' respect for Roosevelt grew during the early days of the New Deal. He went to live in Washington during the first hundred days of the new administration and wrote a series of articles interpreting what he called the President's "program." One day during a long and animated conversation with Roosevelt the President suddenly remarked, apparently with some surprise, "Well, it *does* make a program."

It appeared to Rodgers that the creator of the New Deal was just beginning to see how its various parts fit together. He collected his own articles and published them as *The Roosevelt Program* in 1933. Rodgers was always grateful when Roosevelt praised his editorials. On election day 1934 Roosevelt told visiting newsmen at Hyde Park that they should read the latest Brooklyn *Eagle* editorial for an expression of his own reflection—that America should be grateful that it could face its elections in peace while the rest of the world was in turmoil.

Finally, the 1930s under Rodgers marked an upsurge in the *Eagle's* commitment to city planning, characterized by the close working relationship between the *Eagle* editor and New York Park Commissioner Robert Moses.[9] Some critics of the history of New York City planning might suggest it was too close, like Kinsella's relationship to the builders of the Brooklyn Bridge. Rodgers is credited with having ghostwritten Moses' autobiography, *Working for the People: Praise and Performance in Public Service*, and *Eagle* editorials described Moses as "one of the ablest, most energetic and resourceful public officials. He gets things done."[10] Thus, an evaluation of the *Eagle's* contribution to New York City planning would parallel an evaluation of Moses' career.

The *Eagle's* long-range program for Brooklyn was expressed in a series of ten-year and ten-point plans, all of which had their genesis in the "Forward Long Island" program and the waning stages of the City Beautiful Movement.

Rodgers had played a small role in the planning of the 1912 "Forward Long Island" project, but he had shown no great interest in planning or civic affairs until a 1931 speech by Dr. Nicholas Murray Butler at Columbia convinced him that the important thing about Russia was not communism but the fact that it had a plan. Rodgers, who up to that time had considered the Chamber of Commerce as a bunch of Babbits, now became convinced that the way for Brooklyn to overcome its depression was to stimulate activity, especially public improvements, with the help of federal money. He decided Long Island needed a plan. The *Eagle* sponsored a big luncheon for the Chamber of Commerce and the civic associations on June 30, 1931, and the Long Island Ten Year Plan Committee was launched. The following fall, on October 25, 1931, the *Eagle* devoted its Ninetieth Anniversary issue to the projects. By 1937 most of them were accomplished.

Most of the recommendations of the Long Island Ten Year Plan centered around highway transportation, and their implementation in the long run would reinforce the Robert Moses view of urban

The Brooklyn *Daily Eagle*, Sunday, October 26, 1931.

development that this is the motor age, that men go down to the sea in cars, and that the "sanest, best-balanced people" are those who spend part of the year in cities, part in suburbs, and part in open country.[11] *Eagle* aerial photos of the Shore Road Drive extension and the Sunrise Highway harkened back to the projected grand boulevards of the Brooklyn Beautiful movement of 1911. Of the three fundamental points in the Ten Year Plan—a railroad connection to the South and West, a new series of arterial highways, and rapid transit unification—the highways project, under the direction of Robert Moses, head of the City Parks Department and Long Island State Park Commission, had been expanded beyond all expectations.

Neither the *Eagle* nor the Ten Year Plan Committee could take particular or exclusive credit for this accomplishment, yet Rodgers, in his editorials and lectures, was one of the first to call for the massive federal spending in Brooklyn two years before the New Deal was under way. Furthermore, he did so against the advice of Brooklyn bankers who opposed federal help even for the subway system. Moreover, it was Rodgers' editorial that helped push construction of the Triborough Bridge to completion by urging that a special author-ity be created with Moses as head to get the job done. It seems that Rodgers was one of the *Eagle* editors most willing to see Brooklyn's future development in the metropolitan context. He shared Whitman's expansiveness. His journalistic career was one of continu-ing self-education during which he became increasingly involved in a larger and larger world, both because of his intellectual curiosity and because he was forced to learn about complex problems quickly in order to write about them.

Meanwhile, the depression had shattered Brooklyn neighbor-hoods. It left the neighborhoods in poverty, broke up families, drove citizens to suicide. One Brooklyn writer recalled the depression atmosphere:

> We ate ketchup sandwiches, mustard sandwiches, stale bread
> . . . It was a simple time, but it was not that glorious age that
> phony nostalgia has made it out to be: there was no enormous
> warmth about it all.[12]

Brooklyn's central-city population began to decline in 1930; this was the dangerous turning point in the accelerating exodus of the white middle class who could afford to buy automobiles as their escape ticket from a declining city to a new status in a single house in a new neighborhood, where a family could be raised according to the values the *Eagle* had always espoused. Perhaps if the *Eagle*-Moses effort had been put into an expansion of cheap public transportation, the effects of the shift in population might have been less chaotic and the affluent and the poor might have been distributed more equitably throughout Brooklyn, Queens, and Nassau, but Rodgers' *Eagle* argued against public transportation in favor of the automobile and more express-ways: "We cannot hope to overcome the competition of outlying sections and restore the center of Brooklyn until adequate provision is made for more effective use of automobiles."[13] Today some architec-tural writers and journalists observe that these highways have harmed the very quality that gave Brooklyn its unique charm—its residential aspect.[14] One strong critic is worth quoting at length:

In 1945, Columbia Street was the main shopping street in South Brooklyn. One can still see many of the stores today, but most of them are closed, only a few open on weekends. There was nothing different about Columbia Street—as a matter of fact, the Gallo boys called it home. Then Robert Moses built his Brooklyn-Queens Expressway. In the Heights, he ran it right next to the river, where it cost only some of the oldest, finest, and most historic homes (don't bother to look for the homes Thomas Wolfe or Mary McCarthy lived in). When he got further south, he moved his road a few blocks in from the Harbor, where Hicks Street ought to be. The expressway is built below ground level, but not roofed over. It runs almost the entire length of South Brooklyn, but only three streets cross it. Thus, the Columbia Street community.[15]

Besides promoting the highways and bridges of Robert Moses the *Eagle* inspired a number of lesser but more colorful and human projects that characterized its relationship to the Brooklyn community in the 1930s. When it looked as if the fiftieth anniversary of the opening of the Brooklyn Bridge was going to pass by unnoticed, the *Eagle* published a series of articles on the obstacles that had to be overcome to build it and whipped up enough enthusiasm for a modest celebration of the event. For the centenary April 8, 1934, of the granting of the charter to the old city of Brooklyn, the *Eagle* promoted a big parade and a dinner at the St. George Hotel. When Moses announced in 1935 that the New Prospect Park Zoo was nearing completion but that the federal funds that had built it had made no provision for buying animals, the *Eagle*, which had brought animals from England through submarine-infested waters for the first Prospect Park Zoo in 1914, took on this campaign as well. Another *Eagle* campaign in 1935 saved the old historic Brooklyn Academy of Music from extinction by engineering its purchase by the Brooklyn Institute of Arts and Sciences. Finally, when Long Island reached its tercentenary in the spring of 1936, the *Eagle* promoted a week-long celebration, an all-day Memorial Day parade, and the inevitable banquet at the St. George Hotel at which a message from President Roosevelt was read.[16]

True to the *Eagle* tradition, over 50 percent of the ninety-seventh anniversary issue was given over to letters and recollections from old readers. One in particular was reminiscent of Whitman's *Eagle* description of Fulton Street. Albert H. Marquis, 71, recalled borough scenes of sixty years before in vivid detail. His full-page article led the reader to the corner of Flatbush Avenue and Fulton Street in the late 1870s where little Al sold papers—the *Sun, Herald, Times, Tribune, World, Star, Witness, Truth*, and the only Brooklyn paper worth reading, the *Eagle*. He took us down Fulton Street to the ferry slip with its lifesize statue of Robert Fulton, and up Fulton Street to the *Eagle* building. At the corner of Atlantic Avenue and Clinton Street he showed us the old Atheneum which featured the Booth Dramatic Society, starring the blind actor Thurman T. Hayden.

Marquis remembered walking across the frozen river from the ferry slip to Wall Street. He boarded a horse car, which in winter would have straw on the floor to keep his feet warm and a stove in the middle, and rode out over the cobblestone streets, helping to push the car up the hill of Johnson Street to City Hall. He named the leading politicians—Hugh McLaughlin, who was replaced by Tammany cohort Patrick H. McCarren from Williamsburg, John H. McCooey, and James Kane. He remembered when the 400 room Brighton Beach Hotel was placed on flat cars and pulled by locomotives and moved back five hundred feet from the beach to keep it from being washed away. He recalled that the greatest pleasure in those days was dancing in the parks that are no more, and he ended his meditation in a half-lament:

> And now old Brooklyn, surrounded by the towns of Williams-burg, New Lots, Flatbush, Flatlands, and Gravesend, has burst its bonds, opened its jaws and swallowed up all these towns and has, in turn, itself been swallowed up by the great city of New York. How thankful we are that we still have the name of Brooklyn, even though it is only a borough. . . . I have seen come gasoline, gas, electricity, radios, and telephones. I have seen lager beer come and go and come again and there are other things that I have seen during the 71 years of my life which slip my memory. I belong to the Society of Old Brooklynites, every member of which is a constant and daily reader of the *Eagle*. Wishing the *Eagle* hundreds of years of further birthdays and hoping to meet you at your birthday dinner.[17]

There were those who felt with good reason that the *Eagle* would not have that many more birthdays. The financial crisis begun in the depression was now aggravated by a tragic labor-management dispute that would cause an exhausted and heartsick Rodgers to give up his editorship and accept a post on the New York City Planning Commission.

The Guild

The American Newspaper Guild had come into being during the New Deal under the protection of Section 7-a of the National Indus-trial Recovery Act passed by Congress in June 1933, which guaranteed the right of collective bargaining and freedom of labor union organizations. When it was clear that the provisions of the new voluntary daily newspaper code which had been put together by the American Newspaper Publishers Association did little to further the professional status of working journalists or insure economic security for the workers, reporters and deskmen started talking about forming their own collective bargaining units. In his syndicated column in the New York *World-Telegram* on August 7, 1933, Heywood Broun called for action:

> But the fact that newspaper editors and owners are genial folk should hardly stand in the way of the organization of a newspaper writers' union. There should be one. Beginning at nine o'clock on the morning of October 1, I am going to do the best I can in helping get one up. I think I could die happy on the opening day of the general strike if I had the privilege of watching Walter Lippmann heave a brick through a *Tribune* window at a non-union operative who had been called in to write the current "Today and Tomorrow" column on the gold standard.[18]

Newsmen in Cleveland formed the first local of the American Newspaper Guild on August 20, 1933, and New York newsmen, headed by Broun, published the first number of the *Guild Reporter* on November 23, 1933, and called for a national convention in Washington in December. The Guild began a series of strikes in 1934, starting with the Newark *Ledger* and calling for public boycott of the paper and its advertisers in an effort to get Guild-shop agreements and higher pay scales. By 1938 the Guild had seventy-five newspaper contracts and had signed its first with a press association, the United Press. When the Supreme Court upheld the Wagner Act in April 1937 and held that Associated Press staff man Morris Watson had been illegally discharged for union activity in 1935, the Guild movement was given new and permanent strength. At the same time the New York Guild was split during the recession years from 1937 to

1939 between "pro-Guild" conservative members and left-wing elements who were strong in New York locals.

The 1937 *Eagle* strike was to be the Guild's first test case in New York and a means of putting pressure on the *New York Times*, whose staff had been skeptical of the Guild.[19] It was also a crucial step in the newspaper writer's gradual transformation of his own self-image. Reading through old issues of the Guild *Reporter* and *Front Page*, the organ of the New York Guild, and talking to former *Eagle* employees reveals how much Guild militancy was motivated by a writer's pride and his desire for the same prestige, salary, and security as the other professions. H. V. Kaltenborn recalls that when the Goodfellow group had regained control of the *Eagle* they had begun to cut costs by firing employees, including high-salaried and prestigious writers like himself. The men on the eighth floor, the writers, had no union to protect them. The seventh floor men, the composing room, known as "the Brainery," were protected by a union shop.

An old *Eagle* reporter recalls the months when the *Eagle* Guild was getting started. Management became time-conscious and the managing editor's secretary was sent around to make a survey on the number of hours reporters worked:

Secretary—The managing editor wants me to find out, how many hours a week do you work?

Reporter—Hours? Let's see. About seventy-five, I guess, on an average.

Secretary (slightly embarrassed)—I don't mean that exactly. I don't mean the hours you actually work.

Reporter—You mean the hours I'm supposed to work?

Secretary—I guess so.

Reporter—That would be a lot more. I'm supposed to come to work at 8 a.m. but nobody ever told me when I'm supposed to leave. Officially, I guess I'm supposed to keep right on working until tomorrow, including Sundays—and at times I've done just that.[20]

At the time reporters were often eligible for night assignments and for extra work on the Sunday edition even when they had worked six days a week. In fact, reporters were often proud of the fact that they belonged to a profession where their time was not their own but the paper's. However, when the depression brought on three pay cuts, the writers were moved to organize. Newspaperwork was no longer romantic. Milton Kaufman, secretary of the New York Newspaper Guild, met with about fifty *Eagle* employees and handed out application cards. Within a few weeks the unit had been organized and gradually built up influence in the newsroom.

The group published a shop paper, *The Eagle Reporter*, which was heavily critical of Goodfellow, and the Guild began to take up employee grievances such as the demand of the space reporters on the "night staff" to be put on salary. The spacewriting or piece work night staff was an old *Eagle* institution dating back to the time when the paper was prosperous. Reporters were paid by assignment at a rate of from one to three dollars a column and the assignments were handed out by the city editor. The *Eagle* had always boasted that it was a "school of journalism" and this piece work system was the heart of the school. It also operated at minimum cost. Goodfellow granted that reporters should have more pay but said again and again that he had not any money.

In mid-1936 a meeting of a dozen members of the *Eagle* Guild in Borough Hall, chaired by I. Kaufman, a reporter who had been with the paper since his return from World War I, voted to ask the New York Guild executive committee to open negotiations with the Brooklyn *Eagle* in an attempt to draw up a contract. When the committee came to talk to Goodfellow he would not see them at first; then, after deliberation, he agreed to talk with the Guild at a public meeting in the "old building" with the whole plant present. This conversation became known as "the Goldfish Bowl Conference." The next afternoon he had another meeting in the newsroom without outside observers. Goodfellow's standard speech to both meetings was, "Where am I going to get the money?" As the anonymous Guild chronicler recalls the event:

This company-union gathering was probably the first major mistake by a man who, in dealing with his *Eagle* employees, made all the mistakes in the book. The boys and girls got really angry. Though they had little experience in management-union maneuvering, they sensed, correctly, that this was a maneuver not of an employer who had no money to meet a union's demands—but of one who was chiefly interested in beating down the union.[21]

The next angry issue of the *Eagle Reporter* said it was now plain that nothing would be gained except by "getting rough." Within minutes of reading the Guild threat Goodfellow conferred with his managing editor and published a list of twenty space writers who were being put on salary at twenty-five dollars a week, along with a note testifying that the sudden raises had nothing to do with the Guild demands.

Employee mistrust of Goodfellow accelerated when he bought the Brooklyn *Times-Union* on December 6, 1936. The new *Times-Union* had a greater circulation than the *Eagle*'s and there was a story around the *Eagle* that Goodfellow, who had started his career at the *Times*, had once sworn he would someday control both papers. The *Times* had merged with the *Standard-Union* under publisher Fremont C. Peck, the grandson of wealthy Woolworth partner Carson C. Peck, who had bought control of the *Times*. The *Times-Union* editorial employees had been cautious about joining the Guild because they had been told that the paper, which operated on a deficit that the wealthy owner met reluctantly year after year, would be sold if the Guild came in. When the papers suddenly merged, the anxious guildsmen on both papers joined together to fight for job security and demanded that all old *Eagle* and *Times-Union* people be retained.

The understanding during the merger was that both papers would keep operating as competitors with their original editorial staffs both working in the same editorial office on the fourth floor. Money would be saved by combining mechanical facilities; the type could be set once and used in both papers. Goodfellow apparently hoped he could get around the printer's union "bogus" rule that the type would have

M. Preston Goodfellow, *Eagle* publisher during the 1930s' strike.

to be reset and paid for again, but the printers kept a record of the type which should have been set twice. The wage claims amounted to $62,000. When the issue was brought to an arbitrator, he ruled against Goodfellow. In the months that followed Goodfellow's managerial problems became more complicated; the newsroom was overcrowded and attempts to coordinate the work of the separate staffs merely seemed to add to the confusion. Goodfellow brought in Lyle Dowling, whom one staff member referred to as a "Catholic Communist," as executive editor with authority over both managing editors, and then added a "newspaper doctor" with authority over Dowling.[22]

The *Times-Union* merged with the *Eagle* in June 1937. Meanwhile, the structure of the Guild had changed. A newspaper office workers' union had been formed, technically separated from the Guild but with the understanding that it would merge with the Guild as soon as that became constitutionally possible, as it did in 1937. The *Eagle* Guild was now making its contract demands for the commercial as well as the editorial departments. Management argued that advertising solicitors, because of the "individualistic" nature of their work, were temperamentally not interested in belonging to a union and that circulation branch managers had always worked seven-day weeks without hour limits and that it would be unreasonable to restrict them to a five-day forty-hour week.

In late July the Guild voted that, unless a satisfactory agreement was reached, they should strike. Throughout the rest of the hot summer, pro-strike sentiment grew as negotiations got worse and worse, while Guild membership went up and down as members of the circulation department joined, resigned, rejoined, and resigned again.

At six P.M. on Monday, September 13, 1937, the Guild walked out. Three hundred five people registered for strike duty, including a major part of the editorial department, members of the classified and circulation departments, and Lyle Dowling, who gave up his executive editor's salary to become a strike leader. Although management had threatened the *Eagle* would close never to open again, the paper continued to publish as soon as it was picketed.

This was the beginning of an *Eagle* wound that would never heal. The two things that stand out in the history of this period and in the conversations with the participants are distrust of publisher "Colonel" Goodfellow, which carried over into the management of the next publisher, Frank D. Schroth, and the repeated charge that the union was communist-controlled and therefore more concerned with a political confrontation than with the worker's cause. Both labor and management developed long memories on one another's real or imagined deceptions. It is possible, for example, that when publisher Schroth told the unions in 1955 that a strike would close the *Eagle* the unions did not believe him because Goodfellow had bluffed them in 1937. On the other hand, years after the *Eagle* was dead, some of the Schroths would say the end had come because the leaders of both the 1937 and 1955 strikes were communists.

One witness-participant was Victor Weingarten who, at age nineteen, was chairman of the Guild's grievance committee. He remembers Goodfellow as an autocratic "scoundrel." He also had his differences with Schroth, but he remembers him as the "smartest publisher in New York" who just couldn't overcome the inevitable shift of power and money to Manhattan.[23]

Another witness to the period was Oliver Pilat, who was so angry at Goodfellow for his so-called economies and mismanagement of the paper that he became by his own admission a "fellow-traveler." For a while Pilat functioned as the *Eagle*'s Paris correspondent, but the Paris bureau of which the *Eagle* often boasted was mainly a front for the paper's commercial enterprises, and it functioned as a salon rather than as a real correspondent's office. One of the office's main jobs was to cable back to Brooklyn the news of the safe arrival of Brooklyn rich ladies in Paris. Goodfellow tried to use Pilat to sell ads in Paris; when that didn't work Goodfellow closed the Paris office, sold the furniture, and brought Pilat home.

Meanwhile, the only group at the *Eagle* with a lucid philosophy, presenting a clear alternative to management policies, were the communists led by "spider like" Nat Einhorn.[24]

I. Kaufman, whom later management was to label the archenemy, maintains that he was not a communist and there was no evidence that he was. He acknowledged that the communists had taken him to dinner and asked him to join but says that he refused because he did not believe in totalitarian dictatorships. Yet it seems that he was used by the party; he admits he was slow to catch on to their tactics, particularly their manner of taking over meetings after he was chairman.[25]

On June 29, 1955, CBS newscaster Winston Burdett, who had worked for the *Eagle* from 1937 till 1942, testified to the United States Senate Internal Security subcommittee on the influence of communists in the press and named those who were members of the *Eagle* group. Burdett had joined the party under the influence of former movie writer Alvah Bessie, who had joined the party after leaving the *Eagle*. "I was emotionally compelled to identify myself with a larger cause outside myself, which I believed to be a good one," Burdett said. When he went overseas in 1940 as a roving reporter for the *Eagle*, paying most of his own expenses, Burdett spied for Russia in Finland, Romania, Yugoslavia, and Turkey for two years while also working for CBS.

Burdett named the following *Eagle* employees: Nat Einhorn, Victor Weingarten, Charles Lewis, Hy Charriak, Herbert Cohn, Melvin Barnett, David Gordon, Charles Grutzner, Gladys Bentley, Larry Adler, Lyle Dowling, and Violet Brown, who later married Weingarten. He said he also "assumed" Milton Kaufman and John (Francis) Ryan were communists. Einhorn was called the "leading spirit." The Guild replied that it had gotten rid of communist influence by 1941 and that none of those named had worked for the *Eagle* in recent years. Dowling denied the charges.[26]

The manuscript "Strike History," written by Thomas N. Schroth after the 1955 strike, points out that Lewis, Bessie, Grutzner, Burdett, Einhorn, Weingarten, and I. Kaufman were all Guild leaders at the time of the 1937 strike (pp. 14, 15), thus implying that I. Kaufman was at least under communist influence.

The strike was a long and acrimonious one, lasting fifteen weeks from September till December 21 when it was brought to an end with the help of the state labor negotiator. From the start, considerable pressure was put on the union through the courts. The strike chairman, I. Kaufman, and vice-chairman, John E. Deegan, were arrested for "disorderly conduct" (picketing) the first night. After a series of arrests for picketing after which the charges were dismissed by Magistrate William O'Dwyer, who knew this was an attempt to break the union, there were other arrests for activities like distributing leaflets and making noise.[27]

Simple picketing of the *Eagle* plant was not an effective tactic, so the union developed other means of putting pressure on Goodfellow. The most powerful was the secondary boycott, the picketing and harassment of *Eagle* advertisers. The Guild sent men, many of whom were writers well known to Brooklynites, into the department stores to ask merchants to withdraw their ads. If the managers refused, the strikers talked to the customers to stop them from buying in a store that did business with a paper that was unfair to its employees.[28] The *Eagle* and other papers built up a case against the secondary picketing, and on February 4, 1938, the New York State Court of Appeals ruled against all but "peaceful" picketing, in effect allowing the picketing to continue.

Some of the Guild's tricks were fairly imaginative. One *Eagle* advertiser, a beauty parlor, gained an injunction barring pickets from marching in front of the establishment with signs branding it as "unfair to labor." When the pickets reappeared, the proprietor came out with a pencil and notebook to write down the exact words from the signs and prove violation of the court order; he found the signs blank! When pedestrians would stop and ask the pickets why there were no words on the signs, they would be drawn into a dialogue about the strike. On one occasion strikers wore gorilla costumes into a store with signs on their backs declaring that monkeys advertised in the *Eagle*.

Another pressure device was the "Yell Squad." If the advertiser refused to withdraw his ad, a squad of loud-voiced pickets would walk outside his store and yell till he changed his mind. Meanwhile, to compensate for the lack of strike news coverage in the New York press, the Guild published the "Strikepaper," including a summary of the strikers' educational backgrounds showing that over 50 percent of the strikers had college degrees and many had graduate degrees, making the *Eagle*'s the "most cultured picket line of all time." The communist strikers were always anxious to intensify the conflict by bringing the confrontation to the point of violence. Mrs. Einhorn stuck a policeman's horse with a pin, hoping it would bolt and stir up the crowd.[29]

Meanwhile, an AF of L attempt to organize employees in the summer of 1938 failed. The strike cost the Guild $50,000 and it was only partly satisfied with the contract it won. The Guild won recognition for its own members and those who wished to join, but there were no pay raises and no Guild shop. There was a provision that forty strikers would not return to their jobs, receiving twenty weeks severance pay. Some of the forty were willing to leave, fed up as they were with the way the *Eagle* was going, but their departure increased bitterness in their friends who remained. After the strikers had returned to work, interoffice hostility increased between the Guild members and the nonstrikers who, Guildsmen believed, were being favored by the management as a reward for their "loyalty" during the strike. For weeks strikers and nonstrikers refused to speak to one another in passing.

To further complicate matters, the word was out that the *Eagle* was again up for sale. In March 1938 the *Eagle Eye* predicted that the next publisher of the *Eagle* would probably be S. I. Newhouse, owner of the Long Island *Press*, the Newark *Ledger*, and the Staten Island *Advance*. The story reappeared in June after Newhouse bought the Long Island *Star*. Newhouse had discontinued the Sunday edition of the *Press* and the speculation was that the Sunday *Eagle*, which was now devoting three pages to Queens and Long Island news, would fill the void. On June 25 Newhouse suspended the sixty-year-old *Star* but revived it July 13 when his North Shore edition of the *Press* failed to pick up more than a fifth of the *Star*'s old 30,000 circulation. Other rumors were that the paper would be bought by Brooklyn Democratic leader Frank V. Kelly or "the Scranton syndicate." The Scranton story, although there was no "syndicate," was closest to the mark.[30]

The Eagle Eye

This extremely difficult year, the year of transition from Goodfellow to the new publisher, Frank D. Schroth of Scranton, was also the most vocal one for the Communist party unit at the *Eagle*. From March 1938 till February 1939 the party published its own four-page, five-cent, monthly newspaper, *The Eagle Eye*; biased, propagandistic, and inaccurate as it may have been, it provided an illuminating and sometimes refreshing contrast to the *Eagle*'s view of itself and the *Eagle*'s view of Brooklyn. At most 10 percent of the space in *The Eagle Eye* was devoted to fostering the general national or international Communist party line, and most of its editorial and news space was given to clever and occasionally perceptive internal criticism of the *Eagle* itself. The *Eye*'s main target was always the publisher, first Goodfellow, then Schroth. Then, in a sprightly and slashing column called "Hot Sketches," the *Eye* dissected the personalities and characters of prominent managerial staff members. A colorful contrast to the stiff traditional biographies in the *Eagle* anniversary issues, the sketches exploited all the faults of their subjects as a way of exacerbating the class conflict between labor and capital. Their purpose was to undermine confidence in management by exploiting interoffice jealousies without undermining the pride the workmen may have had in the *Eagle* itself. For example:

Hot Sketches, No. 1: Eddie Martin
When Eddie Martin was a schoolboy decades ago he was a teacher's pet.

"Nobody liked him when he was a kid," a veteran newspaperman says. "He was the same then as now."

Eddie Martin is officially auditor of the *Eagle*. Unofficially he is spat-wearer and cane-carrier.

He has two functions in the production of a newspaper. The first is to save electric light bills by turning off the lights in the plant. The second is to keep printers and other employees from their work by snooping around.

The printers have rarely hesitated to say what they think of him.

His activities also consist of cigarette borrowing and kindergarten work.

He is the personification of the *Eagle* Today.

He is a big shot, president of the New York City Publishers Association. They say he knows all about unions. Unions know all about him.

Eddie Martin is as useless to the newspaper as water in a carburetor. He might be employed as an officeboy but Mr. Preston Goodfellow has always failed to use the talents of those around him.

Of what economic use to a newspaper are the Eddie Martins?

Why do they get the big salaries they are paid?

Eddie Martin represents the screw loose in our economic machinery.[31]

and:

Hot Sketches No. 4: John N. Harman
Them that has—gets. John N. Harman has two useless jobs and gets juicy salaries for both. With a big private office hidden away in the editorial sanctum of the fourth floor, rear, he is under a five-year contract providing $10,000 a year for acting in an "advisory capacity." At the same time he receives $12,000 a year of the public's money as County Clerk of Kings County. And sometimes he doesn't show up at either office for weeks. Harman's real job at the *Eagle* is supposed to be protecting the interests of one Fremont C. Peck, owner of the late *Times-Union*. Also offered as an excuse for his existence here is that he assures the *Eagle* of its share of legal advertising, sort of a bribe from Goodfellow to the Brooklyn Democratic organization. . . .[32]

Hot Sketches No. 5: James D. Garvey
. . . Never a printer, a pressman or newspaper mechanic of any

kind, and never a union man, Garvey (mechanical superintendent) never knew anything about the technique of putting out a
paper—and hasn't learned yet . . .[33]

When the new publisher let five executives go, *The Eagle Eye*
(August 1938) boasted that it had exposed two, Martin and Garvey.
The other three were Thomas Mulherne, circulation manager, Roy
Goodfellow, the former publisher's brother, and A. Haeussler,
Preston Goodfellow's brother-in-law. The *Eye* smiled on all these
departures and, for the time being, withheld judgment on Schroth.

One of the most critical sketches was of Edwin B. Wilson, whom
Schroth named executive editor. Perhaps more than any man in the
later years, Wilson was the personification of the *Eagle* spirit. He had
come to the paper in 1912 and had risen through the ranks, holding
nearly every editorial position, and he remained until the paper's
death in 1955. He was the new publisher's main contact to the old
Eagle and old Brooklyn, a symbol of continuity like the *Eagle* itself.
Wilson was an extremely gentle and gentlemanly man. In his judgment the paper's best period had been the Crist era, and the worst was
the Goodfellow time. Goodfellow, he thought, had ruined the paper
by his bad financial judgments. Later on he regretted the sensationalism that crept in under young managing editor Thomas N.
Schroth. Anyone who knew and admired Wilson would be pained by
this unkind sketch, but he might recognize him:[34]

Hot Sketches No. 9: Eddie Wilson
Edwin B. (Leatherneck) Wilson, editor of the *Eagle*, got his
nickname because he served in the Marine Corps and because it
has been stepped on so often.

For many years, Eddie was a rubber-stamp, Milquetoast city
editor under Harris M. Crist. It was Wilson's voice but the spirit
was Crist's. He joined the Rotary Club. He taught Sunday
School. He was 100 per cent inoffensive, the kind of man so
good you expect him to elope with a choir singer or chorus girl
some fine morning. But Eddie never did.

While Crist was at the *Eagle* no one ever accused him of having a mind of his own.

Everyone knows what newspapers do with men without minds of their own. They make them editorial writers.

Eddie is pleasant. He means well, particularly after a few highballs. Then the romantic Marine emerges and those who look closely see a vine leaf here and there.

When he was city editor the *Eagle* had a big night staff which worked on space. Men and women earned pitifully small sums for long, hopeless hours of work. Eddie kept lots of them on the list so he could cover all assignments. He never had courage enough to decide which stories were wanted and which were not.

Before the days of the Guild it was not unusual for him to ask day men to spend "just a minute" on another story. The "just a minute" came when the man was about to leave for home after a hard day and frequently lasted several hours.

The classic concerns the girl space-writer who worked in a sweatshop for half a week so that conditions might be exposed in an *Eagle* split-page series and then learned she earned more in the sweatshop than from her newspaper. Eddie knew all about such things. If he ever raised his voice in protest no one ever heard it.

Wilson maintains the Cleveland Rodgers tradition of "the balanced editorial" in grand style. Thus he is against vice, tuberculosis, unemployment, intolerance, poverty, dirt and contaminated clams. On the other hand, he is for virtue, health, tolerance, prosperity, cleanliness and uncontaminated clams.

These are days when people know the old ways are not good enough. They want guidance; they seek a newspaper in whose honesty they may believe. The world is alive with movement. It is a battlefield between those who need food and shelter and those who refuse to give them these things—and Eddie Wilson writes mild little editorials signifying nothing.

Really Eddie, it's time you made up your mind. And that goes double for the newspaper which employs you.[35]

*   *   *

Besides expressing the hostilities of a number of employees toward their employers, *The Eagle Eye* served a number of useful functions. It covered the *Eagle*'s coverage—and noncoverage—of the news. It seems to have been a precursor of both the "underground" press and the modern local journalism reviews. A consistent target was old conservative political columnist John A. Heffernan, "the *Eagle*'s white-haired Galahad who rides out daily to slay the Red Camel of Moscow," attacked for his alleged sympathy for Italian fascism and his anti-Semitism.[36] The *Eye* charged that the *Eagle* had an old habit of shielding the public utilities and pointed out that the *Eagle* failed to report the May 16, 1938, Brooklyn Union Gas Company hearings before the Public Service Commission in which consumer representatives presented evidence against the company to head off a rate increase.[37] The *Eagle* also failed to report the suicide of a thirty-three-year-old insurance agent, Chairman of Local 30 of the Industrial Insurance Agents Union in the Metropolitan Life Insurance Company, who killed himself after being told he would be fired if he did not stop his union activities. When Schroth dropped liberal columnist William Weer because of "reader pressure" the *Eye* came to his defense. However, the *Eye* did not mention that William Weer was the pseudonym for I. Kaufman, Guild Unit Chairman. Oliver Pilat claimed Kaufman used the pseudonym because a Jewish columnist would be unacceptable.[38]

The *Eagle* communists continually insisted that they had their own vision of what kind of paper the *Eagle* should be and that they wanted the new publisher to succeed, but they began by trying to throw him on the defensive with a personal attack. They greeted his arrival with a front page letter titled "We Know All About the Past, Boss. But It's the Future That Counts." They charged that in 1936, two years after he bought the Scranton *Republican* and changed its name to the *Tribune*, Schroth went to Germany and returned singing the praises of Hitler. Schroth regretted this, the *Eye* said, but the *Tribune* lost support and was sold. *The Eagle Eye* acknowledged that the new publisher had a reputation as a friend of labor, sometimes paying above scale for good work. The letter warned Schroth about Gannett's and Goodfellow's mistake of making the paper a financial catspaw and the mouthpiece for the Chamber of Commerce:

> We know you are familiar with the *Eagle*'s history. The *Eagle* was once one of the best known papers in the country, with the greatest prestige. It is so no longer. . . . As for us, as communists and as employees, Mr. Schroth, we would like to see you restore the *Eagle* to its former glory. May we point out that many of the people who helped make the *Eagle* what it once was, are still with us.[39]

Schroth was one of the first to put down his nickel for *The Eagle Eye* every month. He read that the communists, while they respected him for his fairness and intelligence, felt he was not living up to their expectations. He had not made an editorial break from the policies of his predecessors.[40]

On October 26, 1938, Schroth made a radio address in the "Forward Brooklyn" series over WMCA in which he gave his own philosophy about Brooklyn as a community and the *Eagle*'s role in the community. The *Eagle*'s function, he said, was to see that Brooklyn retained its neighborly touch.

> The community is merely the family, without the people being bound together by blood ties. In Brooklyn we have common interests affecting the happiness of our people, the safety of our homes, the cleanliness of our city, the education of our children.
>
> Brooklyn's source of power, its loyalty, its character, its reputation, its usefulness, its place among the cities of the country comes from the people who have had their roots in Brooklyn life for many years.
>
> A city succeeds according to the unselfish efforts of its people, and the residents of this borough must have been most unselfish, because no large city in this country so completely retains its neighborly touch. The spirit of old Brooklyn still lives.
>
> It shall be the function of the Brooklyn *Eagle* to revive any

lagging of this spirit and attune it to the trend of these fluxing times.[41]

Schroth promised that the *Eagle* would tell the truth, warts and all, to stimulate civic interest in the affairs of the community. An *Eagle Eye* editorial, "A Tip for Schroth," claimed that ever since the publisher's speech the *Eagle* had been catering more and more to the Chamber of Commerce and machine politicians. When word leaked back that Schroth did not like *The Eagle Eye*, the *Eye* replied that the *Eagle* had nothing to fear from its communists:

> Communists on the Brooklyn *Eagle* want it to become the prosperous paper it was in the past. As the leading community in America's largest city, Brooklyn deserves a daily which will represent it well. We as communists and as employees intend to criticize its failings but for no other purpose than to make it live up to its responsibilities to the people of the borough.
>
> On his side Mr. Schroth must learn that Brooklyn is a community made up not only of a Blum or two, a half dozen clergymen, a Van Sinderen, a few big shots in the Chamber of Commerce, a couple of hundred little old ladies on the Heights who have been tucked away in old lavender since Walt Whitman, but also of 3,000,000 ordinary folk. One by one the little old ladies make their last shopping trip to Loeser's and then die in a respectable hush. Greenwood is filled with them.
>
> The *Eagle* must rid itself of the smell of old lavender or it will die before the last of the little old ladies dies. Brooklyn has changed and its newspaper must reflect the varied lives and interests of its people—not solely the doings of Heights society, high hat Prospect Park West or stuffed-shirt Clinton Ave. The *Eagle* needs circulation and its prospective readers need jobs, want security. They fear war and W.P.A. cuts. Good housing, lowered light and gas rates, decent transportation, cheaper milk—these are some of the things they are after.[42]

Notes

[1]Charles Grant Miller, "The Making of Better Citizens in Brooklyn," *Editor and Publisher* (February 12, 1921): 1.

[2]Daniel J. Leab, *A Union of Individuals, The Formation of the American Newspaper Guild, 1933-1936* (New York: Columbia University Press, 1970), p. 26.

[3]The explanation of the *Eagle*'s financial problem is based on the *New York Times, Editor and Publisher*, and Cleveland Rodgers' *Reminiscences*, pp. 120-125, 185, and those of H. V. Kaltenborn. Rodgers and Crist were also stockholders.

[4]Osward Garrison Villard, *The Disappearing Daily: Chapters in American Newspaper Evolution* (Freeport: Books for Libraries Press, 1969; originally Knopf, 1944), p. 165.

[5]George Seldes, *Lords of the Press* (New York: Messner, 1938), p. 89.

[6]Rodgers, *Reminiscences*, p. 123.

[7]Villard, p. 166.

[8]Rodgers looked back on the *Eagle*'s history in the *Eagle*, October 24, 1937.

[9]Interview with Robert Moses, July 15, 1970.

[10]*New York Times,* May 22, 1956; *Eagle*, January 3, 1933.

[11]Robert Moses, "Are Cities Dead?" *The Atlantic Monthly* 209 (January 1962): 55-58.

[12]Gilbert Sorrentino, "No Radical Chic in Brooklyn," *New York Times*, January 16, 1971.

[13]*Eagle*, February 2, 1933.

[14]Norval White and Elliot Willensky, eds., *AIA Guide to New York City* (New York: Macmillan, 1968), p. 249.

[15]Stephanie de Pue, "Brooklyn Waterfront: Berths or Boondoggle?" *The Village Voice* (December 17, 1970).

[16]*Eagle*, October 24, 1937.

[17]*Eagle*, October 24, 1937.

[18]Emery, p. 692.

[19]Seldes, pp. 86-173.

[20]"A Decade Under the Guild," unpublished MS by an anonymous *Eagle* Guildsman, 1947, from the papers of Frank D. Schroth, Jr.

[21]"Decade," p. 5.

[22]Interview with Oliver Pilat, June 10, 1970.

[23]Interview with Victor and Violet Weingarten, August 4, 1973.

[24]Ibid.

[25]Interview with I. Kaufman, June 15, 1970.

[26]*New York Times*, June 30, 1955.

[27]"Decade," p. 10; O'Dwyer's *Reminiscences*, vol. 1 (Oral History Research Project, Columbia University, 1960-1962), pp. 27-28.

[28]Seldes, pp. 86-173.

[29]"Decade"; interview with Oliver Pilat, June 10, 1970.

[30]*The Eagle Eye*, March, June, July 1938.

[31]*The Eagle Eye*, March 1938.

[32]*The Eagle Eye*, June 1938.

[33]*The Eagle Eye*, July 1938.

[34]Interview with Edwin B. Wilson, February 7, 1970.

[35]*The Eagle Eye*, January 1934.

[36]*The Eagle Eye*, October 1938. The *Eye* claimed that Heffernan's September 14 column had not been critical enough of fascism. Heffernan said Italians he had spoken with respected fascism. "They like the Italy of cleanliness, and strength. . . . the Italy with its chin up. But they like better the free atmosphere of the Democratic Republic of America." In *The Eagle Eye*, November 1938, p. 4, Heffernan is accused of going out of his way to mention that Mrs. Dorothy Bellanca, Labor party-Republican candidate for Congress, is a Jewess.

[37]*The Eagle Eye*, June 1938.

[38]*The Eagle Eye*, February 1938; TNS, "Strike History," unpublished MS, 1958, p. 15; Pilat interview, June 18, 1970.

[39]*The Eagle Eye*, August 1938; *The Eagle Eye* incorrectly reported and retracted the report that one of Schroth's current *Eagle* backers was "a Mr. Roebling," a Trenton, New Jersey financier. Schroth had been an associate of Roebling but he had been dead two years. *The Eagle Eye*, October 1938.

[40]*The Eagle Eye*, October, November, December 1938.

[41]*Eagle*, October 27, 1938.

[42]*The Eagle Eye*, February 1939.

8

A NEW *EAGLE*

It can be argued that Frank D. Schroth was to represent a departure from what Rodgers considered the *Eagle*'s tradition of liberalism, with its Republican owners and independent Democratic editors. He was designated both editor and publisher from the very beginning. More than the Hesters, Gunnison, and Goodfellow, he was a writer with a clear, direct, and forceful style. The publisher would make the policy. He said he was a Democrat and prided himself on being fair with labor, but he had a great deal more love for his friend Herbert Hoover, whom he thought had been unjustly blamed for the depression, than he did for Franklin D. Roosevelt, whom he would support only once, in 1944. In addition, his unhappy conflicts with his unions were to leave him financially and personally wounded for the remaining years of his life.

The transition from Rodgers to Schroth also marked another important shift in the *Eagle*'s editorial policy and in its view of Brooklyn. Under the Hesters the *Eagle* was, at least in its outlook, a Long Island paper. Under Rodgers' editorship the *Eagle* stressed Brooklyn's relationship with the Port of New York and the necessity of improving transportation facilities linking Brooklyn to Manhattan and the farthest reaches of Long Island. Frank Schroth was from two relatively small cities, Trenton and Scranton. He had been selected by the controlling stockholders of the *Eagle* to replace Goodfellow both because of his journalistic ability and because of his reputation as a promoter of civic causes in his previous towns. The Brooklyn business leaders were accustomed to looking to the *Eagle* for civic leadership.

Rodgers had looked outward to a larger metropolitan community;

Schroth would turn inward to Brooklyn as a provincial urban community. The decision to cut back on the *Eagle*'s Long Island coverage had already been made as part of the Goodfellow economies, but Schroth, while a practical man, was a practical visionary. He believed that a borough the size of Brooklyn could support a newspaper of its own.

Schroth began his sixty-year newspaper career in 1904 as a reporter for the Trenton *True American* and had moved within a year to the Trenton *Times* for his first stint of nine years. In 1914 he became secretary of the New Jersey Board of Taxes and Assessments, and he continued as the State House and legislative correspondent for New York and Philadelphia papers as well as a string of New Jersey weeklies. In 1924 Schroth bought the morning *State Gazette* with General Edward C. Rose and Ferdinand W. Roebling, Jr., of the family that built the Brooklyn Bridge. In the same year the *State Gazette*, Trenton *Times*, and Sunday *Times-Advertiser* merged into the Trenton *Times* Newspapers, with Schroth as associate publisher and general manager of the combined papers.

Schroth sold his interest in the Trenton *Times* to James E. Kerney in February 1934 and moved to Scranton, Pa., where he bought the Scranton *Republican*, changing its name to the *Tribune* to stress its political independence. In 1938, with I. W. Killam, Canadian newsprint manufacturer, as his silent partner, he bought the Brooklyn *Eagle* with himself as president, editor, and publisher. Killam, reputedly the wealthiest man in Canada, was one of Goodfellow's creditors.

When Schroth came from Scranton to Brooklyn to take over the bankrupt *Eagle*, he was coming to a community which was in truth no longer a community but a chunk of metropolis regarded as a joke. As *Fortune* magazine described it in a special issue on New York:

> And on Long Island also are two incontrovertible facts. One is the fact of Queens, where live nearly 1,500,000 souls. The other is the fact of Brooklyn, with a population of 2,800,000 souls, second only to Chicago among U.S. urban centers. Queens to

many a smart Manhattanite, is simply a place to be endured on the way to Glen Cove, or Roosevelt Field, or Jones Beach; and some considerable portion of the popularity of New York City Park Commission Robert Moses rests on his having devised highways and bridges to that end. Brooklyn, to the smart Manhattanite, has long been a kind of joke; it is a place that once had a culture and aristocracy, and now is a no-man's land of factories and homes and gigantic tearing avenues—a place to get lost in—an unknown, unexplored land.[1]

Nevertheless, confessed *Fortune*, Brooklyn and Queens were the flesh and blood of the city of which Manhattan was the brain. Five enormous bridges connected the brain with the body—the Brooklyn Bridge, the Williamsburg, the Manhattan, the Queensborough, and Triborough. Eighteen subway tubes plus the tubes of the Pennsylvania and Long Island railroads completed the union. New York was the American continent's largest manufacturing city and nearly a third of its total goods were produced in the factories on the Long Island shore. However, between 1927 and 1937 there had been a drastic decline in production and a significant decline in employment at the same time that the city's population was continuing to rise; Brooklyn had 5,300 factories in 1927 but only 4,100 in 1937. Queens was leading the entire country in residential construction. In 1938, 37,888 apartments and homes sprouted up as opposed to 10,651 in Brooklyn, with two-room apartments renting as low as thirty dollars a month and houses for sale for $5,000.

The mile or so surrounding Borough Hall at Fulton Street, just a few blocks from the bridge, was the closest thing the borough had to an organized center. The *Eagle* building was here, as were Abraham and Straus, the Kings County Trust Company, and the Brooklyn Trust Company. Like the other key men of Brooklyn, Frank Schroth would have lunch at Gage and Tollner's on Fulton Street and at the Brooklyn Club. However, *Fortune* noted, many of Brooklyn's businessmen were too tied up with outside affairs to give much attention to the borough. For example, Walter N. Rothschild, president of Abraham and Straus, lived on East Seventieth Street in Manhattan. Schroth moved into an old town house in Brooklyn Heights.

About 63 percent of Brooklyn's 2,800,000 population were native-born whites. The old neighborhoods of the original towns —South Brooklyn, Williamsburg, etc.—were still cities within cities: Park Slope with its apartment houses overlooking the 526 acres of Prospect Park where families picnicked on Sunday afternoons, Brownsville with half of its 200,000 population living in tenements, and Flatbush, domestic and peaceful. Furthermore, large segments of the population in most of the neighborhoods, especially in the industrial areas, were living at extremely low or substandard levels. Brooklyn's reputation as a cultural center had diminished. Perhaps the one thing it still retained was that atmosphere of separateness, the fleeting peace that night can bring to a community where people live and sleep rather than trade and work:

> When the dusk comes down over Brooklyn, life—instead of tightening as it does in the center of New York—relaxes almost as if one were in the country. Back from Manhattan surge the crowds that have worked their eight hours at high tension and are glad to return to a quieter, slower-going land. To be sure, the lines form around the movie houses along Fulton Street, and the shooting galleries and the roller coasters at Coney continue their thriving trade. The bars along the waterfront also light up, and little groups lounge there smoking, talking. But for most of Brooklyn night means home. The poor scatter to their tenements; the huge middle class to their houses—the businessmen to Clinton Avenue and Albermarle Road. And up along the Heights the old guard of Brooklyn Society—the Livingstons and the Pierreponts—get on with their sedate, staid dinners, oblivious to the huge city at their backs, but cherishing the magnificent view that their homes command over New York Harbor.[2]

Schroth's arrival marked another radical turning point in the *Eagle*'s history. His ownership broke a continuity of control which the

Eagle had had from the beginning and which had been only briefly interrupted by the disastrous Gannett experience. Isaac Van Anden had brought in his nephew William Hester, who had in turn been succeeded by his son William V. Hester, who had served a long and patient apprenticeship. Herbert F. Gunnison had begun as a reporter in Williamsburg and worked his way up, as had M. Preston Goodfellow. During the past fifty years the *Eagle* had had only three editors, McKelway, Howe, and Rodgers. As Rodgers concluded, "Almost without exception, every executive and editor in the ninety-seven years of the *Eagle*'s existence has been developed inside the organization."[3] The new *Eagle*'s main living link with its past would be Edwin B. Wilson. Eventually, Schroth would strengthen his position by bringing his family in; when his sons would return from World War II, Frank Jr. would eventually become assistant publisher and Tom would work his way up from the city room to managing editor. Frank's younger brother Raymond A. Schroth of the Trenton *Times*, who also wrote editorials for the New York *Herald-Tribune*, contributed editorials daily.

There were ways in which the Schroth *Eagle* was both old and new. It was old in the sense that it devoted itself with renewed vigor to the old concept of being a "community service" paper. It picked up some of the old *Eagle* campaigns, thus demonstrating, perhaps, that an institution takes on a certain motion and character of its own and that new personalities have little power to alter it.

In preparation for its Centennial issue the *Eagle* solicited the opinions of a hundred and fifty prominent men and women to help formulate a Ten Point Program for a greater Brooklyn which the *Eagle* would publish and fight for through its editorial columns. To stimulate discussion Schroth called almost half of his hundred together for a special lunch at the Hotel Bossert on September 18, 1941 to give them a chance to talk.[4] As Edwin B. Wilson, editor, wrote in his account of the meeting, ". . . it is the prime function of a newspaper to be a mouthpiece for the community in which it is published. . . ."[5] To the *Eagle*, these assembled judges, bankers, businessmen, and civil servants were the proper spokesmen of the community. The tone of most of the recorded comments suggests that those were quiet days in

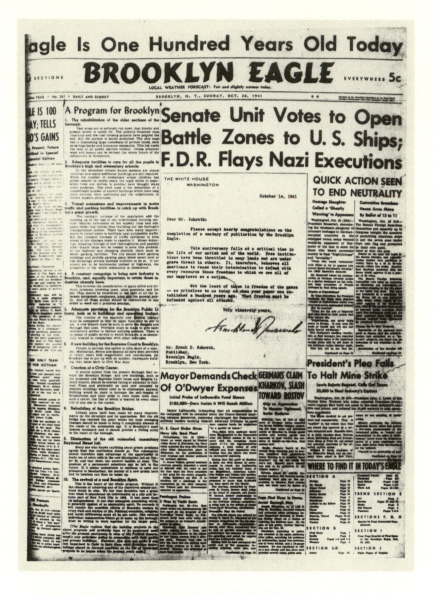

The Brooklyn *Eagle*, Sunday, October 26, 1941. The Ten Point Plan.

Brooklyn, that much of the common philosophy was still tinged with nostalgia for the past, and that the biggest worry was a vague anxiety about loss of "community spirit."

Dr. Joseph Dana Allen, headmaster of Poly Prep, stated that Brooklyn needed three things: a change in its attitude of mind, confidence and pride in itself, and a return to its former status as an independent city. Mrs. Edward C. Blum spoke up in defense of her borough: "We have a real Brooklyn spirit!" She had discovered it when she had suggested a citywide beautification movement, the planting of Brooklyn's own official flower, the forsythia, and had received so much encouragement. Equally hopeful in the face of flagging local zeal was Presiding Justice Edward Lazansky of the Appellate Division. "A majority of residents of Brooklyn have never really been Brooklynites," he lamented. These were men who were satisfied that Manhattan's glory should dim the lights of Brooklyn and who would not even be adverse to a greater centralization of political power in Manhattan at the expense of the other communities. "I do not agree that this lack of community spirit must endure. I am convinced that there must be latent love of the community which may be aroused." Nevertheless, he offered little evidence for this latent love—only the spirit of the Dodgers who had put Brooklyn "on the map."

Only city councilwoman Mrs. Genevieve B. Earle dealt with substantial social issues. The borough's biggest problem, she said, was the absorption and integration of its rapidly increasing population. Furthermore, she said, Brooklyn was a unified community in name rather than in historical fact. It had been formed by a relatively recent merger of old communities with historic names, and the unfortunate competitive spirit between these old neighborhoods was threatening a common unity and spirit. Specifically, she urged the formation of a Brooklyn Civic Council, a Council for Social Planning, and a Church and Mission Federation.

This *Eagle* meeting of Brooklyn's "leaders" should be seen in the context of the *Eagle Eye* charges and the judgment of later critics that the *Eagle* had lost touch with the "real" Brooklyn and was excessively preoccupied with the needs and concerns of a small segment of the borough's population—the old families, "real Brooklynites," the heads of established institutions, and the well-to-do who lived on Brooklyn Heights. As a group, the invited guests seemed most concerned with maintaining a sense of continuity in a community upset by change. On the whole, they were not reactionary or excessively nostalgic. For example, Mrs. William H. Good, who stated that consolidation had been a mistake, argued that a number of changes that had destroyed old Brooklyn landmarks had really brought on greater social benefits. The beloved old Smith mansion on St. Mark's Avenue was now a children's museum, the Country House at the Crescent Club was now a public school, and the Riding and Driving Club, where judges, bank presidents, and business men had enjoyed their Friday night riding classes, was now an apartment building. In short, those "leaders" were concerned with the welfare of the community at large, but there is some question as to whether in listening to them the *Eagle* was in fact listening to Brooklyn.

Robert Moses concluded in retrospect that the *Eagle* was as representative of Brooklyn as the *Atlantic Monthly* was of modern Boston.[6] The *Eagle* archives in the Brooklyn Public Library contains four large manila envelopes with the tag: "These envelopes contain letters of commendation and thanks from Brooklynites, big and little, to the *Eagle*. Together they indicate the influence and role of the *Eagle* in Brooklyn." An analysis of 575 of these letters written between 1942 and 1955 indicates that the *Eagle* was primarily influential with clergymen, charitable agencies, voluntary and civic associations who were conducting fund raising drives, businessmen, and lawyers.[7]

The New Plan and "Divorce"

When the results of the talks were published in the *Eagle* Plan, most of the proposals were for building projects:

1 The rehabilitation of the older sections of the borough.

2 Adequate facilities to care for all the pupils in Brooklyn's high schools and elementary schools.

3 Transit extensions and improvements in motor traffic and parking facilities to catch up with Brooklyn's great growth.

4 A constant campaign to bring new industry to Brooklyn and, equally important, to retain those industries already here.

5 Adequate provision for the Brooklyn Public Library both as to buildings and operating budget.

6 A new building for the Supreme Court in Brooklyn.

7 Creation of a Civic Center in Brooklyn.

8 Rebuilding of the Brooklyn Bridge.

9 Elimination of the old, outmoded, unsanitary Raymond Street Jail.

10 The revival of a real Brooklyn spirit.

A page one editorial argued that the tenth point was at the heart of the whole program:

> Without it the chances of achieving any of the objectives already outlined would be slim. We feel that Brooklyn lost a great deal when it abandoned its individuality as a city and became part of New York City in 1898. It lost more than its independence. It lost that intangible something which is generally spoken of as community spirit. To recreate it will require the unselfish efforts of Brooklyn leaders in every walk and station of life. Political, economic, religious and racial differences must all be put aside. The various individual communities which go to make up the borough must be willing to work together for the larger good.[8]

In devising and promoting the Ten Point Plan, which was revised and renewed ten years later and was largely completed by the time the paper closed, the *Eagle* was returning to the unfinished business begun in the "Brooklyn Beautiful" movement of 1911.[9] In his second major project Schroth returned to a theme that old Brooklynites had never allowed to die—regret over consolidation.

One of Frank Schroth's techniques in pressuring governments into paying attention to community problems was the sponsoring of independent surveys. When he had been with the Trenton *Times* he had commissioned the political science department at Princeton University to study the tax and financial problems of the state of New

Jean Raeburn photo, Brooklyn Public Library *Eagle* Collection

Frank D. Schroth, last publisher of the *Eagle*.

Jersey and the efficiency of the state government. The report was printed in the *Times* and became the basis of government reform legislation for several years. In Scranton he had commissioned another group of experts to see how the city's economy could be built up. Aware that many Brooklyn citizens felt that their borough was not getting a fair share of New York City funds and conscious of the longing expressed in its own centennial issue for a return to independent status as a city, Schroth approached the Princeton University Research Center and had them make a survey of what Brooklyn was getting in the way of city services. He announced beforehand that if the survey found Brooklyn was actually being neglected, the *Eagle* would recommend divorcing Brooklyn from New York. The survey was "mischief making" as Schroth acknowledged many years later. The *Eagle* never saw separation as a real possibility, but it was a good way of pressuring city hall and educating Brooklyn citizens to the realities of urban economics. In a sense, the *Eagle* was exploiting one of the borough's weaknesses, its nostalgia, in order to catch its attention and make it reflect on its present condition.[10]

The Princeton report, issued in May 1942 and published in the *Eagle* in serial form, recounted the history of consolidation, emphasizing how Brooklyn had been driven into union largely by the threat of bankruptcy and how every new city charter from 1901 to 1941 had moved toward greater centralization of city services. The economic interdependence, it said, had worked to Brooklyn's advantage. In the first year under the new charter the tax rate in Manhattan had gone up forty-seven points, a 25 percent increase over its former level, while in Brooklyn the tax levy was the lowest in seventeen years, $1,680,627 less than in 1897.[11]

Between 1890 and 1940 Brooklyn's population had risen from 838,547 to 2,698,285, a jump from 33.4 percent to 36.2 percent of the total population of Greater New York, with the biggest percentage increase between 1900 and 1910. By 1941 Brooklyn was considered by the survey scholars to be rather fully developed with a population density of 33,332 per square mile. They judged that new transit facilities might increase land values but not the population. Brooklyn had the largest population of any borough, although the population growth rate in Queens during the past four years had surpassed Brooklyn's, which had dropped slightly. Brooklyn was an outstanding foreign trade center, the second largest borough in land area, and had the second largest valuation of taxable real estate.

Brooklyn was doing so well, the survey concluded, that there was no reasonable basis for separation. There was no evidence of anti-Brooklyn discrimination on the part of the New York administration. If Brooklyn wanted more intensified community development it could get it by separation if it wanted to pay for it, but separation would cause disaffection on the part of those Brooklynites who looked to the larger city for values, and it would increase the tax rate and bring with it a number of other economic and legal problems.[12]

If separation were therefore out of the question, Brooklyn and the *Eagle* had to make other plans for civic improvement. The survey suggested setting up a public works reserve to handle postwar unemployment and an orderly replacement of public facilities that would suffer hard use and lack of repair during the war. Meanwhile, the City Planning Commission had earmarked $628,000,000 for long-range improvements, 30 percent of which was designated for Brooklyn, plus an additional $91,000,000 for low-cost public housing, $29,000,000 of it for Brooklyn.

The Eagle's Brooklyn After the Second World War

Like the depression, the Second World War dealt a devastating psychological blow to economic and family life in Brooklyn. Its immediate impact, as the young novelist Gilbert Sorrentino describes it, was "glory." The young were free, off to adventure; the older men got richer than ever before on pay checks from the Brooklyn Navy Yard, which were paid in down payments for houses in Queens. However, the war demanded its own payment in the blood and neurosis of the community. It was a decade of drift and disillusionment; Sorrentino recalls:

Then the troops returned from *the* slaughter, ready to take their places. But how strange that so many of them had become drunkards, brawlers, bums content to stand on the corner with the boys, who had been just too young to get into it. They fought, they ogled the high school girls, drank wine, shot crap, played the horses. Some disappeared into psychiatric wards, got married to neighborhood girls, got jobs—even though they had not skills. [13]

As Pete Hamill remembers those years:

The first cracks in that stability showed up during the war, when a lot of fathers were away fighting and a lot of mothers were working in war plants. Some Brooklynites had been shocked at the revelation about Murder, Incorporated, the brutal Brooklyn-based Jewish-Italian mob whose members killed for money. But when the teenage groups started roving Brooklyn during the war, then some citizens thought the end was near (you could abide Murder, Inc., of course, if your other institutions—family church, jobs—remained stable). In Bedford-Stuyvesant, the first black gangs, the Bishops and the Robins began to assemble down on Sands Street; the Navy Yard Boys were already rolling sailors and shipyard workers; the Red Hood Boys came out of the first projects and the side streets around the Gowanus Canal; the Garfield Boys, from Garfield Place in South Brooklyn, expanded into the South Brooklyn Boys, and became the training ground for many of the soldiers who are now in the Brooklyn chapters of the Mafia. In my neighborhood, the Shamrock Boys became the Tigers, and they fought the South Brooklyn Boys with the expertise in urban guerilla warfare (on both sides) that the Black Panthers would be advised to study. I don't know if there ever really was a gang called the Amboy Dukes (I am told by buffs that there was), but Irving Shulman's *The Amboy Dukes* became the bible for a lot of these kids; they studied the Sayings of Crazy Shock the way the motorcycle gangs later studied Lee Marvin and Brando in *The Wild One*.

The gangs were wild, often brutal; there were more than a few knifings and gang rapes, and a number of killings, especially after the war, when veterans started bringing home guns as souvenirs; in shop classes in high schools, students spent more time making zip guns out of pieces of pipe than they did making bookcases or pieces of sinks. The gun—especially if it was a *real* gun—became a thing of awe. The first time I ever saw Joe Gallo (they called him Joe the Blond in those days) he was in the Ace Pool Room upstairs from his father's luncheonette on Church Avenue; someone, I think it was an old friend named Johnny Rose, whispered to me, "Don't ever say nuthin' about him: he's packin.' "[14]

The gangs broke up during the fifties, partly because their membership was depleted by the Korean War but also because they lost a lot of men through heroin. Brooklyn became a city of fear and the citizens talked about getting out. The Long Island which Brooklynites saw thirty years before as an extension of their city now became another country, an escape. Therefore, it was the *Eagle*'s role during Brooklyn's greatest period of instability to assure Brooklyn citizens that its institutions really were still stable.

In the last stages of the war Frank Schroth toured the Pacific war zone with Henry Luce, met with General Douglas MacArthur, and sent home human interest stories highlighting the contributions of Brooklyn boys. On June 7, 1945, he wrote from a carrier off Okinawa: "There has never been a finer group of young men aboard any ship in any fleet. And a good portion of them are from Brooklyn." At the end of the war the *Eagle* published a special booklet—though not as elaborate or thorough as the ones it had put out at the end of the Spanish-American War or the First World War—called *Staging Area Brooklyn*, describing the port of Brooklyn's contribution to the national effort. The *Eagle* then turned its first postwar efforts to sponsoring a competition for the best design for the Brooklyn War Memorial and to promoting a campaign to build it.

On the question of juvenile delinquency during the period described in Pete Hamill's vivid and terrifying recollections, the *Eagle* took a positive and reassuring approach. Rereading the *Eagle*'s special series on Juvenile Delinquency published between September 29, 1943, and September 24, 1944, it is hard to escape the conclusion that the *Eagle* was overaccentuating the positive; yet the series followed from the paper's basic presuppositions that the salvation of the community was in supporting its civic, religious, and voluntary institutions, that social problems were to a large degree the result of a breakdown in religious observance, and that idleness was one of the main causes of crime. It seems as if the "self-help" themes of the Emma Bullet *Autobiography* and the old biographical sketches of *Eagle* editors and nineteenth century "prominent Brooklyn citizens" had carried over to the treatment of this ghastly wartime social catastrophe.

The first article was by J. Edgar Hoover, an old *Eagle* friend who sent the paper a letter every time its editorials said a kind word for the FBI.[15] The second piece, by John E. Wade, New York City Superintendent of Schools, stressed the need for religious instruction. In the rest of the articles there was frightfully inadequate treatment of the extent of the crime, the organization of the gangs, or the other changes in the social living patterns that were shaking the community. The emphasis was on the fine things already being done to care for Brooklyn's youth by farm workers, the Italians, the Big Brothers, the Public Library, the Bureau of Charities, the Park Department, settlement houses, parents, Boys' Clubs, Boy Scouts, YMCA, Catholic Charities, the Salvation Army, Camp Fire Girls, Girl Scouts, the Dodgers' Knot Hole Club (watching baseball combats idleness), and the Knights of Columbus. The final article, the most constructive, called for a new Social Planning Council to unite the borough's efforts.

One of the *Eagle*'s most popular contributions to Brooklyn's pride and self-awareness after the war was the publication of a series of six booklets in the Sunday paper, beginning with October 13, 1946, on the histories of Brooklyn's six original towns. Just as the juvenile delinquency series served to restore the community's confidence in its institutions, the history pamphlets served to restore a feeling of neighborhood belonging and a sense of place to a borough on the verge of a new migration. Publisher Schroth wrote in the foreword:

It is the hope of the Brooklyn *Eagle* that printing of these histories of the original settlements will interest not only our adult residents but—and this is more important—will also serve to make the youth of the Borough conscious of the stirring events that have transpired in the past 300 years on the very ground over which they pass each day about their appointed tasks.

For this reason sufficient copies of these booklets have been printed for distribution in the public parochial and private high schools in Brooklyn.[16]

Although it was not an expressed purpose, the texts also built up the confidence of a community that had suffered a long and costly war. When read today, alongside other descriptions of postwar Brooklyn, these "historical" pamphlets can be seen not simply as records of a once great city's "stirring events" but as evidence of a frightened community's efforts to recapture its poise by rediscovering its roots. The *Eagle* and Brooklyn shared the American faith that somehow education was the solution to all its social problems. Somehow if the young people of Brooklyn could appreciate that the Soldiers and Sailors Memorial Arch at Grand Army Plaza was the "most beautiful arch in the world" and that their basketball courts at Fourth Street and Fifth Avenue had once seen the fiercest fighting of the Battle of Long Island, their civic virtues would be reinforced. If a stroller at Fulton Street and Dock Street, now in the shadow of the Brooklyn Bridge, could appreciate that this was the spot depicted in Francis Gay's popular 1915 painting "Snow Scene," he could project himself back into a simpler and cleaner life. In its final pages the *Eagle* repeats the creed which more and more Brooklynites were finding hard to believe:

Brooklyn takes pride in its industrial supremacy but prefers to stand forth as the finest place in the world in which to live and go to church and send the children to school.

Brooklyn is still growing, but despite its size, its heterogeneous population, and its cosmopolitanism there is a community solidarity and a spirit of hometown neighborliness that exists nowhere else in the world.[17]

There is a special irony in the *Eagle*'s last assertion that "Brooklyn takes pride in the fact that the mayor of the City of New York, the Hon. William O'Dwyer, is a Brooklynite."[18] Within five years O'Dwyer and the *Eagle* would be locked in a battle that would end in the Mayor's resigning and leaving the country under a cloud to be Ambassador to Mexico.

The Crime War

One of the things that changed at the *Eagle* was its style. In March 1940, when the managerial reorganization was complete, the *Eagle* adopted a more "modern" format with a bolder type face. Now it called itself the Brooklyn *Eagle* rather than the Brooklyn *Daily Eagle*. Now an "independent" rather than a Democratic paper, it endorsed Wendell Wilkie for President. Eventually it made more and more dramatic use of headlines, splashing them boldly across the page in the largest available type. It developed its technique on its civic service campaigns—maximum, daily, page one, dramatic exposure of an issue. The *Eagle* became a livelier and more sensational paper.

A contributing factor in the *Eagle*'s new life was the publisher's son, Thomas N. Schroth, who came to the *Eagle* after the war and after experience in the Washington Bureau of *Time* and the Boston office of the United Press. At the *Eagle* he was a reporter, copyreader, rewriter, city editor, news editor, and managing editor. As a young man, he had a number of ideas about what was wrong with the *Eagle* and how to improve it. Like others, he was dissatisfied with the cautiousness of Mr. Wilson's editorial page. As managing editor he sent a flood of memos to the staff praising good work and criticizing mistakes. He had discovered Brooklyn by wandering around its neighborhoods and had quickly learned to love it. He was intelligent, imaginative, idealistic, more liberal than his father, ambitious, and a good man to work for.[19]

What was by some standards the best year of the new *Eagle* began in

September 1949 when *Eagle* reporter Ed Reid overheard a man at a bar say "A new boss has taken over the bookie joints in town. Guy called Mr. G. They say he was put in business by three top coppers." "Mr. G." was Harry Gross, a flashy young gambler who had contributed to O'Dwyer's campaigns in 1945 and 1949. It had been common knowledge in Brooklyn for years that the nation's underworld had merged into a crime syndicate called The Combination, and that the headquarters of the assassination gang, known as Murder Inc. and led by Joe Adonis and his chief executioner Albert Anastasia, was in southern Brooklyn. District Attorney William O'Dwyer had begun to make progress in the prosecution of the syndicate in 1940, but his investigation had faltered when his key witness, Abe "Kid Twist" Reles, died in a mysterious fall. Now O'Dwyer had just been reelected Mayor of New York with *Eagle* support—and a scandal was about to end his administration. In fact, the *Eagle* had uncovered evidence of police bribery before election time but had held off till after the November election because it didn't want to embarrass O'Dwyer.[20]

The *Eagle* had heard that bookmaking had reached such proportions in Brooklyn and throughout the city that it was being protected by the city police department to the amount of $20,000,000 a year in payoffs to crooked cops and officials. Managing editor Robert M. Grannis relieved Reid of other duties and assigned him to the crime story. He visited Brooklyn district attorney Miles McDonald, who urged him on.[21] The *Eagle* prepared its readers for a shocking exposé with large ads and editorials. On December 11, 1949, the *Eagle* splashed its headlines across the page and began a relentless war that was to culminate in a New York grand jury investigation, the resignation of the Mayor, the New York sessions of the Estes Kefauver Senate Crime Committee in the spring of 1951, and the Pulitzer Prize for the *Eagle*.

While the *Eagle*'s manner of presentation was flamboyant and calculated to shock, its central theme was fundamentally conservative—the preservation of home and civic virtue. It was careful not to undermine civic pride by strong attacks on named individuals. O'Dwyer, a Brooklynite, was not initially the *Eagle*'s target.

Two weeks before Christmas, Brooklynites picked up their Sunday morning *Eagle* and read, in Reid's emotional prose:

LUCRATIVE BOROUGH RACKETS
FEED VAST CRIME SYNDICATE

Brooklyn is a mailed fist on a scabrous arm of crime that stretches from California to New York.

The brains behind that arm and fist which holds hundreds of thousands of Americans in thrall is known as the Combine.

The Combine is a monstrous fusion of criminal brains built on the bloody ashes of Murder, Inc. Its agents are found in almost every big city in the United States.[22]

The front page editorial was milder, almost stepping gingerly away from what the news columns had screamed:

The cure is not in the hands of this newspaper. Public co-operation in the form of evidence turned over to the law enforcement agencies is the first step in the solution.

We do not presume to dictate a code of moral conduct for any adult. But we do hope this series will pave the way for a cleaner Brooklyn and eliminate all possibilities of alliances between law enforcement agencies and the underworld.

Monday afternoon Reid renewed the attack:

Racket Expose Reveals
HUGE PAYOFF FOR PROTECTION
Bookies kick in $225,000 a Week
30 Betting Districts Here
Furnish $7,500 Each to
Keep Wheels Grinding

The Combine rides Brooklyn rackets with an iron hand plated with 24-karat gold.

Reid explained how the Brooklyn Combine had bought into the trucking and liquor industries and how both protection money to policemen and the section No. 399 in the County Courts Code of Criminal Procedure, barring the uncorroborated testimony of an accomplice, had protected criminals from prosecution:

> It is this section that saved from the electric chair the man whom the *Eagle* learned is now rackets boss in the United States, the man to whom even Frank Costello tips his hat. He is Vito Genovese, former darling of the Italian Fascists.[23]

WHO IS THE TOP BOSS OF BROOKLYN'S RACKETS?

The grotesque and hybrid camaraderie that enables racketeers to seek out and mingle with persons high up in Brooklyn's social strata finds its fulfillment in the person of the borough's present rackets boss, whom we will call Mr. X.

He is a highly respected member of society—charitable, palpably religious—well thought of by people who are not in the know. He is the kind of fellow who shows at public ceremonies—was at one recently connected with the construction of a new wing on a well-known institution.

Mr. X, wrote Reid, had a farm guarded by an electric eye and savage dogs. He had been a black market operator during the war. He contributed thousands of dollars to charity and almost received a high decoration from the church. The *Eagle* did not name Mr. X, although Reid's *Shame of New York* has a chapter on a "Mr. Big" who meets Mr. X's description; he was businessman William J. McCormack. (McCormack's name later figured prominently in the United States Senate investigations of crime on the Brooklyn waterfront.) Reid's style betrays some of the animus a number of *Eagle* staff members felt toward Brooklyn's so-called "prominent citizens" who were usually treated with such respect by the *Eagle*. However, Reid's later book, *The Grim Reapers* (New York: Bantam, 1969), names Joseph Profaci as the *Eagle's* "Mister X."

That very day the *Eagle* reported that Brooklyn Congressman Emanuel Celler was calling for an FBI investigation in response to the *Eagle*'s revelations. "It sounds fantastic," said Celler. Nevertheless, if a "reputable paper like the *Eagle*, with a long reputation for fair conduct," published the charges, the matter should be checked. On the same page was a story about recently reelected Mayor William O'Dwyer's recuperation in seclusion in Florida, where he was preparing to marry thirty-three-year-old model Sloan Simpson.

Nothing, apparently, angered the *Eagle* more than the corruption of children:

GAMBLERS INFEST SCHOOLS, PREY ON KIDS' LUNCH MONEY

Students Hired
By Ring to Take
Wagers on Games

The crime bosses are infecting our school children with the gambling fever.

They are reaching into the schools, into the dark corridors, into the shadows behind the buildings where the ivy, bright green in the sun, turns to ugly purple.

They are taking our children, their pennies, nickels, dimes and quarters. They are planting the gambling fever in them and they are hoping that it burns forever.[24]

In a five-column front-page spread the *Eagle* reproduced copies of the betting cards on basketball, football, and baseball games circulated in the schools by "runners" for the syndicate. A page one editorial urged the Board of Education to "safeguard our decent young people from the most insidious of temptations, the promise of a rich reward for the illegal investment of a few of their pennies." One boy at Brooklyn College made $1,000 taking bets in the previous football season. The next day the *Eagle* banner headline cried:

SCHOOL CHIEFS LAUNCH WIDE PROBE OF RACKET-LED STUDENT GAMBLING

and the editorial page cartoon depicted a Pied Piper gambler leading Brooklyn's children out of their schools and over a cliff. Reid's next stories detailed corruption on the waterfront and a conversation with a bookie who was paying off the police.

As the series progressed, the *Eagle* front page gave more prominence to Brooklyn's reaction to the exposé than it did to the crime series itself. The school gambling report seems to have stirred up the greatest anxiety—although in retrospect it seems the least significant—probably because it threatened Brooklyn where it thought it was strongest, in the homes and schools. The Sunday, December 18 headline announced the outrage of the borough's religious leaders, who hailed the *Eagle*'s exposé of the combine, while Reid's installment disclosed that Carlos Tresca, the militant anti-Fascist editor who was killed in New York in 1943, had been gunned down on an order from Italian Fascists.

Meanwhile, the *Eagle*'s editorials were curiously mild and uncrusading. They said again and again that the *Eagle* was not a prosecuting agency nor did it intend to preach to people or legislate adult morality. The *Eagle* just wanted to protect young people and eliminate corrupting links between criminals and police.

On December 22, Miles F. McDonald asked for and received extension of the 1949 Grand Jury till March 31, 1951. This was granted by Judge Samuel Leibowitz, who praised the *Eagle*. McDonald's statement on the Reid articles, which had prompted his decision, was not unconditional praise:

> Despite the fact that these articles have been of a general nature and contained little or no facts of any evidentiary nature, they were written in a rather flamboyant style which would undoubtedly cause concern among the general public, particularly the article which averred that a nationwide gambling syndicate was preying upon the youths attending educational institutions in the country.[25]

McDonald's probe, conducted by forty young "uncorrupted" police right out of the academy, continued through the winter, spring, and summer, making progress in May with the indictment of a few policemen and the convictions of three bookies who had preyed on student bettors.[26]

In the meantime, Mayor O'Dwyer's troubles had been increasing. When he announced that the Brooklyn Civic Center building funds had been curtailed indefinitely, the *Eagle* responded with a front-page cartoon showing Father Knick crushing the child Brooklyn's toys with his foot.[27] When his plan to legalize gambling was defeated in Albany, the *Eagle* reminded its readers that although O'Dwyer meant well he was dead wrong. The law had an educational function; it is "a guidepost telling children what path to follow."[28]

O'Dwyer responded with a campaign of personal intimidation against Schroth.[29] The *Eagle* was reminded that the city owned the *Eagle* building, having bought it to make way for the Civic Center, and might want to use it for civil defense. He said privately that the *Eagle* had campaigned for the Center to make money on the building sale. O'Dwyer also told newsmen off the record that a "certain publisher" had received a free trip to Germany on the Hindenburg at the invitation of Hitler. Schroth replied that the *Eagle* had lost on the building sale and he had paid for his own trip. The *Eagle* was also anonymously informed that O'Dwyer had also sent an agent to Scranton to investigate Schroth. To O'Dwyer, an ex-policeman, the *Eagle* investigations were a "witch hunt" to embarrass good cops.

The O'Dwyer-Schroth feud is one of the more mysterious and tragic episodes of the *Eagle*'s final years. The two men do not seem to have had any personal contact after December 1949 and they were communicating with one another in the worst possible way. The *Eagle* pounded away on the crime issue, increasing O'Dwyer's embarrassment; O'Dwyer continually made private remarks that he must have known would be repeated to Schroth. At one time he would complain how the *Eagle* was "getting lousier" every day; at another he would talk warmly of his "old friend" Frank Schroth and pass the word that they should get together. Meanwhile, O'Dwyer's feud with Schroth was paralleled by a similar erratic battle with Brooklyn Borough

President John Cashmore over control of the Brooklyn Democratic party.

O'Dwyer became convinced the *Eagle* was under the control of his enemies in the Democratic organization because the *Eagle* was living off advertising, legal notices, etc., from the organization, and that his old friend Schroth was out to "get" him.[30] Schroth, who resisted suggestions that the two "get together" on the grounds that there were no differences to be adjusted since the *Eagle* coverage had been objective and fair, saw O'Dwyer's remarks as an assault on his integrity.

O'Dwyer's most desperate charge, that Schroth had remained silent on the persecution of the Jews following his 1936 trip to Germany and Russia, was made just a few days before his own resignation in August. It recalls the *Eagle Eye*'s 1938 charge that Schroth had been friendly to Hitler. Perhaps O'Dwyer, who had been a Brooklyn magistrate at that time, had heard the accusation when Schroth first came to town and had harbored some unknown grudge for over twelve years; it is tragic that this slander stayed alive so long. In actuality, Schroth wrote in the September 18, 1936, Scranton *Tribune* that the German Olympic games were not sporting events but Nazi propaganda, that Hitler's treatment of the Jews was "unconscionable," and that Nazi policies were "ruthless" and could lead to war. He said that the German and Russian people backed their governments because they had been deceived by a controlled press, and ended up with a condemnation of Fascism, Nazism, and Communism. It is possible that O'Dwyer's poor health—he had spent part of the year in the hospital suffering from severe hepatitis—explains at least part of his strange behavior.

As the year went on, the *Eagle* found room on its already overcrowded front page for the Korean War, Red China, the "revelations" of Senator Joseph McCarthy, a New Hampshire mercy killing, Ingrid Bergman's baby, and another lurid crime exposé by Bert Hochman on crime in the streets. Every day from February 21 to March 6, the *Eagle* cried across the top or bottom of its first page, "PUT COPS BACK ON THE BEAT."

The tragic climax of the *Eagle*-O'Dwyer fight came with the *Eagle*

July 17, 1950 headline, "Quizzed in Rackets, High Cop Is Suicide. Note Denies He Shot Self Over Gambling Probe."

Captain John G. Flynn, commanding officer of the Fourth Avenue police precinct, had shot himself in the head at the station house. The note said, among other things, that he was tired of commuting in from Queens. His wife cried, "Haven't they done enough in Brooklyn . . . They murdered my husband."[32] O'Dwyer seized on the Flynn funeral to make a public display of his resentment. Singling out the *Eagle*, he said that "Captain Flynn's babies shouldn't have to carry the disgrace contained in that headline," and he passed the word that every available policeman should march in Flynn's funeral parade to the requiem mass at the Roman Catholic Church of the Ascension in Queens. Meanwhile, the *Eagle* reprinted the headlines of the *Post, News, Mirror, Journal-American, Herald Tribune, Times* and *Compass* to demonstrate that all the papers had said virtually the same thing.

The Mayor and Police Commissioner William P. O'Brien marched at the head of 6,000 police into the church to say that Captain Flynn was, in O'Dwyer's book, "a clean man." The *Eagle* responded with a blistering Sunday editorial, "Politics Unwelcome Intruder at Solemn Requiem Mass," calling the funeral ceremony a shocking and sacrilegious display that discredited the police department and the Church. The editorial was secretly written, at Frank D. Schroth's request, by a Jesuit labor priest, Father William Smith. Smith was a blunter writer than Wilson, and Schroth wanted criticism of the Church to come from a priest.[32]

Within a month, Mayor O'Dwyer had resigned to become Ambassador to Mexico. The *Eagle*'s editorial, "The Evolution of Mr. O'Dwyer from Mayor to Ambassador," described his career in kindly terms, noting that he had become a "different man" after his illness, "attacking some of his warm friends . . ." The editorial concluded, "The *Eagle* wishes Mr. O'Dwyer well in his new post and is confident that he will do a fine job for his country."[33]

By the end of 1950, the *Eagle*'s war on crime had won it seven awards, including the Pulitzer Prize gold medal "for the most distinguished and meritorious public service rendered by an American newspaper."[34]

BROOKLYN EAGLE

LATE NEWS
★★★★

WEATHER
Today cloudy and humid; scattered showers tonight.

109th YEAR—No. 195—DAILY and SUNDAY BROOKLYN 2, N. Y., MONDAY, JULY 17, 1950 **5 CENTS EVERYWHERE**

REDS REACH TAEJON

Smash on 3 Fronts to Encircle City

Quizzed in Rackets, High Cop Is Suicide

Note Denies He Shot Self Over Gambling Probe

GUNMAN KILLS BOROUGH MAN AFTER HOLDUP

Shoots Car Owner Objecting to Use Of Auto in Flight

THEY MADE IT TOUGH—Although U. S. Army mortar squads like one shown above along south shore of Kum River took heavy toll of Communists crossing from north, they were forced to retreat shortly after this picture was taken. Yanks retired to Taejon under heavy assault.

EXPECT TRUMAN TO REJECT PEACE BID FROM NEHRU

To End Korea War if UN Admits China Reds

Report Stalin Willing

Massed Tanks Push GIs Steadily Back —Abandon Airstrip

TOP BRASS SEES LONG, HARD PULL BEFORE VICTORY

United Press Correspondent Gene Symonds reported from Korea that bee reports indicated Red forces were just a few miles from Taejon on the north and west and were driving down on the city from the east.

N. Y. National Guard Seeks 3,000 Recruits

Enlistments Reopened to Bring Force Up to Full Strength of 30,000 Men

Fog and Rain Again in Store For Brooklynites

Queen Mary May Carry U. S. Troops to Korea

'Courtroom'

Dead Reds Piled Like Cordwood As Hordes Screamed in Attack

By ROBERT C. MILLER

Anti-U. S. Rallies Ordered

WHERE TO FIND IT

Front page of the *Eagle*, July 17, 1950.

Notes

[1]"Brooklyn and Queens," *Fortune* 20 (July 1939): 145.

[2]Ibid.

[3]*Eagle*, October 25, 1937.

[4]Participants in the *Eagle* September 18, 1941, lunch at the Hotel Bossert: Dr. Paul D. Shafer, president, Packer Collegiate Institute; Walter Hammitt, vice-president, Loeser's; Walter Holcombe, vice-president, Brooklyn Edition Company; Jacob C. Klinck, president, Kings County Savings Bank; Oscar Lewis; Frank W. Miller; Charles E. Murphy; Tristram W. Metcalfe, dean, Long Island University; Clifford E. Paige, president, Brooklyn Union Gas Company; Howard Shiehler, secretary, superintendent of schools; Mrs. Clarence P. Waterman; William O'Dwyer, district attorney; Dr. Joseph Dana Allen, headmaster, Poly Prep; Philip A. Benson, president, Dome Savings Bank of Brooklyn; Robert E. Blum, vice-president and secretary, Abraham and Straus; Joseph W. Catharine, president, Brooklyn Rotary Club; Mrs. Mary E. Dillon, president, Brooklyn Borough Gas Company; Dr. Milton J. Ferguson, chief librarian, Brooklyn Public Library; Henry J. Davenport, president, Downtown Brooklyn Association; James G. McDonald, president, Brooklyn Institute of Arts and Sciences; Louis G. Wills; Reverend Edward E. Swanstrom; Grover M. Moscowitz, federal judge; Samuel S. Leibowitz, county judge; Edward A. Richards, president of East New York Savings Banks; Daniel J. McVarish, president of Brooklyn and Queens Board of Business Agents, AFL; George H. Trumplet, Society of Old Brooklynites; John Cashmore, borough president; Joseph O. McGoldrick, controller; Mrs. William H. Good; Edward Lazansky, presiding justice of Appellate Division; Lewis J. Valentine, police commissioner; Michael F. Walsh, secretary of state; Genevieve B. Earle, councilwoman; John H. Delaney, chairman, Board of Transportation; David L. Tilly, president, Brooklyn Chamber of Commerce.

[5]*Eagle*, October 26, 1941.

[6]Interview with Robert Moses, July 15, 1970.

[7]Nearly all are brief, polite, routine notes of appreciation for complimentary *Eagle* editorials supporting various civic causes, fundraising drives, etc. One hundred and seven are from clergymen, church groups, religious and quasi-religious organizations such as the YMCA, National Conference of Christians and Jews, and various Jewish organizations. One hundred and five are from charitable agencies, voluntary associations, and semi-public in-

stitutions such as hospitals, the Red Cross, the Girl Scouts, the Children's Aid Society, the ASPCA, and the Industrial Home for the Blind.

Fifty-eight are from businessmen, bankers, insurance men, and real estate dealers. Forty-five are from agencies of the New York City and Brooklyn city governments, such as the Brooklyn Council on Social Planning. Forty-four are from judges and thirty-four from lawyers. Forty-one are from New York State and City and Brooklyn political leaders. Thirty-three are from educators, fourteen from federal agencies, and six from congressmen.

J. Edgar Hoover wrote to the *Eagle* eight times, thanking the editor for the *Eagle*'s support of the FBI. The largest group of letters from a single source is from the Joint Conference of Affiliated Postal Employees. Fifty-five workers sent in postcards around June 2, 1945, and twenty-six around February 17, 1948, thanking the *Eagle* for support of higher salaries for postal workers.

Very few letters discuss national or international political or social problems. Only one is from a labor union, and one says, "Your recent editorials on the labor situation were splendid. They showed clear thinking and fairness." (J. H. Szymanski to Editor, May 20, 1947). Hardly any are from so-called "little people," except the postcards from the postal employees (which were probably written at a meeting), a few cards praising the *Eagle* in general terms, and two letters thanking the *Eagle* for its efforts in finding lost dogs. (Mrs. C. Hyams to Editor, August 5, 1949; Beatrice Moehler to Editor, March 14, 1949).

An examination of the editorial pages during a representative year shows that only about one-third of the editorials were on these "complimentary" topics. Yet the collector, probably Mr. Wilson, found these letters significant enough to preserve.

I shall reproduce four typical letters as examples of how leading Brooklyn citizens felt about the *Eagle*.

(1)

45 Plaza Street

March 28, 1940

Dear Mr. Wilson:

That was a perfectly splendid article on Forsythia Time in Brooklyn. Your cooperation in this civic movement is magnificent.

Please accept my appreciation of all you are doing to help, and also convey my hearty congratulations to the writer for her clever and effective story.

Cordially,
Florence A. Blum
(Mrs. Edward C. Blum)

(2)

Supreme Court of the State of New York
Justices' Chambers
Mineola, N.Y.

November 9, 1950

Dear Ed:

You certainly took care of Mary's engagement party. The whole family joins in thanking you.

You will never realize how much relieved I was when I learned that a settlement had been arrived at with the Union. I can think of nothing more disastrous for the City of New York than the Brooklyn *Eagle* or the New York *Times* to suspend publication even for one day. Of course, the New York *Times* was not involved, but the community would receive an awful setback.

I will be in Brooklyn in December and I am looking forward to seeing you.

Sincerely,
TOM(S)
Thomas J. Cuff
(Justice)

(Cuff was a former *Eagle* employee. He took night assignments as a reporter while in law school).

Mr. Edwin Wilson
Executive Editor
24 Johnson Street
Brooklyn, N.Y.

(3)

Supreme Court of the State of New York
Justices' Chambers
Brooklyn, N.Y.

September 17, 1951

Mr. Frank D. Schroth
The Brooklyn *Eagle*
24 Johnson Street
Brooklyn, N.Y.

Dear Mr. Schroth:

It seems that I am forever writing thank you notes to you and Ed Wilson.

The editorial comment of the *Eagle* on my being selected as the Men's League Award was most heartwarming. Many many thanks. I hope I may always merit a pat on the back from my neighbors, among whom I am so happy to live.

Cordially yours,
Emil M. Barr (s)
(Justice)

(4)

Brooklyn Public Library
Grand Army Plaza
Brooklyn 17, N.Y.

November 2, 1951

Mr. Edwin B. Wilson
Executive Editor
The Brooklyn *Eagle*
Brooklyn, N.Y.

Dear Ed:

Recent coverage of Library news in the *Eagle* has been splendid, the "Library Day" spread in particular—and now comes your grand editorial, top of column too, supporting Mr. St. John's wholly reasonable arguments for the same per capita appropriations for the Brooklyn Public Library as the New York and Queens Borough public libraries receive.

This is unquestionably one of the things to keep hammering at through this year, and I know we can depend upon the *Eagle*, to do it as the occasion arises.

The *Eagle* has come up so fast in the last years, has built up into such a civic-minded and crusading newspaper, and interesting through and through, that it makes a former associate very proud.

With warm personal regards.

Cordially,
Tom (s)
Thomas G. Brown
Editor

[8]*Eagle*, October 26, 1941.

[9]For detailed reports on the progress of the Brooklyn Civic Center see *Brooklyn Progress: Annual Report*, Hon. John Cashmore, president, Borough of Brooklyn, 1951-1956; "Brooklyn Alters Basic Character," *New York Times*, December 19, 1959; and Robert S. Bird, "Whatever Happened to Brooklyn?" New York *Herald-Tribune*, February 15, 16, 19, 20, 21, 1962.

[10]Interview with Frank Schroth, November 27, 1969.

[11]*Brooklyn's Relation to the City of New York* (Princeton Surveys: *Eagle* Press, 1942), p. 7.

[12]*Brooklyn's Relation*, p. 47. In its study of the various city services, the survey team concluded that Brooklyn schools were up to standard, that playgrounds would have to be increased by 6 percent to meet the other boroughs, and that the libraries were good but that the branches were too remote from their customers. Low-cost housing was judged satisfactory. Since the beginning of the New York Housing authority in 1934 twelve low-cost housing projects had been completed in New York: five in Manhattan, four in Brooklyn, two in Queens, and one in the Bronx. Of these, 42 percent of the total dwelling units were in Brooklyn.

The housing needs had been judged by the number of old-law tenements in the area and the number of violations of fire, safety, health, and building regulations, while the areas themselves were rated according to other parts of the master plan, the permanent residential character of the area, the oppor-tunities for walking to work, and the proximity of rapid transit and other facilities.

[13]Sorrentino, *New York Times*, January 16, 1971.

[14]Pete Hamill, "Brooklyn: The Same Alternative," *New York* (July 14, 1969): 27.

[15]The series was republished in a special booklet, *Juvenile Delinquency in Brooklyn* (1944).

[16]*Brooklyn* (Breukelen) (Brooklyn: *Eagle* Press, 1946).

[17]*Brooklyn*, p. 58.

[18]*Brooklyn*, p. 58.

[19]TNS letter to FDS, September 10, 1949; interviews with TNS and friends.

[20]*Newsweek* (October 16, 1950): p. 63.

[21]Ed Reid, *Shame of New York* (New York: Random House, 1953) in an expansion of his *Eagle* articles; Edward Robb Ellis, *The Epic of New York City* (New York: Coward-McCann, 1966) has a chapter, pp. 565-578; *Reminiscences of William O'Dwyer*, 8 vols. (Oral History Research Office, Columbia, 1965) has only a few references to the *Eagle*. These volumes can be seen only with the permission of Paul O'Dwyer.

[22]*Eagle*, December 11, 1949.

[23]*Eagle*, December 12, 1949.

[24]*Eagle*, December 14, 1949.

[25]*Eagle*, December 22, 1949.

[26]*Eagle*, May 8, 10, 12, 23, 1950.

[27]*Eagle*, January 13, 1950.

[28]*Eagle*, January 18, 1950.

[29]This is detailed in Thomas N. Schroth, *Responsibility of a Newspaper*, pp. 6-7, and Wilson, "History," pp. 15-17.

[30]*Reminiscences*, vol. 1, pp. 132-133; vol. 6, p. 210. John Kelly, who conducted the Oral History interviews, told O'Dwyer he had not seen this advertising in the *Eagle*. In an examination of 1949-1950 *Eagles*, neither did I.

[31]*Eagle*, July 17, 1950.

[32]FDS interviews, August 12, 1950.

[33]*Eagle*, August 12, 1950. Schroth occasionally hired outsiders for controversial religious editorials. The *Eagle*'s anti-Father Coughlin editorials were by Michael Williams, founder and former editor of *Commonweal*.

[34]For the year 1950, the *Eagle* won the following awards: Brooklyn Chamber of Commerce silver plaque "for distinguished service to the Com-

munity in the best tradition of American journalism," December 18, 1950; Citizens Union City of New York citation of merit "for awakening public interest and measuring up to the finest traditions of journalism," May 7, 1951; Brooklyn Businessmen's Award "for integrity of purpose in serving the best interests of Brooklyn, its homes and its people," October 11, 1950; Grand Lodge of Masons, New York State plaque in appreciation "for constant cooperation and devotion to charity and Brotherhood," May 4, 1950; Brooklyn Bar Association citation "for distinguished and outstanding service to the people of Brooklyn," November 12, 1950; Brooklyn Civic Council scroll commending the newspaper "for its crime expose and 109-year-old fight for the betterment of Brooklyn," November 15, 1950; and the 1950 Pulitzer Prize gold medal "for the most distinguished and meritorious public service rendered by an American newspaper during 1950," May 7, 1951. *Editor and Publisher*, August 11, 1951.

The *Eagle* had won three previous Pulitzers, for Nelson Harding's cartoons on the Lindbergh Flight in 1927 and on the League of Nations in 1928, and for a Charles B. Macauley cartoon on war reparations in 1930.

9

THE END OF
THE *EAGLE*

The last year of the Brooklyn *Eagle* recapitulates and draws to a climax the principal themes of the institution's history. First, the *Eagle* continued to project a philosophy of optimism in the face of apparently overwhelming social and economic forces. The office memoranda of Tom Schroth, the new managing editor, were a steady flood of exhortations, congratulations, stern corrections, and bright ideas for new features and stories; for example: "The time of the year has come when we should be at a peak of our performance, when circulation potential is highest, and when, perhaps, the tide can be taken at its flood."[1] He urged his reporters to do more interpretive articles and more in-depth research. He instituted more front-page promotion of the *Eagle*'s editorial features. Concerned about Brooklyn's economic future, he increased business coverage and planned a special section on "Brooklyn's Vast Future" for January 6, 1955.[2] The *Eagle*'s 1954 decision to build a new plant, like the publisher's decision to concentrate on the borough rather than on Long Island, was an act of faith in Brooklyn's future. His final task was to convince Brooklyn's business leaders that his faith was justified and to persuade organized labor that it should postpone immediate gains for the long-range good of a future Brooklyn.

Second, the *Eagle* intensified its efforts to understand and analyze Brooklyn as a *changing community* by calling attention to its social problems without shaking the confidence of its citizens. Brooklyn's biggest problem was race; in April 1954 Schroth ordered Sidney Frigand to prepare a comprehensive series on the Negro in Brooklyn:

> The approach would be to present the positive and constructive role which the Negro plays in this community, with historical background and sociological undertones. . . . It should attempt to establish an intellectual and emotional basis for accepting the idea of brotherhood as related to the Negro in Brooklyn.[3]

While positive in tone, the stories were to deal frankly with evidence of intolerance. The fourteen articles, which won the Guild's Page One Award and the Christopher Award, were published between July 25 and August 7 and were called "Three Centuries of Pioneering." They set out to fit the Negro into older Brooklyn traditions and the Protestant work ethic to show that the Negro belonged in Brooklyn, that he had always been there, and that the typical Negro did not match the stereotype of the "lazy shuffle-footed black man that is etched in the minds of other Brooklynites."[4] The articles were a curious blending of the century-old *Eagle* formula and enterprising journalism, in that they contained one of the first exposures of the unscrupulous real estate dealer's practice of "block-busting." They emphasized the prominent Negro citizens, the leading Negro artists, musicians, and intellectuals, and Brooklyn Negroes working hard to improve themselves in the borough of Negro homes and churches. Frigand had gone out looking for good things to write about. He had found black and white people working together since the 1930s to avoid tension in Bedford-Stuyvesant and a Negro assistant superintendent of schools who said that Negroes lived in Bedford-Stuyvesant simply because they wanted to be with their own people.

However, he knew he could not write about the "Jim Crow" school system and the "slum makers" in real estate and be complimentary. His criticisms were mild by present day standards, but they were too much for some Brooklyn businessmen. The *Eagle* lost twenty-seven advertisements because of the Frigand series. Today Frigand recalls that he was very proud of the *Eagle* for resisting the pressure of real estate advertisers, and he believes that if the *Eagle* had survived the strike it would have become the real voice of Brooklyn's disadvantaged populace.[5]

Third, the final chapter in the *Eagle*'s history is the story of a *conflict between individual personalities*, each of whom had his own concept of Brooklyn and of Brooklyn journalism. To the publisher, the *Eagle* was Brooklyn; a rise in the *Eagle*'s fortunes would herald a better future Brooklyn, its fall would cast Brooklyn in Manhattan's shadow. In the eyes of the publisher, the leaders of the Guild were willing to destroy the *Eagle*, and hurt Brooklyn, because their loyalty lay elsewhere —with the labor movement, or perhaps even with international communism. The Guild members were also intensely aware of their Brooklyn citizenship but they did not see Brooklyn through the eyes of a venerable institution. They saw it as workingmen who were being paid less for the same work as their fellow journalists across the river. Many remembered the pre-Guild and pre-Schroth days when the *Eagle* had been a sweatshop. Now they had to either continue to accept a slightly lower salary scale than Manhattan newsmen, thereby implicitly admitting they actually were worth less pay, or demand an increase. In short, the decision to strike would be influenced by their need to prove that Brooklynites were not second-rate, that they were not men who couldn't "make it" in New York. In the eyes of the labor leaders the publisher was willing to destroy the *Eagle* because his loyalty lay elsewhere, to his class or to his own financial ambition.

On October 10, 1954, the *Eagle* raised the price of its Sunday edition to ten cents and Tom Schroth, in a little interoffice promotion gesture, sent each of his staff members a dime Scotch-taped to a note urging, "Let this dime be a symbol of the beginning of a new period of progress for the *Eagle*." He was after "superior" reporting and editing and was calling for the cooperation of the whole staff; the Guild agreed.[6] Actually, the *Eagle* was to have only five more months of publication. The Guild contract with the seven other New York papers was to expire November 1, and negotiations were under way that would win for the Guild, without a strike, a pay increase package of $5.80 over two years—a demand the strengthened Guild would then make the basis of its negotiations for a new *Eagle* contract, which had a later expiration date.[7]

Eagle employees around managing editor Bob Grannis' desk in 1952.

Brooklyn Public Library *Eagle* Collection

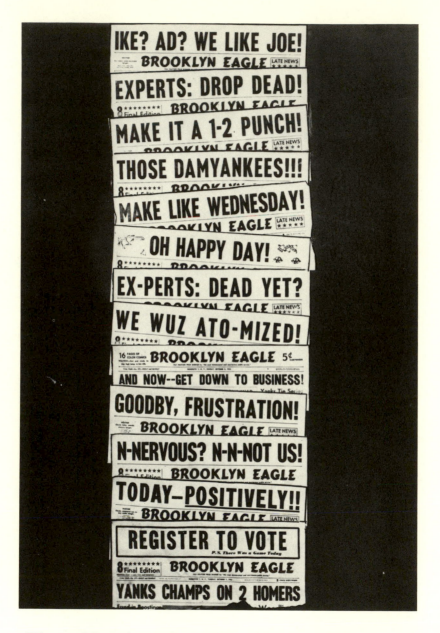

Winners of the *Eagle* interoffice headline-writing contest during the 1952
Brooklyn Dodgers-New York Yankees World Series.

The previous spring Frank D. Schroth had invited a group of Brooklyn business leaders—merchants, manufacturers, bankers, utility operators—to the Hotel Towers to give them his own estimate of the state of Brooklyn and of the *Eagle*. His talk, while affirmative and hopeful in tone, had an air of "crisis" to it in that he implied that if these business "leaders" did not assume greater responsibility for the borough's new civic projects, the future of the borough and its newspaper could be questioned.[8]

Schroth had almost left publishing in September and October 1953. He had tried to sell the *Eagle* to the New York *Herald-Tribune* for a reported $3,000,000.[9] The Reid family, owners of the *Herald-Tribune*, had made a verbal agreement to buy the *Eagle* and planned to publish it as a Brooklyn section of the *Tribune*, but the unions had sworn that they would picket and close both papers at any attempt to economize, even the laying off of one person. Mrs. Reid therefore considered her moral and legal obligation to Schroth cancelled. *Tribune* publisher William Robinson discussed the possibility of leaving the *Tribune* and buying the *Eagle* with his own financial backing, but he did not follow through.[10] This attempt to sell the *Eagle* intensified the Guild's bad feelings toward Schroth and strengthened its charge that he was in publishing for the money. Then, in the same year, he made an unpublicized attempt to sell the *Eagle* to the New York *Daily News*. Money was a factor in Schroth's decision to sell, but he was also weary of conflict and willing to retire. He had also proposed to the members of the Guild that the employees buy the *Eagle*, but his suggestion had been taken facetiously.[11]

Since the publisher could not sell the *Eagle*, he had to convince the Brooklyn advertisers they needed the paper. He said that his Hotel Towers address was not an appeal for more advertising linage but a plan for a renaissance for Brooklyn, one that would be possible only with *Eagle* support. He quoted Robert Moses, City Coordinator, who said, "I can't image Brooklyn without the *Eagle* and without Frank Schroth," and Brooklyn Borough President John Cashmore, who added, "Brooklyn without the *Eagle* would be an oddity, without a newspaper voice of its own, and without a champion of its best public interest. Such a state of affairs would be unthinkable."[12] If it had not been for the *Eagle*, Schroth said, the Veterans' Hospital would not be located at Fort Hamilton, the State University would not be locating its new medical school on Clarkson Avenue, the Nostrand Avenue subway extension would not have been approved, the Gowanus Creek channel would possibly not now be actually finished, switchblade knives would still be legal, and there might not be any additional cops back on the beat. All the other Brooklyn papers—the *Times*, the *Standard*, the *Times-Standard*, the *Union*, the *Standard-Union*, the *Times-Union*, and the Brooklyn *Argus*—had passed into history. All had become part of the *Eagle*.

The borough was now in the first stages of planned rebirth. It anticipated $781,828,493 for building projects such as the new Civic Center, for which the *Eagle* had editorialized for years, at the same time that many of its preeminent citizens were losing interest in the borough and when the future of its indispensable newspaper was in question. Schroth criticized some of his listeners for being "nine-to-five" Brooklynites, for making their money from Brooklyn citizens then returning to Manhattan without facing the fact of the borough's deterioration or lifting a finger to help solve Brooklyn's economic and social problems. He was shocked to find, for example, that the buyers and department heads of the various stores who were given *Eagle* tours of historic and beautiful Brooklyn knew nothing about Brooklyn and went home to Manhattan and Long Island reading Manhattan papers on the subway. In short, due partly to social change and partly to indifference on the part of citizens who should be most concerned, Brooklyn and the *Eagle*, the borough's "last hope," were in danger.

The publisher had spelled out the paper's critical situation in the testimony to the arbitrators over the Guild contract in March 1954.[13] The heart of the Schroth argument during all his labor battles was that the *Eagle* was a "fringe" paper, a local Brooklyn paper and not a Manhattan paper like the *Times, Herald-Tribune, Mirror, Journal-American, World Telegram* and *Sun*, or *Post*. Schroth listed the circulations of the New York newspapers at that time as *Herald-Tribune*, 340,806; *Post*, 406,395; *Times*, 542,680; *The World Telegram and Sun*, 536,021; *Journal American*, 659,410; *Mirror*, 889,616; *Daily News*, 2,111,830; *Eagle*, 125,339.

Schroth claimed the *Eagle* should therefore not be subjected to the same economic pressures as those papers in the so-called "Manhattan Pattern" or forced to pay the same wage scales as papers backed by family fortunes or a national chain. He argued that the *Eagle*, along with the Long Island *Press, Newsday*, and the Newark *News*, was considered a fringe paper by the Manhattan papers and by the Guild. He thought the *Eagle*, with its 1953 circulation of 125,339 and advertising linage of 12,022,045 lines should be entitled to the same consideration as the Long Island *Press*, with its circulation of 195,000 and advertising linage of 19,811,232 lines, which the Guild did not require to match the Manhattan patterns.

While the *Eagle* did pay the Manhattan pattern wages to the craft unions, the management did have complete control over the number of craft union members it needed. When management reduced the size of the paper it could also cut down on printers, pressmen, stereotypers, and photoengravers, but the number of Guild members (317) was not susceptible to change.

In Schroth's mind, the Guild had been a persistent foe of all his attempts to economize, and he had made numerous economic steps during his own ownership, some of which radically affected the nature of the paper. He had first discontinued the neighborhood inserts which were part of the *Eagle*, the "Island News," and "Home Talk." Next the paper had abolished its home delivered circulation on Long Island and followed by discontinuing its financial page and stock market prices. It then "risked its very existence" by disposing of its membership in the Associated Press to the Hearst newspapers. The *Eagle* had also abandoned the service of the Standard News Association, an agency that covered Brooklyn and Queens much like the Associated Press covered the Bronx and Manhattan, several months before the service went out of business. In 1953 the *Eagle* had also withdrawn from the New York Newspaper Publishers' Association so that it would not be bound by citywide negotiations in dealing with the unions.[14] Finally, in April 1954, the paper reluctantly had gone into a one-press operation, meaning there would be a continuous running of the press instead of a number of new editions at stated times. This meant that those who received home deliveries would get a less complete paper; it also meant laying off at least seventeen employees.

There is some question as to the wisdom of these decisions. Some staff members felt the economizing measures were hurting the paper, particularly by cutting down on coverage. At night there were sometimes only one or two reporters on duty from 4 P.M. until 12:30 A.M. Costly efforts to boost Long Island circulation and pick up additional advertising failed; the *Eagle* did not have the staff to cover the Island properly. Now, by deciding against competing for more Long Island circulation, the *Eagle* locked itself in more firmly as a local Brooklyn paper, isolating itself from the centers of expanding population and betting its future on a "renaissance" for Brooklyn. Within two years the civic improvement programs Schroth mentioned in his Hotel Towers address would be composed of 325 projects involving an estimated investment of approximately $900,000,000 in funds, principally from municipal, state, and federal sources. It was not certain, however, that government funds poured into schools, hospitals and transit would bring on the kind of economic recovery that would save the *Eagle*.[15] In each decision, however, the publisher was convinced that without the cutback the paper could not possibly survive.

At the same time, the publisher, who knew he was taking an enormous risk when he bought the *Eagle*, had decided to increase his risk and his investment in this crucial year. Schroth once told his employees:

Life for my *Eagle* began with the culmination of the fourteen weeks Guild strike; the abortive effort to make the paper a great national institution by Mr. Gannett; the various promotions and financial fenegling of the immediately preceding management; the complete loss of reader interest; labor unhappiness; dwindling circulation and a debt of upwards of $4,000,000. The smart operators told me—with tears in their eyes—that I was just a little this side of being nuts.[16]

Now he was telling them:

> This year will be for the *Eagle* a year of decision. It starts by giving us the two worst months we have had in years. January and February were tragic months, opening a year when we must face the alternative of obtaining a new plant or completely discontinuing the paper.[17]

The famous old Johnson Street *Eagle* building that had become a Brooklyn landmark in the very heart of what was old Brooklyn had been bought by the city to make way for the new Supreme Court building of the new Civic Center for which the *Eagle* had campaigned since 1911. Thus, ironically, the *Eagle* was to become the victim of its own campaign. The cost of moving the machinery from the old to the new plant, along with the cost of the new building, would be enormous. *Eagle* circulation was just about holding its own. While weekday circulation of the New York City papers had dropped 6.2 percent, Sunday circulation had dropped 12.6 percent and suburban papers had gone up 24.5 percent on weekdays and 118.6 percent on Sundays. *Eagle* advertising rates, the highest in New York and the highest of any comparable paper in the country, could not reasonably be increased.[18]

The *Eagle* spent 60 percent of its total operating expenses for wages and salaries for 630 employees, and the Guild payroll came to $27,292.68 per week. Finally, to further complicate matters, the contingent liability of the *Eagle* for Guild severance pay was $694,782, which curtailed management's opportunity to borrow large sums of money for moving and improvement. In the publisher's judgment, the Guild contract had not only made the newspaper's position economically hazardous, it had seen to it that it would be impossible to obtain new money. All this was true despite the fact that there was a Guild shop at the *Eagle*, something the Guild had been able to gain at only one major Manhattan paper, and in spite of

The *Eagle* building in the 1940s, next to the Brooklyn Post Office.

Jules Geller photo

Managing editor Thomas N. Schroth, publisher Frank D. Schroth, and assistant publisher Frank D. Schroth, Jr., breaking ground for the new *Eagle* building, 124 Johnson Street, May 17, 1954.

the fact that the *Eagle* was among the top eight papers in the country on the Guild's list for the highest pay for reporters. The only papers ahead of it were the seven Manhattan papers; the Long Island *Press* and *Star-Journal* ranked 107th and 108th on the list.[19]

On the other hand the economic status of the newspaper industry was sound on a national basis. The general trend in publishing for the prior thirty years had been one of suspensions and mergers, but the population explosion of the 1940s had given papers a wider base of support, and circulation increase had kept pace with the rise in population. The number of daily newspapers decreased between 1930 and 1960, then leveled off near 1,750.[20] Although the number of daily papers had declined during 1954, the nation was still far from its saturation point in circulation, and there had been a net increase of twenty-one in the total number of daily papers between 1944 and 1954.[21]

Despite the fact that the daily newspaper business had attained the highest degree of stability in its history, and even though this economic soundness had allowed the press to raise its standards, the industry was perplexed by a number of economic problems. The price of newsprint was rising steadily and did not level off to $135 a ton until 1957. Production costs were rising, particularly with increased wage demands from unions, and there were dramatic losses in national advertising to television. As a result of the intermedia competition between 1945 and 1960, newspapers became more and more a local advertising medium.[22] Furthermore, although dying dailies were often replaced by new ones, competition killed papers in the big cities while new papers started in the suburbs. By 1954 only 6 percent of American cities with daily newspapers had competing dailies, and—to indicate the trend—by 1962 only four cities (New York, 7; Boston, 5; and Houston and Washington, 3) had three or more daily newspaper owners. The dramatic circulation gains went to the small suburban dailies, especially in Los Angeles, Chicago, Philadelphia, Detroit, and New York.

New York had special problems. Hearst's *American* had been lost in 1937 when it merged with the *Journal*. The evening *Sun* was sold to Scripps-Howard in 1950 for a merger with the *World-Telegram*. The

Brooklyn *Citizen* succumbed to its financial troubles in 1947. Meanwhile, out on Long Island, the tabloid *Newsday*, founded by Alicia Patterson in 1940, had made a circulation leap from 24,834 in 1941 to 167,933 in 1952 when the *Eagle* was just holding its own around 123,000.[23] After Brooklyn lost the *Eagle*, New York lost the *Herald-Tribune*, the *Mirror*, the *World-Telegram*, and the *Journal-American*.

New York papers, like the *Eagle*, were destroyed by their financial and management problems and above all by the change in urban living patterns. Former Manhattanites who had moved out of the city now read suburban papers. Brooklyn, which had once been the residential suburb of New York, had become a decaying industrial city with a new population struggling to rebuild its pride with civic projects like the monumental Civic Center rising at the end of the avenues leading to the Brooklyn Bridge.

Three of the seven New York papers were losing money. Some papers experimented with contests, sprightlier headlines, "modernized" layout, and more entertainment to recapture lagging circulation.[24] But often enough their experimentation and flamboyance were symptoms of deeper insecurities—warnings of some deadly disease. The *Eagle* too had modernized and economized, and had become more sensational under its last publisher. It had also done what the New York papers were failing to do for their own city; it campaigned vigorously for the "community." Nevertheless, the *Eagle* had been overtaken by a series of events that were bringing it to its end.

Negotiations and Personal Tensions

When the Guild negotiators, a team of about eleven members led by John Deegan, an organizer from the New York office, and *Eagle* unit chairman I. Kaufman sat down with management representatives Frank D. Schroth, Jr., Advertising Director John Dean, and Managing Editor Thomas N. Schroth in the assistant publisher's office on November 15, 1954, they must have had the feeling they had been through all this before.[25] Every winter since he had come to

Brooklyn, Frank D. Schroth had been snatching the *Eagle* from the jaws of death. He had convinced the Guild that the paper was too poor to meet their demands and they had settled without a strike. As the years went by, however, antagonisms increased.

Looking back on these discussions and the several minor feuds that preceded them, it is clear how much the negotiators must have been hampered by the personal antipathy that had grown up between Frank D. Schroth and I. Kaufman. Throughout the years their relationship had been marked by a number of squabbles. As a Guild leader since its founding, Kaufman had been brought into constant conflicts with management not only in contract negotiations but also in grievance procedures. Some of the grievances concerned himself. In 1947 Kaufman wanted extra pay for writing the script of the *Eagle*'s daily news broadcast and Schroth claimed Kaufman was trying to provoke a conflict with him. In a March 6 letter to Guild unit chairman Paul Rubin, the publisher mentioned the many favors he had done for Kaufman and Kaufman's assurances to him that he did not feel discriminated against; then, however, Schroth went on to question Kaufman's competence and objectivity as a writer and implied that Kaufman put Guild work ahead of the *Eagle*. The letters were posted on the bulletin board. The Guild *Reporter* defended Kaufman against the publisher's criticisms, replying that the *Eagle* had printed all of Kaufman's seven-months World War II overseas reports and that none of his labor stories were turned down for lack of objectivity. The *Reporter* editorialized:

> At any rate all their sniping at a single employee hardly adds to the status of the publisher of the Brooklyn *Eagle*. Obviously, he is not comfortable in the position he is in. In our opinion, in the opinion of most *Eagle* employees, he ought to stop it. (LET'S BOTH STOP).

Schroth replied in a public notice:

> Don't worry about my comfort.
> You have shown me very little respect

in the past and I expect nothing better
from you now.[26]

There are other examples of the publisher publicly criticizing the
poor work of his employees and personalizing issues by singling out
individuals such as Nat Einhorn and the Weingartens in addresses to
his workers.[27] (In 1941 Victor Weingarten told Schroth he had
listened to his "guff" long enough.) It is indeed possible that he failed
to appreciate how much this approach simply increased worker solidarity against him even when his critical judgments may have been
correct. In the judgment of at least one fairly prominent Guild
member, Schroth was a small town paternalistic "Lord-of-the-manor"
type who did not know how to deal with more sophisticated and more
independent New York workers and thus alienated them by his
manner and aloofness.[28] Yet as I. Kaufman recalls his old opponent
today, he says he "rather liked him" as a person and that Schroth had
done him several personal favors, and particularly recalls the time
they both gave to the blood drive together, lying on tables next to one
another. Violet Weingarten, looking back on the *Eagle* days, says
Schroth was "a great man."[29]

In the midst of an earlier labor-management conflict, one Guild
member, Gertrude McAllister, wrote a public letter to her associates
on the *Eagle* in which she attempted to bring some reason and
objectivity into the dispute. The Guild had voted to strike if its
demands were not met but, said the writer, some members were
having second thoughts. Her letter puts a great deal of blame for the
bad feelings in the plant on the Guild for its unsparing personal
attacks on the publisher:

> In spite of the fact that I have sometimes disagreed with the way
> in which management has done things, I would like to say that
> at no time have I agreed with the vilifications the head of this
> management has been subjected to in the shop paper. He has
> been ridiculed to a point where it is sickening, where it is unfair
> and where it goes beyond the bounds of decent, duty-conscious,
> modern-thinking unionism.[30]

I. Kaufman, chairman of the *Eagle* unit of the New York Newspaper Guild.

She described the publisher as a generous man, "quite a *gentleman*," (italics, Gertrude McAllister's) who had made great efforts to improve relations but was still misunderstood. Her description of the psychological atmosphere in the newsroom is reminiscent of the *Eagle* in its worst years when Goodfellow was trying unsuccessfully to operate the *Eagle* and *Times-Union* out of one room and the newly formed Guild was working up tensions for the first strike:

> On the fourth floor we're supposed to be concerned with news-paper work but there has been such a tension that it is almost impossible to do any kind of a job. . . . Look—are we so badly treated, so badly paid that an actual strike is a better choice? Is the owner of this newspaper really such a dreadful person that we must spend our time militating against him, all the time? He never comes out to the city room any more and I can't say I blame him.

Publisher Schroth assembled all the employees to listen to his story only four or five times in his career at the *Eagle*. The speeches he gave to the *Eagle* unit of the American Newspaper Guild on April 10, 1941, and eleven years later, to all his employees in the *Eagle* news room on November 24, 1952, were quite similar in their basic themes: the publisher described the gains made by labor during his ownership and defended himself against anti-labor charges in the shop papers, the *Eagle Reporter* and the *Guild Reporter*, warning that unless employee-management war at the *Eagle* stopped, there would be no *Eagle*. Occasionally he personalized the argument:

> I invite all in this room to look out the windows and see what has happened to the buildings on Adams, between Johnson and Myrtle. Next week ground is to be broken at Johnson and Adams, on the very corner opposite this building, for the new Domestic Relations Court.
> I do not say that it is up to the Guild employees to buy us a new building. I merely contend that the *Eagle* cannot exist

without a new building. For employees not to be concerned about the future of the paper mystifies me.[31]

The Contract

The contract which the Guild wanted improved was made between the Guild and the *Eagle* on November 30, 1952; it was to expire on November 29, 1954. It contained a reopening clause on the first anniversary for purposes of renegotiating wages. Minimum wages being paid during the second year of the contract ranged from $36.50 a week for inexperienced clerks to $131.50 a week for experienced reporters (this represented a differential of $2.00 to $3.00 from the scale being paid by the Manhattan dailies.). On the Long Island *Daily Press* an experienced reporter received $100.00 a week.[32]

The *Eagle* contract also granted a 100 percent Guild shop, a voluntary dues checkoff, and strict job security with dismissals to reduce the size of the staff in inverse order of seniority except in those cases where it would "substantially prejudice operations to the injury of the publisher." In management's view, the Guild's strict interpretations of this clause meant that the talented men and women brought in by the present management had to be dismissed while others who could not carry their part of the load had to be kept.

The severance indemnity clause entitled persons dismissed to severance pay at the rate of one week's pay for each six months continuous employment, with a maximum of fifty weeks' pay. A man could be dismissed without severance for dishonesty, repeated drunkenness after warning, gross neglect of duty, or gross insubordination, but not for incompetence. The extent to which Schroth felt hampered by the Guild contract is indicated in a letter to George N. Dale, chairman, Special Standing Committee, American Newspaper Publishers Association, May 9, 1555:

> If the Brooklyn *Eagle* could have economized with its staff and dismissed the drones and incompetents, and not be committed to priority, where the young and efficient must go first, with severance pay, it would have been a marvelous contract. This

would have permitted management to reduce the number of Guild employees from 315 to about 200; it would have saved a million dollars a year in salaries; and it would have made the difference between success and failure.[33]

A person employed fifteen years or more received four weeks vacation. There were eight holidays a year and employees worked a standard five-day, thirty-five hour week. All time over regular hours was paid time and a half with certain provisions for double time.

The Guild demanded that the *Eagle* agree to the $5.80 package granted by the Manhattan papers: $3.40 the first year, $2.40 the second year of the contract. They also wanted the *Eagle* to bring minimum wages up to Manhattan standards, raising some reporters' salaries from $131.50 weekly, to give four weeks vacation after twelve years instead of after fifteen years, and increase severance benefits to fifty-six weeks maximum. The Guild based its demands on two major grounds. First, workers in Brooklyn doing similar jobs as workers in Manhattan should be paid similar scales; they should not be "second-class citizens." Second, the *Eagle* had agreed to the $5.80 package with the craft unions; the Guild should get the same treatment. Management had requested several contract revisions which would make the operation of the paper more efficient and strengthen its ability to manage, but it stated it was willing to continue for a year with the same contract.

Throughout all the negotiations there was general agreement on both sides of the minor issues: the sections in the contract on checkoff, holidays, assignment from home, call back, individual bargaining, syndicate rights, leaves of absence, service clause, and outside work. Yet whenever they returned to the money issues they were "eyeball-to-eyeball." Furthermore, management became irritated by what it considered the Guild's delaying tactics. At one point there was a two-week pause between meetings because the Guild negotiator, Mr. Deegan, said that he was tired from negotiating some Manhattan contracts and needed a rest.[34]

Once again, management had begun by reciting the paper's financial difficulties and the problems it faced. The *Eagle* had lost

$168,980 in the first nine months of 1954. They had suffered severe advertising loss, particularly since the closing of the Loeser store and since more Brooklyn stores were directing their linage to the suburban market. The move to the new plant of the presses, conveyors, ink tanks, linotypes, stereotype equipment, generators, etc., would cost nearly $500,000. To economize, management had not filled the posts of business manager or promotion manager. It had dropped the travel bureau. It had raised the price of the Sunday *Eagle* from five to ten cents while Sunday circulation was going down.

The Guild negotiators, however, were unaffected by management's arguments. They also refused to accept management's contention that the *Eagle* should receive the same consideration as the Long Island *Press*. The Guild would have struck the Long Island *Press*, but it wasn't strong enough there.[35]

Management tried another approach on Monday, January 10, 1955. It reminded the Guild of the death of the Los Angeles *News* a few weeks before in which 300 Guildsmen lost jobs and called attention to the story in the press section of *Time*, "Trouble in New York," pointing out that only four Manhattan newspapers were making money. Management then proposed that the *entire contract* be submitted to an arbitrator. It felt sure that an arbitrator would award wage rates and working conditions for the *Eagle* Guild members comparable to the rate paid on other comparable newspapers with which the Guild had contracts, and that any risk the *Eagle* was taking on increased wages would be compensated for by improvement it would receive in other phases of the contract such as overtime and security, where the *Eagle* contract was more generous. The Guild negotiators caucused briefly and said they would not recommend this to the unit.

The next day they met again. Management let the Guild see the *Eagle* payroll to figure the cost of its proposals but the Guild would not let management see its contract with the Long Island *Press*. Schroth Jr. made another plea for the Guild to put the welfare of the entire paper ahead of the Guild's own interests for just one "year of grace" to give the paper a chance to make some economic gains, but on January 13 at the Guild unit meeting attended by about 150 of the

Guild's 315 members, with about 15 persons voting "no," the unit elected by a voice vote to strike if further efforts to produce an acceptable contract failed.[36] A union, the *Eagle Reporter* had said, "is required by law to do more than say 'yes sir' when the employer says he can't pay. If that were all, no employer would ever pay a union raise."[37] The Guild felt that management had outbluffed them two years before and it was not going to let that happen again.

A federal mediator, Thomas G. Dougherty, was brought into the negotiations on January 17 but to no avail. At the next meeting on January 27, management made its last concession: a two-year contract with a general across-the-board increase of $1.40 and a further automatic increase of $1.00 at the beginning of the second year. All other contract conditions such as severance, holidays, hours (35 a week), vacations, and Guild shop were to remain the same. The Guild turned it down. At 2:30 P.M. on January 28 Dougherty called an eleventh hour meeting which lasted three and a half hours. No progress was made. Just before the strike deadline the Guild's New York office, through Thomas J. Murphy, sent a telegram to the *Eagle* offering to arbitrate wages, vacations, and severance. All other Guild demands would be dropped. Management replied that it stood by its offer to arbitrate only the entire contract. Kaufman says this was one of the saddest days of his life.

At midnight January 28 the Guild put a picket line at the *Eagle* entrance on Johnson and Adams Streets, and in the early morning hours it became clear that the craft unions had decided not to cross the line. This was the crucial decision; the *Eagle* had been prepared to publish without the Guild. Many galleys of editorial copy had been set in advance and the work had been divided among thirty executive and secretarial employees, but without the New York Typographical Union No. 6 honoring its own contract, the *Eagle* could not appear.[38] For the first day in 114 years, the Brooklyn *Eagle* failed to publish.[39]

The Last Eagle

The "eight star" final edition of the Brooklyn *Eagle* on January 28, 1955, was the last copy of the newspaper ever published.[40] An

WEATHER
Cloudy today; light snow tonight.
High today, low tonight.
Hot snap, sunlight, 16.

BROOKLYN EAGLE

A Pulitzer-Prize-Winning Newspaper—Champion of Its Community

116th YEAR—No. 27—DAILY and SUNDAY

BROOKLYN 1, N. Y., FRIDAY, JANUARY 28, 1955

5 CENTS EVERYWHERE

LATE NEWS
★ ★ ★ ★

Body of Woman, 58, Found in Cellar

LANDLADY BEATEN TO DEATH

Speed Senate Formosa Vote; Opposition Ebbs

Washington, Jan. 28 (UP)—Senate leaders of both parties today drove for a quick final vote of approval for President Eisenhower's "fight-if-armed" resolution for defending Formosa.

Fleet Off China Ready for Job, Navy Chief Says

Washington, Jan. 28 (UP) — Navy Secretary Charles S. Thomas today assured Congress the Navy is on ripe with "any local naval action" in the Formosa strait.

Red Ball Up in Prospect Park

KEY, KIDS, GET YOUR SKATES! — Red ball is up and there's skating today on Prospect Park Lake for first time since 1949. Skating area runs from boat house to near Terrace Bridge. Among first to enjoy the big freeze are three Midwood High students, Sara Plotzman, left, 1641 50th St., Diana Stone, 1099 E. 10th St., and Nina Shapiro, 1316 Avenue J.

12° COLD WAVE DESCENDS ON CITY

Coldest weather of the Winter gripped the city today.

Money, Jewelry In Her Apartment Left Untouched

Her skull and face bones battered and crushed by repeated brutal blows, a 58-year-old Borough Park landlady was found beaten to death early today in the cellar of her home, 2131 60th St.

BOROUGH PARK VIOLENCE

2 Boys Methodically Loot School, Nabbed By Cops in Getaway

Cops Are Convinced Rubinstein Was Slain By a Trusted 'Friend'

A close and trusted friend chiefly slew the 60th [...] strangler [...]

Tot Survives 11-Story Fall, Mystifies Docs

BEDFORD-STUYVESANT CHASE FATAL

Woman Killed as Stolen Car Crashes Into Cab

Taxi Driver, 2d Passenger Injured as Thieves Escape

DEATH CAR—Rammed by stolen car, this taxi crashed into tree at Park Place and Kingston Ave. last night. Woman passenger was killed, cab driver fatally injured and another passenger received head cuts.

No Winner in 4 Weeks Puts $500 in PRUZZLE Kitty

The Brooklyn *Eagle*, Friday, January 28, 1955. The last *Eagle*.

examination of its contents indicates to some extent what Brooklyn lost when the *Eagle* died. The last *Eagle* presents an uneasy blend of parochialism and sensationalism. The publisher, who had been arguing his case against the Guild in a first page box all during the week, described the silencing of the *Eagle* as another instance in which Brooklyn was being dominated by Manhattan:

> The borough has been a stepchild in government service, charity, social activities, and indeed in every phase of community life. The Manhattan Pattern now closes, at least temporarily, the last voice that is purely Brooklyn.

The extent to which the *Eagle* was purely Brooklyn is evident in an analysis of the news stories. The *Eagle*'s last headline is spread across the top of the page in bold type:

Body of Woman, 58, Found in Cellar
LANDLADY BEATEN TO DEATH
Money, Gems Untouched in Apartment
Tenant's Neighbors Quizzed by Cops Tell of Hearing Screams

> Her skull and face bones battered and crushed by repeated brutal blows, a 58-year-old Borough Park landlady was found beaten to death early today in the cellar of her home, 2131 60th Street.
> Tillie Bernstein, who lived with a brother, Jack Bernstein, on the first floor of the three-family, two story brick house, was either beaten with a heavy clublike instrument or knocked down and kicked to death, police said.

The second most prominently featured story concerned a two-year-old Negro boy, Richard Padgett, who had fallen eleven stories from a bedroom window of the Van Dyke Houses and "confronted doctors in Beth El Hospital with two unsolved mysteries: 1 How did the child escape alive, with no injury more serious than a slight scratch on the head? 2 and at what point did he pick up a small upholsterer's nail in his throat?" Throughout the paper, which was only 22 pages long, six news stories concerned international events, eleven national, four state, and forty-eight examined local Brooklyn affairs. The local stories were roughly divided into two categories: "community news" and crime.

On the day the *Eagle* died thirty-six Brooklyn deaths were listed. That same day police questioned Patricia Wray, pretty secretary of "multi-millionaire draft dodger" Serge Rubinstein, in connection with Rubinstein's murder the day before. In Manhattan, a Brooklyn armored truck guard, Stephen Tarallol, 39, foiled a "10G Payroll Snatch" by firing one shot. "The accoster escaped in an unknown manner." A fast moving thug roughed up a Bedford-Stuyvesant baker and fled with $90 in a taxicab. A man and his wife were convicted in a TV repair racket and another husband and wife team was found guilty in a "weird forgery plot." Two teenagers looted P.S. 105. A redhaired thug robbed two druggists in one night. A Bedford-Stuyvesant woman shot herself to death when she learned she had cancer. Two people died in four auto accidents.

The editorial page was neatly laid out—more attractively than the rest of the paper where the alternating plain and bold type gave the page an uneven quality. The lead editorial praised Great Britain and France for rejecting Soviet warnings that fulfillment of the policy of arming West Germany would mean annulment of existing treaties of friendship. The other editorials approved Mayor Robert Wagner's move toward economy, discussed President Dwight D. Eisenhower's responsibilities in the defense of Formosa and the Pescadores, and congratulated sixty-three-year-old former Dodger pitcher Dizzy Vance on his election to the Hall of Fame. The editorial cartoon depicted Mayor Wagner holding out a big hat to request $136,700,000 more revenue for the city from an embarrassed Governor Averell Harriman. The two syndicated columns on the page were by Ray Tucker on Washington politics and Eugene Lyons on Russia's return to the "hard line."

The other *Eagle* columns included Harold H. Harris' "Politics and People," Bob Farrell's gossip on "New York at Night," Al Salerno's uncritical restaurant appraisals in "Going Places," and a "humor" piece by Leslie Hanscom called "What is a Jerk?" There were a woman's page, an entertainment page, and two and a half pages of sports along with the extremely popular Jimmy Murphy column on school boy athletics and a half-page of comics. There were also miscellaneous features such as a bridge column, a puzzle, news of Brooklyn GI's, and "Meet Your *Eagle* Carrier Boy." Advertising was sparse—four and a half pages of classified ads and only five ads from department stores, the largest a full-page from Abraham and Straus.

The *Eagle* editorial columnist was former managing editor Robert M. Grannis, who had been at the *Eagle* for many years and was, like John Heffernan before him, a conservative and one of the *Eagle*'s representative men. His cliche-ridden essay scoffed at those who favored disarmament and reflected *Eagle* anti-communism and moralism.

. . . The Commies are not satisfied to limit their practice to home territory. The entire globe is their happy hunting ground.

But they are incapable of accomplishing their ends without the use of force and equally incapable if we are ready to fight for what is ours by tradition and choice. Under no circumstances would I accept the word of a Red that he would lay down his arms if others did. He'd hide them in the cellar or in hay piles just in case. He is essentially a liar and essentially an aggressive person without morals or religious beliefs.

However, although Grannis could be described as a political conservative, he was far from happy with the editorial direction of the paper under Edwin Wilson. Late at night in the office during the strike he wrote two long memos to Tom Schroth, his successor as managing editor, describing what the future *Eagle* should be. He felt the *Eagle* editorials should stop backing away from issues and stop praising the obvious. He particularly regretted the *Eagle*'s silence during the McCarthy era.

"The population of Bro̊klyn has changed and there is a great necessity to put the accent on mass appeal which is evident in what you are doing in the news columns. And I say hooray for that. But why can't we get out of the horse and buggy age on the editorial page and write with vigor and courage instead of hiding behind evasive and pedantic phrases and incidentally wasting valuable space." Grannis felt the "new" *Eagle*, after the strike, should be a tabloid that would appeal to the "little guys" who were Brooklyn's new majority; "we are no longer living in a conservative age and there are not enough die-hards in our community to support a conservative paper."[41]

The Strike and Its Aftermath

Snow fell on the picket lines and freezing strikers huddled around an ashcan fire in zero weather, cheering one another up. The Guild was set for a long battle. The *Frontpage* editorial told Guildsmen that, more than money, a principle was at stake: "Guild members are not to be dealt with as second class citizens, orphans of the publishers' storm." Morale was high and it was for the most part a polite strike with strikers and management people saying "hello" as they passed. One day an elderly man put his arm around a picket and said, "I remember your last strike very well. I was a cop assigned to strike duty then . . . Good luck!"[42] Negotiations went on, but with each day recovery became more difficult. Advertisers and readers were already shifting to other papers.

A Brooklyn Citizens Committee was formed, met in the Hotel Towers on February 24, and on February 28 ran large advertisements in several Manhattan papers signed by about 150 citizens and organizations exclaiming, "We Want Our *Eagle* back! We Want the Voice of Brooklyn!" The group offered to set up a fact-finding committee to look into the dispute; the publisher accepted, the Guild refused. Meanwhile, workmen could not cross the picket line to move the *Eagle* machinery to the new plant. The financial position of the *Eagle* was worsening; even if the paper were to resume publication it would take at least three months to build its circulation up to 100,000.[43]

On March 16, 1955, the publisher sent a letter to the Guild and issued a statement:

> As of today the Brooklyn *Eagle* has not published for 47 days. So, after 114 years without ever having missed an edition, we are giving up. . . . Faced with the choice of accepting terms that would have doubled the great financial loss of 1954, or of suspending completely, we have chosen to quit. In these circumstances there is no hope for us. The Newspaper Guild problem is malignant. . . . So the Pulitzer Prize-Winning paper of Whitman, Van Anden and McKelway has been silenced forever, and Brooklyn, the largest community in America without a voice, will indeed be doomed to be cast in Manhattan's shadow.[44]

The Guild would not believe it. At Guild headquarters off Times Square about thirty-five persons were playing cards, sipping coffee, and staring out the window. A picture of Heywood Broun hung on the wall.[45] They still said Schroth was bluffing, but as the months passed the picket line was reduced and Guildsmen struggled for jobs on the New York papers. The largest number, fifty, went to the *World Telegram and Sun*, which had put out an elaborate Brooklyn section within two days of the *Eagle*'s closing. But by May, while the Guild kept up the picket line, only one-fifth of the 630 employees had found other jobs. A series of attempts to sell the *Eagle* fell through. The management "History" says prospective buyers could not meet Guild demands even when the Guild would make generous concessions to prospective publishers which it denied to Schroth. The Guild version is that Schroth did not really want to sell.[46]

On May 11, 12, and 13, an auction sale was scheduled to dispose of the assets as a complete unit or in three component parts: (1) copyrighted names and goodwill, including complete files of papers since 1841, library, morgue, and circulation lists; (2) machinery and printing equipment; and (3) office equipment and furnishings; or piecemeal, if the first two attempts were not successful. The highest bid for (1) was $8,000, so they were not sold. Although there was no bid for the presses at the auction, eventually every physical item was disposed of until the old *Eagle* building contained nothing but a few desks and filing cabinets. The *Eagle* made only $127,000 on the auction. In June, Frank D. Schroth joined the staff of the New York *News* to develop its Long Island section. In July, demolition of the old landmark began. The two-hundred pound bronze eagle with the eight-foot wings which had surmounted the *Eagle* building was taken down and given to the New York City Community College on Pearl Street. The new *Eagle* building, a sleek two-story brick and glass modern structure which never housed a newspaper, was turned into a school for the city's sanitation workers.

Perhaps partly through the personal antipathy that had been building up in recent years and partly out of the shock of finding themselves jobless when they expected the strike to end in victory, the Guild launched a personal attack on the publisher. In June they published a pamphlet, *Who Killed the Brooklyn Eagle?*, unsigned and undocumented, accusing Schroth of killing the *Eagle*.[47] Schroth's strategy, said the Guild, was to sell the paper and merge it. During the recent contract negotiations his objective had been to get arbitration by the American Newspaper Publishers Association to weaken the Guild contract and then fatten up the paper for sale. Or, if the Guild struck, the publisher "would collect $350,000 in strike insurance and run away with $750,000 severance pay owed the employees."[48] What the publisher had called "losses" up to $111,000 in 1954 the Guild called "investment," the costs of getting a new building. The cost of granting the $5.80 package would have been $150,000 in two years, in which increased revenues would have topped $600,000.

The Guild said its evidence came from a prospectus put forth by a group of former *Eagle* executives who wished to start publishing a Brooklyn newspaper of their own, headed by a man who was *Eagle* business manager and secretary-treasurer from 1940 to 1954. The man, unnamed, was William F. ("Frank") Crowell. Crowell clarified this statement in an interview. Crowell was not business manager when the paper closed. He thought the *Eagle* management should have compromised in its bargaining and that the *Eagle* could have survived paying higher salaries, but *not for long*. Crowell believed that increased union demands and other expenses still would have forced the *Eagle* to close after a few years.[49]

Now, claimed the Guild, the publisher might be secretly planning to publish the *Eagle* again in his shiny new building without the Guild. At any rate, the Guild said Schroth was just a profit-hungry publisher who, like the publisher of the old pre-Guild papers which had been merged out of existence (the *World*, the *American*, the *Herald*, and the *Sun*), was more interested in money than in the welfare of his employees or in journalism itself. Yet throughout the negotiations management had offered to open its books for inspection, and the union had not examined them.

Actually, Schroth's intention throughout the negotiations and at the time of his decision to suspend production was that he would permanently retire from the publication of the paper but that the *Eagle* would reappear under entirely new auspices. Running through all his thinking was the basic belief that he was "protecting the Brooklyn *Eagle* from disappearing from the community life of Brooklyn."[50] He had suspension insurance to carry him through the period of crisis. He had hoped that once he had suspended publication the pickets would leave and that the contractors could quickly move the machinery from the condemned building to the new building so that the *Eagle*, under new ownership, could quickly reappear and recapture its circulation and advertising. Tom Schroth, in particular, was most reluctant to see the *Eagle* die. In the week before suspension he had speculated about breaking negotiations and announcing suspension with the hope of starting all over again in a year with new capital.[51]

The evidence indicates, therefore, that management did at least think of suspension as a strategic move to disarm the Guild with the very slim hope that a new *Eagle* could rise from the ashes with a more favorable contract, a new plant, and a more economical operation. Yet there does not seem to be sufficient evidence for the Guild charge that the Schroths were both operating and killing the *Eagle* for personal gain. Their private memoranda and conversations, as well as their public statements and policies in operating the *Eagle*, indicate that they were primarily concerned with the good of Brooklyn and the preservation of a 114-year-old cultural institution which they saw as linked with a unique intimacy to the past and future character of Brooklyn. Ironically, if the Schroth management is to be faulted it is in its interpretation of that very "spirit" that made the *Eagle* a unique institution in a unique urban community. They overestimated the city's demand for its paper.[52]

The Willard Wirtz Decision

Although the *Eagle* was gone, the battle that precipitated its death continued for four more years. The Guild, along with its other claims, sued for $750,000 in severance pay and asked the Special Terms Court to compel the *Eagle* to arbitrate the claim. The case went up to the Court of Appeals, which ordered arbitration. After considerable consultation, Schroth accepted Northwestern University Professor W. Willard Wirtz of Adlai E. Stevenson's law firm as the arbitrator. He later regretted the decision, for Wirtz not only ruled against management but perhaps unintentionally, in the course of his decision, delivered an epitaph for a once great newspaper that, taken out of context, left a bitter taste with those who had loved it.

During the long and arduous hearings which began on March 26, 1958, the Guild fought to recover nearly a million dollars in severance pay while the publisher was suing the Guild for two million for the destruction of the paper. At the conclusion of four days on the stand, Schroth himself was led by his counsel into personalizing his testimony to answer the charge that he had desired the strike as an excuse for closing the paper. He replied by recounting his whole career of fifty-four years in newspaper work which he had hoped would end with his sons carrying on the *Eagle* tradition. To his surprise, the Guild counsel did not cross-examine him on this point; it merely insisted that it had acted legally in striking for the Manhattan pattern.[53]

Wirtz rendered his decision on February 2, 1959. He ruled that the *Eagle* was under contractual obligation to pay 315 of its former employees approximately $1,000,000 in severance, vacation, and other back pay and denied the publisher's counterclaim for $2,000,000 damages. In short, Wirtz's decision was that severance pay constituted fully earned wages and that termination of the contract does not terminate the publisher's obligation. However, the arbitrator went on to answer the publisher's broad claim that the employees had forfeited their rights by the strike, concluding that the strike, though disastrous, was essentially only a strike for higher wages. Then he added the epitaph:

> No one could be insensitive to the tragedy of what happened here. A century-old newspaper went out of existence. The valiant fifteen-year effort of a dedicated newspaperman and his sons to revive a dying newspaper was defeated. Over six hundred employees and their families were put to a crisis in their lives. The borough of Brooklyn was left, probably forever, without a major newspaper of its own.
>
> It is equally clear that the root cause of this tragedy lay neither in the motivation nor in the tactics of the employees or their union, but in the harsh fact that the *Eagle* had outlived its economic usefulness.
>
> The most sympathetic attention to the depressing chronicle of the last fifteen years of the *Eagle* compels the conclusion that it was the victim of inexorable economic pressures—of which wage demands of its employees represented only one part. It had gone through bankruptcy in 1940. In each succeeding year it had been necessary to impose increasingly spartan economies, to cut one feature and service after another, to feed its fires with its own substance. The Publisher's description of the advertising preferences of most Brooklyn merchants, the reading preferences of most Brooklyn residents, and the financial advantage of the other New York metropolitan papers, makes poignantly clear the central fact that the time had come when the *Eagle* could no longer meet its competition. The Schroth family was willing, for reasons beyond financial profit, to fight the inevitable. The employees of the paper were not.

To feel strongly that the diminishing number of papers in this country is a danger sign for democracy, to resent the forces which cause this, even to confess economic nostalgia—none of this is warrant for charging the employees of a particular newspaper with a responsibility to continue working for it at wages they consider inadequate and less than they can get elsewhere. The claim that the Guild's 1954 wage demand was "outrageous" does not consist with the facts that the demand was for the scale being paid by the other metropolitan newspapers, that this comparison had been held valid in three previous arbitration cases, that the Publisher was paying all of his employees in the craft bargaining units the "New York rates," and that the Guild offered to arbitrate the issues which were in dispute. The "strike" on January 28 was not the result of one decision, but of the conflict of two: the employees' decision that they would not continue to work for the wages they had been getting, and the employer's decision that he could pay no more. If some of the picketing tactics used by the Guild during the strike were "ruthless" (particularly in the refusal to permit the moving of the *Eagle* to its new building), they were nevertheless within the bounds of the law and of the practices of bargaining.

The epitaph of the Brooklyn *Eagle* will have to be that it died not at the hands of the Newspaper Guild of New York but rather because it had become an economic anachronism.[54]

The Schroths were stung by the "economic anachronism" phrase, feeling that the decision had in fact come not so much from the justice of the union's case as from the arbitrator's economic philosophy. Tom Schroth insisted with typical brave optimism that the *Eagle* had actually been "on the threshold of renewed vigor. . . ." A year later his father wrote to him, "So, fifty-five years of newspaper effort goes down the drain."[55] Today, almost twenty years after the event, the more one thinks of the final strike the more the *Eagle*'s closing seems a very dismal event with elements of personal tragedy. Both labor and management made mistakes; the biggest mistake seems to have been that each side looked at the other in terms of some pre-given conceptual framework. Neither Frank D. Schroth nor I. Kaufman was as the other saw him to be. The Guild was not out to destroy the *Eagle*, but Frank D. Schroth was not bluffing when he said he would rather close than accept what he considered the Guild's unreasonable demands.

Notes

[1]TNS memo to the editorial staff, April 8, 1953.

[2]TNS memo to Hank Connors, January 6, November 8, 1954.

[3]TNS memo to Hank Connors, April 7, 1954.

[4]*Eagle*, July 26, 1954.

[5]*Eagle*, August 10, 1954; Frigand interview, October 23, 1970.

[6]*Frontpage*, October 18, 1954.

[7]*Frontpage*, December 15, 1954.

[8]Talk by Frank D. Schroth, Publisher of the Brooklyn *Eagle*, to his guests at Hotel Towers, May 5, 1954, TNS.

[9]*Editor and Publisher*, March 19, 1955.

[10]Private memoranda in FDS paper, October 2, 5, 6, 1953, TNS. FDS interview, November 27, 1969.

[11]FDS statement to Arbitration Proceedings on the Guild contract, March 22, 1954, TNS.

[12]FDS, "Hotel Towers Talk," pp. 8-9.

[13]FDS, "Statement to Arbitration Proceedings . . . Guild Contract," March 22, 1954, TNS.

[14]FDS, "Statement to Arbitration Proceedings," p. 3, TNS; Don Malafronte, "Brooklyn *Eagle* Blends Optimism and Economy," *News Workshop* 5, No. 1 (December 3, 1953): 3.

[15]John Cashmore, *Brooklyn Progress* (Brooklyn: Borough of Brooklyn, June 20, 1956), p. 10.

[16]Undated MS in TNS papers.

[17]FDS, "Statement to Arbitration Proceedings," p. 3.

[18]The *Eagle* minimum daily milline rate (the rate per line that an advertiser would pay if that newspaper had exactly one million circulation and charged relatively its current rate) for general advertising was $3.46. The *New York Times'* was $2.95. Advertising linage in suburban newspapers had increased 30 percent since 1948 while linage in New York City papers had remained stationary or fallen slightly. FDS, Statement, p. 4.

[19]FDS, Statement, p. 4; the *Guild Reporter*, November 27, 1953.

[20]Edwin Emery, *The Press and America* (Englewood Cliffs, N.J.: Prentice Hall, 1962), pp. 672-673.

[21]Raymond B. Nixon, "Who Will Own the Press in 1975?" *Journalism Quarterly* 32 (Winter 1955): 11.

[22]Emery, pp. 674-676.

[23]Earl Josephson, "Are New York Dailies Losing Readers?" *News Workshop* 5, No. 1 (December 1953): 1.

[24]*Time* 64 (December 20, 1954): 42-44.

[25]During negotiations, management issued regular bulletins to all employees giving detailed accounts of the meetings. The TNS "Strike History" is based on these bulletins and his personal notes on the meetings.

[26]*The Eagle Reporter*, March 18, 27, 1947; Letters, FDS to Paul Rubin, March 6, 1947 (FDS).

[27]FDS "Address to the *Eagle* Unit of the New York Newspaper Guild," April 10, 1941; "Address to All *Eagle* Employees, in the *Eagle* News Room," November 24, 1952.

[28]Interview with Al Salerno, November 6, 1969.

[29]Interview with I. Kaufman, June 15, 1970; Violet Weingarten interview, July 19, 1973.

[30]Gertrude McAllister, "I'm for a New Look!" *Eagle Job Press* Friday, May 14. Internal evidence suggests that the letters were written before 1950 since the author says Schroth had been at the paper for ten years.

[31]FDS "Address," 1952.

[32]*Agreement between the Brooklyn Eagle and Newspaper Guild of New York*, November 30, 1952, pp. 6-9; TNS, "Strike History," p. 17; *Agreement between the Long Island Daily Press, Publishing Company, Inc., and the Newspaper Guild of New York*, Local #3, May 20, 1954.

[33]TNS.

[34]"Strike History," p. 30.

[35]Interview with I. Kaufman, June 13, 1970.

[36]*Eagle Reporter*, January 17, 1955, puts the "No" votes closer to five. The management's version of the strike emphasizes that "This was the only time when the 315 members of the *Eagle* unit of the Guild had an opportunity to express themselves on the strike issue. No further vote was taken before the strike actually was called by the committee. There were never any secret votes." "Strike History," p. 47.

[37]*Eagle Reporter*, January 13, 1955.

[38]The *Eagle* and the typographical union had agreed to observe the same

contract which the union had with the New York Publishers Association, December 8, 1954, containing the clause, "the union agrees that it will not support a strike or work stoppage under any other circumstances." ("Strike History," p. 52).

[39]It is significant that the circulation of Manhattan dailies increased very little in Brooklyn with the *Eagle* gone. Most *Eagle* subscribers already read Manhattan papers. *Editor and Publisher*, March 19, 1955.

[40]The *Eagle* came back briefly as a weekly from October 23 to November 26 in 1960 and daily in 1962 under the ownership of Robert W. Farrell, a flamboyant gentleman who had been an *Eagle* columnist for seven years. Farrell bought the morgue and right to publish the paper for $25,000 in November 1959. The Guild, which had become legal owner of the *Eagle* on January 22, 1960 as a result of the Guild's suit for severance pay, approved the Farrell sale. During the New York newspaper strike the circulation went up and his income exceeded $1,000,000. The paper cost five cents and was sold only in Brooklyn. Due to a number of financial difficulties, he suspended publication June 26, 1963. Letter from Farrell, *Editor and Publisher*, July 25, 1964; *Frontpage*, February 16, 1960; *New York Times*, November 20, 1959, p. 20; Farrell returned in January 1971 with a resurrected New York *Daily Mirror*.

[41]Bob Grannis memo to TNS, February 16, 1955.

[42]*Frontpage*, February 16, 1955.

[43]"Strike History," p. 62; a confidential memorandum circulated within the management during the strike gives an analysis of the earnings and expenses of the *Eagle* for 1954 and concludes that it would be possible to survive if operations were resumed. It indicates that the Schroths were certainly not anxious to kill the paper, as the Guild later charged.

In 1954 there had been no predominant downward or upward trend but rather a seasonal pattern similar to most years. Advertising was down. Expenses were up; but so was circulation.

The Schroth strategy remained one of economies plus risk-taking with the hope that the investment would pay off. There were still possibilities for cost-cutting in the mechanical department, particularly in overtime costs. The greatest loss in 1954 had been in advertising revenues, first in classified advertising, then in national advertising. The hope was that they could increase local advertising and classified display advertising. However, the analysis was loaded with "ifs." If reader and advertiser support was forthcoming, a prudent and tight operation might get the paper to a breakeven point after the first two months. ("Confidential Analysis", TNS).

[44]*New York Times*, March 17, 1955.

[45]*Editor and Publisher*, March 19, 1955.

[46]"Strike History," pp. 70-71; *Frontpage*, June 14, 1955; *New York Times*, May 10, 1955; *Time*, May 23, 1955.

[47]*Who Killed the Brooklyn Eagle?* (New York: The Newspaper Guild of New York, Local 3, American Newspaper Guild, CIO), June 7, 1955. John Deegan, Guild organizer who had worked at the *Eagle* in the early 1940s, said at the closing that the *Eagle* situation was the most mystifying he had ever seen. "How can he just throw away three million dollars worth of property?," Deegan said of Schroth. *Editor and Publisher*, March 19, 1955.

Today Deegan maintains the union was "mousetrapped" into the strike and that the publisher was willing to close the paper because he mistakenly thought he could make a good profit selling the machinery. Deegan interview, June 17, 1970.

[48]*Who Killed the Brooklyn Eagle?*, p. 5.

[49]Interview with Crowell, December 20, 1970.

[50]FDS letter to John R. Blades of Blades and Macaulay, Newark, New Jersey, March 31, 1955, TNS.

[51]TNS, confidential memorandum to FDS and Frank D. Schroth, Jr., March 10, 1955.

[52]The Manhattan dailies moved quickly to fill the gap left by the *Eagle*. Circulation figures for Manhattan dailies in Brooklyn at that time are not available; according to the Audit Bureau of Circulation, New York newspapers did not break down their city circulation by counties during the *Eagle*'s lifetime. However, an *Editor and Publisher* survey indicated that in the forty-seven days that the *Eagle* had been unable to publish because craft unions honored Guild picket lines, the Manhattan dailies picked up very small circulations in Brooklyn. One circulator, whose paper had added about 4,000 sales daily, explained that much of the *Eagle*'s home delivered circulation was duplicate buying by "hometown folk." *Editor and Publisher*, 88 (March 19, 1955).

The Manhattan papers were very interested in the Brooklyn want ads and began a competitive campaign to re-educate Brooklynites who had been dependent on the *Eagle* to use Manhattan papers as an advertising medium. Manhattan papers also increased their Brooklyn coverage. Within two months the New York *World-Telegram* claimed to be providing twenty-four columns of borough news daily, in contrast to the eighteen columns formerly provided by the *Eagle*. *Editor and Publisher* 88 (March 26, 1955): 42; (April 9, 1955): 32; (May 7, 1955): 15.

In short, it would seem that the core of Brooklynites faithful to the *Eagle* learned fairly quickly to reorient their reading and advertising habits and loyalties across the river.

Meanwhile, in the last weeks of its history, the *Eagle* had been predicting a bright future for Brooklyn: "Dynamic Future of Boro Industry Shown in Eagle Business Review." "On the basis of the facts and opinions here given and of our own first-hand knowledge, we have complete confidence in the future of Brooklyn as an industrial, shipping, and population center."

The Brooklyn labor market average take-home pay per family was $5,538, high compared with other cities, and the mass annual buying power was $4,738,398,000. However, the *Eagle* acknowledged that Brooklyn was threatened by competition from the St. Lawrence Seaway, industries moving to the South, and the population shift to the suburbs. *Eagle*, January 6, 1955.

[53]FDS letter to family, March 31, June 5, 1958, TNS.

[54]W. Willard Wirtz, *In the Matter of Arbitration Between Newspapers Guild of New York and Brooklyn Eagle, Inc.* (Chicago, February 2, 1959); *Editor and Publisher* (February 7, 1959): 59.

[55]TNS letter to J. Russel Wiggins of the *Washington Post*, February 5, 1957; FDS letter to TNS undated.

10

THE *EAGLE*

AND BROOKLYN

A number of years ago—he is not sure how many—Robert Moses was on his way to see Mrs. Blum in her penthouse apartment in the Brooklyn Heights' charming old Hotel Bossert. In the elevator he encountered a bearded old man who recognized him and invited him for a visit and a drink. The old man was a former Brooklyn politician, so the two talked about the mysterious city they both loved and worried a bit about what was happening to it. As Moses left, his host stopped him for one last word and offered the phrase that in Moses' mind summed up more than any other expression what was the trouble with Brooklyn.

"The trouble with Brooklyn," the old man said, "is that everyone is the same size."[1]

Brooklyn, by its geographical situation, by its historical relation as "underdog" to the city of New York, and by its provincialism and small town atmosphere, had made the terms "greatness" and "Brooklynite" incompatible. A look at Brooklyn, its resources, its history, and its community spirit, particularly as these attributes are reflected in the Brooklyn *Eagle*, demonstrates both the truth and the inadequacy of the old man's statement.

An examination of the 114-year history of the interaction between this growing urban community and its most representative newspaper indicates that this extremely varied and complex interrelationship is not subject to any one single interpretation. This narrative has been held together by three threads—the history of the *Eagle*, the history of Brooklyn, and the newspaper's continuing attempt to both interpret and influence its community until the community did not seem to need it any more. At the same time, this study has stressed the importance of a community's need for a clear image of itself and the importance of people's feelings about their surroundings. The *Eagle* understood to an extraordinary degree that its readers had to relate in a familiar way to neighborhoods, to dead heroes, and to sturdy old buildings. It knew that some kind of face-to-face relationship and some kind of public acknowledgment for otherwise forgotten men, women, and children was imperative for human living in a rapidly changing urban milieu.

Perhaps more than any comparable American urban community, Brooklyn has steadfastly defied analysis. Although the borough has always been called a "community," it is also appropriately described as a collection of independent communities, each with its own tradition, hanging together under a common name as its area grew and grew. This illusiveness is particularly characteristic of modern Brooklyn, the conglomeration of changing and in many cases fading neighborhoods that hold historic and ethnic roots in long half-forgotten eighteenth and even seventeenth century towns.

Brooklyn was not always this mysterious, nor was it always uncertain about its identity. In the nineteenth century and even in the first decades of the twentieth century, Brooklyn knew itself as the city of homes and churches. Sometimes Brooklyn saw its neighbor Manhattan as an adversary or a threatening rival and sometimes as a breeding-ground for materialism and corruption; yet Brooklyn retained its sense of moral and even economic superiority. Its politics were cleaner, its water was fresher, its landscape and beaches were lovelier, and its real estate was cheaper.

This sense of well-being which old Brooklyn enjoyed was both attributable to and reflected in its press, particularly in its greatest paper, the Brooklyn *Eagle*, which either absorbed or survived all of Brooklyn's other newspapers. The *Eagle* thrived during Brooklyn's century of growth and died when the community it served was likewise in an unexpected and almost traumatic period of decline.

Just as Brooklyn itself has been described through the metaphor of a riddle, a mysterious labyrinth known, in Thomas Wolfe's story title, only to the dead, so has the Brooklyn *Eagle*, remembered in the years after its death, been described as a contradiction, a journalistic and cultural mixture of timeless qualities and fleeting trivia. While acknowledging the influence of Kinsella, McKelway, Crist, and Schroth, the history of the Brooklyn *Eagle*'s relationship to its community seems to indicate that the lifespan, influence, and prosperity of an urban community newspaper are determined by the economic, political, and cultural health of the community itself. At the same time, it is the paper's job to discover and to define what are the distinguishing characteristics of its community and its principal readership. The paper must ask what unique spirit unifies the geographical area, the institutions, homes, and persons it would address.

The great editors and publishers, therefore, are those who can sense and share the attitudes and aspirations of their readers, who can feel the common emotional and intellectual yearnings of the citizens and articulate them in an uncommon way. This was especially true of Joseph Pulitzer of the New York *World* and William Randolph Hearst of the New York *Journal*, both of whom had considerable influence on the *Eagle*'s concept of community service and its later use of sensationalistic techniques. Once this special resonance between the newspaper and its community is lost, the paper no longer serves its purpose.

Most newspapers die because they can no longer make money. Since the price of newsprint went up during the Second World War, since unionization and inflation have forced labor costs steadily upward, and since both publishers and unions have failed to modernize their equipment, financial problems have killed some of the finest and most venerable papers in the country, particularly in New York. Yet death comes to these institutions not simply because they have run out of money, but rather through a complex interaction of a number of causes all related to how well the paper fulfills its several community roles. A newspaper's prosperity or decline, for instance, is related to its coverage, its advocacy, its political philosophy, and its entertainment values as well as to the publisher's managerial skill.

These rules are all related to the paper's unifying purpose of unraveling the mysteries of community living, teaching people threatened by a changing and apparently hostile society how to survive, reassuring them when it seems that their institutions may have failed, and telling people who they are. In short, the essence of a successful newspaper is its clear and distinct image, projected by a firm institutional identity that partakes of the identity of the community it reflects.

The *Eagle*, like all newspapers, had several community functions. First of all, it was a means of communication, a source of information for the citizens of a historic, highly diversified, and industrialized area who needed news about themselves that would reinforce their own self-image. In this way the *Eagle* resembled the suburban and small-town weekly community papers. It publicized local people who would be passed over by the large metropolitan dailies. Events at the Brooklyn Museum and the Academy of Music, for instance, were well covered, as were the comings and goings of Brooklyn "society," which was distinct from New York Society. The letters from the interviews with former *Eagle* employers and readers stress this *Eagle* characteristic, local news coverage, above all others. Irwin Shaw recalled that when he was a boy his team could schedule its baseball games through the *Eagle*. "Fat Club, 13 to 15 class, uniformed, traveling, looking for games. Call Brighton 2033, any evening after six and ask for Al."[2]

The *Eagle* was a business enterprise. Although it was founded as a temporary paper for the temporary purpose of promoting the political fortunes of its owners, the Democratic law firm of Murphy, Vanderbilt, and Lott and the family of the first printer, Isaac Van Anden, turned it into one of the wealthiest newspapers in the United States and played a significant role in Brooklyn's economic and political life for over eighty years. The business drive of Colonel William Hester's family and the managerial genius of Herbert Gunnison tied the *Eagle* to the economic progress of other Brooklyn businesses and industries, particularly Long Island real estate, waterfront warehouses, and travel.

In the course of its rise to wealth in the 1880s and 1890s, the

Hester family and the *Eagle* also came to embody the materialistic aspect of the American Dream, the Gospel of Wealth, and the worship of what William James called the bitch goddess success. The *Eagle*'s prosperity paralleled that of Pulitzer's New York *World*; its success was another manifestation of the Gilded Age in which both the *World* and the *Eagle* had to display their wealth by building magnificent new plants and topping them with golden domes. Edward Bok, who had begun his rise to success at the *Eagle*, rejoiced, "We live in a country where every success is possible, where a man can make of himself just what he may choose."[3] The *Eagle* preached the Gospel of Wealth in the late nineteenth and early twentieth centuries in various direct and indirect ways. In its coverage of the rich, with particular emphasis on their palatial homes and clubs, it held them up as objects for emulation. For example, all the heavy volumes—*The Eagle and Brooklyn*, celebrating the opening of the new *Eagle* office in 1891, and the ornate Seventy-Fifth Anniversary Issue in 1916—can be seen now, in the context of the *Eagle*'s whole history, as extravagances, as a distorted picture of Brooklyn, as characteristic projections of the *"Eagle* Spirit," projections of the gospel of success, and as ultimately harmful to both the *Eagle* and its community.

The pictures, biographies of prominent men, and local histories in these landmark publications so reinforced one another and so forcefully propagated the belief that Brooklyn *was* these institutions, clubs, and personalities—to the silent exclusion of lower classes —that when the myth of the socially prominent and successful Brooklynites faded both the *Eagle* and Brooklyn were left groping for a new self-understanding. It is particularly significant here that Edwin B. Wilson, who was at the height of his influence as executive editor and chief editorial writer under the last publisher, Frank D. Schroth, when the *Eagle* most needed to adapt to a changing urban situation, was formed in the *"Eagle* Spirit" under the Hester-Gunnison regime when the *Eagle* was most devoted to Brooklyn's successful elite.

Meanwhile, the *Eagle*'s mentor, the *World*, avoided this trap. Pulitzer consciously catered to the poor and immigrant masses, lambasting the wealthy for their venality, particularly when the millionaires of the New World aped the corrupt aristocracies of

Europe, without undermining the Horatio Alger mythology of American life. Both Pulitzer and Hester coveted wealth and enjoyed the symbols of their triumph, their buildings that dominated their respective skylines from opposite sides of the Brooklyn Bridge and their personal yachts. The *World*, however, retained a democratic egalitarian base of support until its death in 1931, while the *Eagle*, under St. Clair McKelway and Arthur M. Howe, rejected the blatant sensationalism which linked Pulitzer and Hearst to the masses and prided itself on being a "class" newspaper that, unlike its cheaper rivals, sold for three cents.

In a time of great social ferment when the class lines were beginning to harden, in the era of the Haymarket trial, the Pullman Strike, and the slow building up of racial tensions in urban ghettoes, the *Eagle* expressed its "democratic" tendencies by supporting Grover Cleveland and Woodrow Wilson and treating the poor and the blacks with, at best, *noblesse oblige*. Two books on classic American social conflicts use the *Eagle* as an example of the reactionary press. Henry David's *The History of the Haymarket Affair* quotes the *Eagle*'s editorial on the conviction of the accused anarchists:

> Let the great Western community be congratulated upon the wholesome example she has set, . . . the precedent will be faithfully observed . . . the people that fought each other four years . . . in order to settle conflicting ideas as to the best way in which to perpetuate own institutions, are back of these Chicago Verdicts—in Chicago, in New York, in Boston, in New Orleans, and everywhere else.

Arthur I. Waskow, in *From Race Riot to Sit-In: 1919 and the 1960's*, cites the *Eagle*'s reaction to the 1919 Washington race riot:

RACE WAR IN WASHINGTON SHOWS BLACK AND WHITE EQUALITY NOT PRACTICAL.

The *Eagle* blamed the riot on the full employment, high wages, and increasing independence that Washington Negroes had won from the war.[4]

The *Eagle's* commitment to the gospel of success is also evident in the encouragement it gave to the myth of the self-made man and self-help literature so prominent at the end of the nineteenth century. Self-help literature was largely a product of Protestant theology, a historical outgrowth of Puritan teachings and the Protestant doctrine of the calling. Success was to be won by self-discipline and by marshalling the resources of the will, by frugality, hard work, sobriety, and perseverance.

The *Eagle*, in spite of the fact that New York and Brooklyn were ever teeming with new waves of Italian and Jewish immigrants, was mainly a Protestant paper, and its Monday morning sermon page—a few of which (legend has it) were written by reporters who had slept through the services—were predominantly Protestant documents. As Reverend Maurice Ambrose Levy of Brooklyn's Green Avenue Baptist Church emphasized on the eve of the *Eagle's* seventy-fifth anniversary, the *Eagle*, through the "gospel of the press"—"a man must save himself, work out his own salvation" by leading the "square life"—was spreading the Kingdom of God.[5]

For example, *The Autobiography of Emma Bullet*, the life story of the *Eagle's* Paris correspondent, was written at management's request and printed at the *Eagle* Press as a Brooklyn woman's contribution to self-help literature and the *Eagle* spirit of aggressive individualism. She wrote it, she said, after twenty-five years of never missing a letter, with only one idea in view:

> . . . that some un-named women who will read these lines, and who have ambition to make a position for themselves, will be encouraged . . . and whatever happens, whatever adverse winds blow, however great the storm of life may be, will keep on "paddling their own canoe," as I did, until they reach a goal, at which each one may say, "By my own efforts, by my own work, I have an independent position, and I am ready to quote the words of Byron: 'I stand alone, but would not give my place for a throne.' "[6]

"Standing alone" was also a dominant theme in the Seventy-Fifth Anniversary *Eagle* Pageant at the Brooklyn Academy of Music in 1916. Examined now in the context of the *Eagle*'s whole history, this series of episodes on the key moments in the institution's inexorable rise to wealth and prestige, written largely to glorify the independent individualism of the Van Anden-Hester family, presents clear evidence that the institution was more interested in preaching its own somewhat narrow spiritual doctrine than in objectively portraying its own traditions.

Walt Whitman was gently ridiculed because he allegedly preferred to loaf in the grass than to work, although the recent scholarship indicates that the young *Eagle* Whitman was very industrious. At the same time, according to the skit, the *Eagle* owner recognized Walt's hidden genius. His boy companion, "Hen" Sutton, was portrayed by way of contrast as a zealous teen-age toiler, perhaps as a model for the nonunionized, underpaid, and overworked employees of 1916.

The scenes built around William Hester stressed the Horatio Alger element in his life, with his starting as a printer's apprentice in his uncle's office and working his way to the presidency. Other scenes illustrated other elements of the *"Eagle* Spirit" such as the moral superiority of *Eagle* editors to common politicians, the paper's preference of moderation to radicalism before and during the Civil War, and its avoidance of sensationalism when a prominent citizen's—Henry Ward Beecher's—reputation was involved.

The Pageant, in its selective view of the *Eagle*'s history, passed over the facts: that history has found Walt Whitman, who was fired for his Free Soil doctrine, more enlightened than his publisher on the slavery question, that rather than acknowledge Whitman's genius, the *Eagle* management unfairly criticized him and misunderstood him for over eighty years, that even though the *Eagle* was faithful to the Union during the Civil War it was a fidelity marked by great hostility to Lincoln, and that the Kinsella *Eagle* was not as supportive of Henry Ward Beecher as the Pageant suggests. In short, the 1916 Pageant and Anniversary Issue, like the *Eagle and Brooklyn* and the *Consolidation Issue*, indicate that the *Eagle*'s concept of its own role in Brooklyn history was becoming pompous.

When Colonel Hester died in 1921 and when the inflated American economy built partly on myth of inevitable progress fell apart eight years later, the *Eagle*'s piously materialistic interpretation of the American Dream would also begin to fade. The *"Eagle* Spirit,"* based as it was on an alliance between the Protestant work ethic, the wealth and prestige of a limited Old Brooklyn Society, and uninterrupted economic prosperity, could not withstand cracks in any of its pillars.

For a long while, newspapermen went along with the idea that newspaper work itself was its own reward. Talented young men like Hans Von Kaltenborn and Cleveland Rodgers and hundreds of others took low-paying *Eagle* jobs because men still believed that journalism was a romantic way of life. For them, standing outside the Metropolitan Opera House on a cold night to catch the names of Brooklyn Society ladies who had seen "Aida" that night was the first step in a glamorous globetrotting career. For Kaltenborn this was true, but he eventually left the *Eagle* with some bitterness. The founders of the *Eagle* unit of the American Newspaper Guild were in several instances Brooklyn Jews with Marxist leanings, "new" Brooklynites from the swelling, crowded Brooklyn Jewish ghettoes. They had no inclination to accept the value system of a Brooklyn Heights society that had long excluded them and they had no taste for a theology that in the face of Depression poverty found merit in work itself. I. Kaufman, particularly sensitive to the old *Eagle*'s neglect of the Jewish community, remembers that Crist had told him there was no Jewish society in Brooklyn. The employees were particularly slow to accept the virtues of austerity when they were convinced that management, with its frequent turnovers between 1921 and 1939, was draining the paper for its own profit.[7]

When Old Brooklyn Society began to die, the *Eagle* was slow to bury it. The biographies in the commemorative issues, the list of prominent citizens invited to advise the *Eagle* readers on the borough's future, and the letters to the editor preserved as a measure of the *Eagle*'s influence all suggest that the *Eagle* measured social importance in terms of leadership in long-established and stable civic institutions such as the Brooklyn Institute of Arts and Sciences and the Brooklyn Museum, exclusive clubs, old homes, and churches.

When representatives of the new Brooklyn minorities such as the Jews gained social acceptance, it would be because of the stability and prosperity of their institutions, such as the Edward C. Blum family's department store, Abraham and Straus.

There was certainly no conscious anti-Semitism during the Frank D. Schroth administration, and the private accusation in 1950 by the sick and angry Mayor William O'Dwyer that the pre-Brooklyn Schroth had once been friendly with Adolph Hitler was particularly ugly in view of the Schroth *Eagle*'s efforts to be open to Brooklyn's Jewish community. Yet Schroth had come to the *Eagle* as a stranger to Brooklyn. With that predilection toward successful people which a defender could call honest ambition and which a critic might call snobbism, he may have been too quick to accept the prevailing though nonviable *Eagle* management consensus as to what Brooklyn was and who were its leading citizens.

Stages of Brooklyn History

In examining the relationship between the community of Brooklyn and its most characteristic newspaper we could divide the community's history into three periods: a period of growth and confidence, a period of change and decay, and a period of gradual reawakening. The first era began with Brooklyn's incorporation as a city in 1835 and continued throughout the nineteenth century into the first three decades of the twentieth. This period is distinguished by accelerating territorial expansion, growth in population, industry, commerce, education, cultural, and civic institutions and, with notable exceptions, an increase in the pride and sense of well-being of its citizens. This interpretation of Brooklyn's history dominates the best contemporary journalistic histories of the city such as the twenty-fifth anniversary issue of the elite magazine *Brooklyn Life* (May 29, 1915). There Samuel B. Moore could write with confidence:

Brooklyn has worn seven-league boots in its growth and in the matter of purely material gains. Nobody would have the temerity to even faintly utter a denial of this assertion. It is too palpable and plain. Not only "he who runs may read", but he who is blind can see it with his mental vision. From the materialistic standpoint the onward march has been a mighty and realistic progress. [8]

The *Eagle* shared this vision of its sister publication and taught this doctrine to its readers again and again in its histories and commemorative issues.

There is a problem in pinpointing the beginning of the period of decline. The first stages of any historical process, particularly the disintegration of the nation's fourth-largest city, remain obscure. Even in a period of remarkable growth there are a number of events which can be interpreted both positively and negatively depending on the values at stake. The completion of the Brooklyn Bridge in 1883 was one of the greatest technological and cultural achievements in American history, but by physically joining Brooklyn to Manhattan it foreshadowed and ultimately caused the end of Brooklyn's independence and distinct community character. Consolidation with New York in 1898, now often referred to as the "Mistake," meant that Brooklynites could consider themselves members of the greatest city in the world, and the move brought on an improvement in real estate values and in city services. Nevertheless, if, as one writer says, many of the problems of the American city are emotional, 1898 was the beginning of the end of community spirit in Brooklyn. [9]

The other new bridges connecting Manhattan and Brooklyn—the Williamsburg Bridge in 1903, the Manhattan Bridge in 1909 and the Queensborough Bridge in 1909 linking Manhattan and Queens—all contributed to Brooklyn's population but also changed the character of the population, bringing more poor Irish, Italians, and Jews into the older parts of the city. The bridges, in conjunction with the expanding rapid transit system, tended to make Brooklyn people culturally more dependent on Manhattan and the Bronx than on downtown Brooklyn.

Finally, 1930 could be designated as the year of decline since it marked the beginning of a continual population fall-off, particularly in the oldest neighborhoods. This was the change, I believe, that most affected Brooklyn's self-image and the future of the *Eagle*. Brooklyn's worst period of change and uncertainty seems to have come at the end of the Second World War. The war period had brought more money with the expansion of the Brooklyn Navy Yards and its seventy-one thousand workers, but it also brought more poor Negroes looking for jobs, gangs of juvenile delinquents, and Murder Incorporated. One would judge by reading other publications as well as the *Eagle* that the community was coming apart in the 1950s; the police were being paid off by mobsters, teen-agers roamed the streets killing old men for thrills, and violence was the order of the day. Some typical front page banner headlines in the fall of 1954 were:

THRILL KILLER TURNS ON PALS[10]
PSYCHO SLAYS COP, WOMAN[11]
TEEN REVENGE BATTLE NIPPED[12]

The *Eagle* closed in January 1955 and the community was without a voice. Within a year two other symbols were gone; Ebbetts field was sold for a housing site and the Brooklyn Dodgers left for Los Angeles. The Navy Yard, which had been languishing for years, was abandoned in 1966.

The tone of absolute certainty so pronounced in earlier writings was gone from Brooklyn's postwar interpreters. No longer able to conclude as McKelway could that the essence of Brooklyn was homemaking, they tried to evoke the varied experience of the place by naming its parts and stringing together personal life episodes on the thread of an artist's memory. Irwin Shaw, struggling to define his home town in 1950, had to confess that he did not recognize it any more. He saw two Brooklyns, the city of the historians and census takers, and the private and personal Brooklyn "which haunts the memory and sharpens the behavior of all her sons no matter where they roam." He was reduced simply to cataloguing its many faces by paraphrasing Walt Whitman, who had celebrated the city a century before:

I sing of Brooklyn, city of myth, stone mother, whose cobbled caress shaped me, for better or worse, into the man I am today.

Heroic stepdaughter of the metropolis, water girdled, iron-voiced, at the far end of all high bridges, subway empire, barracks for the millions, port for the humbler vessels of the seas, bargain playground for the sweltering masses of the city, borough of homes, borough of churches, borough of schools, borough of cemeteries, borough of back gardens, borough of thugs, borough of poets, borough of Capone, borough of O'Dwyer, anybody's borough, everybody's borough, nobody's borough.[13]

Norman Rosten, writing in 1960, was also overcome by the mystery of the city, but he did discern the pathetic characteristic that also struck Robert Moses as the key to Brooklyn:

We always knew, unconsciously, that this was a "beginning" place. We know, today, that those on their way up the ladder never move into Brooklyn; they move out of it to Manhattan, Westchester, Queens, or the reaches of Long Island. But some of us have in our blood, I think, the fierce pride of Those Who Stayed. And many stayed all their lives.[14]

The maintenance of the "fierce pride" can be an awesome task. It seems to belong preeminently to the community newspaper. A community unconsciously aware that all its citizens are "the same size" and that they owe their eminence as "old Brooklynites" not to having competed for a prize and won but rather to the fact that they have held their ground in the face of a revolutionary population shift, is bound to need regular reassurance that it is not second-rate, that it *is* competitive, that it is unique.

Nineteenth century Brooklyn was competitive in a number of ways. Brooklyn really was outstripping New York in the quality of its real estate and in its rate of territorial expansion. In the first two decades of the twentieth century Brooklyn was competitive as it expected to dominate Long Island economically and to build international seaports at Montauk Point and Sheepshead Bay. In its period of decline Brooklyn could only be symbolically competitive. The cult of the underdog grew, the *Eagle* called its own teen-age baseball program "Brooklyn Against the World," and the 1953 Dodgers-Yankee World Series in daily *Eagle* banner headlines took on the dimensions of the classic nineteenth century struggle between Brooklyn and New York. With the two institutions, the *Eagle* and the Dodgers, that were the prime weapons in the symbolic struggle gone, Brooklyn has had to look for a new way of defining itself. It could also be argued that the loss of the Dodgers was good for Brooklyn in that the Dodgers' mystique encouraged a fake "Dem Bums" image of Brooklyn. They saw that Dodgers' owner Walter O'Malley was motivated more by money than by the love of the borough. This "loss of innocence" might encourage Brooklynites to think more realistically about their community.

The Eagle and Social Change

Perhaps the best way to evaluate the *Eagle*'s understanding of an impact on Brooklyn would be to move through Brooklyn's history and assess some of the newspaper's major interests and campaigns. In general, I believe the *Eagle* made a great contribution to the welfare of Brooklyn and a substantial though not spectacular contribution to American journalism. Yet ironically, a number of factors that contributed to the *Eagle*'s prestige in Brooklyn also contributed to its mediocrity. By being so provincial, it also became part of a culture where everyone was the "same size." The *Eagle* also made a number of mistakes in judging which way Brooklyn was going. It lost touch at a time when it was most needed—not drastically, but enough to make one speculate, in retrospect, that if the *Eagle* had handled things a little differently, the "Brooklyn Spirit" might have suffered a little less.

Its nineteenth century campaigns against bossism, particularly its war against John McLaughlin and John Y. McKane, along with its support for Seth Low and William J. Gaynor, were truly campaigns in Brooklyn's best interests, even though the lack of emotional detachment on the part of the *Eagle* editors may have detracted from the *Eagle*'s achievement. The *Eagle* was largely responsible for William

O'Dwyer's resigning as Mayor of New York. It must be recorded that one reporter who took part in the *Eagle*'s 1950 crime investigation does not now feel comfortable about his participation. He feels that O'Dwyer was personally honest and did not view police payoffs as immoral in the way the *Eagle* did.[15]

Seen in retrospect, the *Eagle*'s effort to prevent consolidation with New York seems to have been a fight against the inevitable, against the very trend of urban history toward the greater centralization of city government. The *Eagle*'s policy was not mere obstinate political foot-dragging, however. The city itself was fairly evenly divided on the issue, and all points of view were well represented in the New York and Brooklyn press. The *Eagle* correctly wanted to protect Brooklyn's basic character of civility and order, qualities every American city might wish it had retained. Insofar as the *Eagle*'s opposition to joining New York was sterilely nostalgic, and insofar as the *Eagle* was slow to psychologically accept the fact of consolidation long after the event, the *Eagle*'s influence may have been harmful. A new community is not fortified by longing for an independent city that has disappeared.

Forty years later, at the beginning of the Schroth management, the *Eagle* resurrected the idea of a separate Brooklyn, not because Schroth really believed the clock could be turned back but because he saw it as a tactic to pressure the New York City government into giving Brooklyn better service. In a 1938 *Eagle* series on Brooklyn's needs, A. M. McKay, a "born and bred Brooklynite," suggested that Brooklyn should secede from the Greater City and that Long Island should become a separate state because the borough had not received its share of services. The snow was not being scraped off the ice for skating in Prospect Park, and there were no more Brooklyn regiments for parades.[16] In the *Eagle*'s centennial issue in 1941, some prominent citizens still expressed regret over the union.

The Princeton University Survey *Brooklyn's Relationship to the City of New York* made it clear that the joining of the two cities had been an economic necessity and that Brooklyn had profited financially from consolidation in its tax rate and real estate values. Furthermore, except for park and playground space, Brooklyn was on a par with the other boroughs in receiving services from the city. It may be that this constant agitation, this constant spirit of conflict marked often by resentment, was important in keeping up Brooklyn's pride, but the Princeton Survey indicated that Brooklyn's fears of being slighted were largely imaginary. I would judge that the *Eagle*'s continued attention to the consolidation issue was for the most part unproductive.

Long Island

One of the *Eagle*'s major miscalculations regarded the future of Brooklyn in its relationship with Long Island. City planning was one of the *Eagle*'s main concerns in the twentieth century but its interest began when planning was still a relatively young science and the work not of the central government but of private groups and individuals. New York City did not have a Planning Commission until its new charter in 1938 and there was no comprehensive City Plan until 1969. The *Eagle*'s earliest contribution, on the fading end of the City Beautiful movement in 1911, was a grandiose vision of downtown Brooklyn coupled with a projection of the future of Long Island as the rural extension of downtown Brooklyn. The vestiges of the downtown ideas were carried on in a more realistic form through the several *Eagle* Ten-Point plans for rebuilding the city. From St. Clair McKelway to Frank D. Schroth, when the *Eagle* took up a cause it did not let it die.

Downtown Brooklyn and the waterfront have not been redesigned along the lines of classical Rome, but a number of the elements of the Brooklyn renaissance during the last ten years were part of the *Eagle* 1952 Ten-Point Plan—the rebuilding of the waterfront, the clearing of slums and the building of new housing, and the attracting of new industry. Thanks to the *Eagle* Gowanus Creek channel was deepened, the blight-spreading Fulton Avenue "L" was demolished, and the Brooklyn Bridge was remodeled by 1955. There seems little doubt in the *Eagle*'s brief histories of its own campaigns, in the letters from *Eagle* employees and readers both to the *Eagle* and to me, and in the judgment of Robert Moses that the *Eagle*'s influence in these and other campaigns was real and often decisive.

The *Eagle*'s 1911 conception of Long Island as an economically and culturally isolated entity with Brooklyn as its "capital" was a common one until an unforeseen series of bridges, such as the Triborough, Bronx-Whitestone, and Throgs Neck, linked Long Island with Manhattan, the Bronx, and Westchester. A two-page color advertisement in a 1920 promotion booklet for Brooklyn subway ads depicted Long Island as a bottle with Brooklyn as its neck. The Island was the "playground of New York's Rich . . . tap the neck and you tap the contents."[17] In this frame of mind, the *Eagle* played a major role in the development of Long Island through its real estate promotion and through Robert Moses' highway building programs during the New Deal. However, it did not—and could not be expected to—foresee the massive population shift that would take place in the 1930s and during and after the Second World War, when the very pride in individual home ownership which the *Eagle* encouraged would lead Brooklynites to flee the old city and look for homes in Queens and Nassau.

By the end of the nineteenth century the good single family house survived only in the northernmost reaches of Manhattan and on the edge of Brooklyn. In Flatbush, Flatlands, Bensonhurst, Queens, the Bronx, and New Jersey, promoters were converting farms into lots. The remoteness of these areas and the expense involved in commuting isolated them from the new groups of foreign-born poor, particularly the Italians and East European Jews, who were streaming into New York between 1880 and the First World War. The 1920s seemed to be a period of stability in New York, as large-scale immigration subsided and the population growth leveled out, and civic groups gave more attention to regional planning. Robert Moses, then Park Commissioner, used the great inpouring of federal talent and money during the New Deal to expand his park, bridge, and highway system linking New York with the "playland" of Long Island—coinciding and cooperating with the *Eagle*-sponsored Long Island Ten-Year Plan.

The *Eagle* published its analysis of Brooklyn's problems in a series of editorials in early 1933. Rodgers saw many of Brooklyn's needs in terms of transportation. Long Island needed a railroad tunnel to the

South and West.[18] Above all, said the *Eagle*, the future of downtown
Brooklyn depended on the automobile; New York was spending too
much on public transportation when people were moving to the
suburbs because New York had failed to provide adequate facilities for
the automobile. As a result, business and industry were following the
people out, leaving the heart of the city a "dead area." The answer,
said the *Eagle*, was in a great system of expressways, the extension and
completion of the Interborough Parkway, Grand Central Parkway,
Eastern Parkway, and Southern State Parkway.[19]

Brooklyn now has a network of express highways connecting it
with Long Island but it remains nearly impossible to drive and park in
the central city. It is strange to read in the 1970s a 1933 editorial
arguing that more cars rather than expanded public transportation
should bring people into the central city. Furthermore, the express-
ways have injured the way we look at Brooklyn:

> The physical objects themselves do not really undergo the trans-
> formation. With certain notable exceptions they only seem to
> age and get grimier. It is, rather, the way in which we *see* them
> that changes. Brooklyn today, even to many of its residents, is
> very often the image of Brooklyn absorbed from driving the
> limited-access highway: the industry of north end, the products
> of American industry awaiting shipment on the docks below
> Brooklyn Heights, the spin along the Narrows with the Ver-
> razano Bridge punctuating the contrast between man and na-
> ture. Motorists remember the intricate spider web of Coney
> Island's Wonder Wheel, the endless stretches of swampland at
> Jamaica Bay, or the 25-mile-an-hour curves in a
> 50-mile-an-hour car in Verdant Interboro Parkway. The place-
> ment of our highways and the speed of our cars tend to play up its
> other attributes.
>
> What a different image Brooklyn must have provided in other
> periods.[20]

World War II was a period of renewed expansion and prosperity for
New York and for Brooklyn. The rapid expansion into the suburbs

which had slackened during the 1930s quickened once again. For the most part, those who fled the city did so because they could no longer fulfill their middle-class ideal of rearing their children in a single-family home in a good neighborhood in the urban milieu. However, this movement from Brooklyn to Queens and Nassau was not accompanied by a great extension of public transportation like the one that had contributed to Brooklyn's population growth. As the new struggle for status became a race for better housing, only the well-to-do, those with cars, could make their escape and take advantage of the outburst of new construction on Long Island after 1950. As the middle-income families moved out their places were taken by the new disadvantaged, the Negroes and Puerto Ricans, particularly in the older areas of Brooklyn such as the neighborhood around the dying Brooklyn Navy Yard, which was becoming one of the most depressed areas in the country.[21]

By the time the *Eagle* died, Brooklyn had gone through such a drastic demographic transformation that the old Brooklyn it had been addressing existed only as a remnant. The old neighborhoods had completely changed and new ones had developed blurring the lines of the old. A study of the population trend between 1930 and 1957 shows a population drop of 178,863 in nine northern, long established, and densely populated communities counterbalanced by a gain of 213,531 in eleven less central and more outlying communities. Only the most remote areas, Canarsie and Sheepshead Bay, those least accessible to downtown Brooklyn, showed continued growth. The sharpest deterioration was in the Bedford-Stuyvesant area after 1950; it was rapidly becoming a new black ghetto. Between 1950 and 1957, 344,000 whites, 13.8 percent of the white population, left Brooklyn, while the black population rose from 208,478 to 307,796 to become 11.8 percent of the populace; at the same time the Puerto Rican populace went from 40,299 to an estimated 160,000.[22] Queens became the most rapidly growing borough.

Did the *Eagle* realize what was happening? The *Eagle* was certainly aware that Brooklyn was changing, but the management, in contrast to some of the staff, did not appreciate the depth of the change.[23] From the beginning of the twentieth century Brooklyn's imperialism, its desire to dominate Long Island, kept it from realizing that Long Island was developing economic and cultural ties with the rest of the metropolitan area. Cleveland Rodgers' concept of Brooklyn's economic future being tied to freer world trade and the development of the Port of New York seems farsighted and correct, but his acceptance of the Robert Moses reverence for the automobile to the neglect of rapid public transit contributed to the decline of the central city.

Perhaps no one could foresee how much the Second World War would bring on the Long Island industrial population and housing boom, but the *Eagle* management should have foreseen that with Brooklynites moving out there, the Island was an *Eagle* market. In 1937, against the protests of some of his staff, Colonel Preston Goodfellow pulled the *Eagle* back from Long Island by eliminating the Island News section of the paper circulated in Nassau and Suffolk Counties. Said Goodfellow, "There is no future for the *Eagle* on Long Island."[24] A few years later *Newsday*, now the most powerful paper on Long Island, began its remarkable circulation rise.

Considering how drastically the borough was changing, the *Eagle's* understanding of the social problems associated with the new minorities now seems inadequate. The Juvenile Delinquency series in 1943 served more to reassure Brooklynites as to the strength of their institutions than to alert them to a critical problem. Moreover, it is questionable whether the nostalgic historical booklets on the original Brooklyn towns gave gang-ridden postwar Brooklyn youths a sense of belonging to a stable society.

A 1949 series on Brooklyn's housing crisis by Major Joseph Caccavajo did educate the *Eagle's* readership on the population shift, the need to halt the spread of blighted areas, and the need to rehabilitate old houses in Park Slope,[25] and the 1950 crime stories did help awaken the borough and eventually the nation to the sinister power of the Mafia. Yet the moralizing, oversimplification, sensationalism, and the occasional vendetta-like tone of the exposés reveal a negative aspect of the prizewinning series.

Perhaps with equal justification, Sid Frigand considered the *Eagle's* refusal to submit to its real estate advertisers' protests during his 1954 race articles the paper's finest hour. In the years following the Kerner Report when we are supposedly more sophisticated and less patronizing in our racial attitude, the *Eagle* series looks like mild material; yet, for its time, it was a bit ahead of a good part of its readership.

Finally, even if the *Eagle* was at least partly aware that Brooklyn was changing, it can be faulted for not recognizing the extent to which its potential readership was changing. Bob Grannis' memorandum during the strike suggested that a resurrected *Eagle* become a tabloid with a broader appeal. If the *Eagle* had survived the strike, there was a fair chance that it would have recognized the demographic change and addressed itself to the blacks and Puerto Ricans and become a voice for the new Brooklyn, but by then the weight of its 114-year history had grown heavy enough to become a burden. A newspaper, by its very nature, can least afford to lose touch with the temper of its community, but it seems that time had passed the *Eagle* by.

The last publisher, acutely aware of the effect of the population shift on the downtown business district and on advertising revenue, struggled to rekindle the spark of the old "Brooklyn Spirit" in New York businessmen who made a good deal of money in Brooklyn but lived and spent it across the river in Manhattan. He does not seem to have considered changing the *Eagle* to fit his new potential readership. The new Brooklyn Civic Center was to be the focal point, the symbol of a reborn city and its new prosperity and, because the *Eagle* had campaigned for it for over fifty years, a concrete sign of the *Eagle*'s continuing power. A walk through downtown Brooklyn today is a depressing experience for anyone familiar with some of the literature on a former Brooklyn and the rhetoric on what the Civic Center should be. The Center has no focal point, no character. If it is a symbol of anything, it is a symbol of a promise unfulfilled.

The focal point of this part of town used to be a great bronze eagle soaring from a turn-of-the-century gilded dome.

Brooklyn Public Library *Eagle* Collection.

The great bronze eagle lowered from the *Eagle* building's gilded dome to prepare for the building's demolition in 1955.

Notes

[1]Interview with Robert Moses, July 15, 1970.

[2]Irwin Shaw, "Brooklyn," *Holiday* (June, 1950): 45.

[3]Edward Bok, "The Young Man in Business," *Cosmopolitan* 16 (January 1894): 338, quoted in George Juergens, *Joseph Pulitzer and the New York World* (Princeton: Princeton University Press, 1966), p. 177.

[4]Henry David, *The History of the Haymarket Affair* (New York: Collier, 1963), p. 272; Arthur I. Waskow, *From Race Riot to Sit-In: 1919 and the 1960's* (Garden City: Anchor, 1966), p. 37.

[5]*Eagle*, October 23, 1916.

[6]*The Autobiography of Emma Bullet* (Brooklyn: *Eagle* Press, 1906), pp. 3-4.

[7]William T. Rose, "The *Eagle* Strike," *The New Republic* (September 29, 1937): 210-211.

[8]Samuel B. Moore, "Brooklyn—Past and Present," *Brooklyn Life* (May 29, 1915): 35.

[9]Pete Hamill, "Brooklyn: The Same Alternative," *New York* (July 14, 1969): 26.

[10]*Eagle*, November 15, 1954.

[11]*Eagle*, December 4, 1954.

[12]*Eagle*, October 7, 1954.

[13]*Holiday*, p. 35.

[14]Norman Rosten, "The Meaning of Brooklyn," *Holiday* 27 (March 1960): 136.

[15]Interview with Sidney Frigand, October 23, 1970.

[16]*Eagle*, January 20, 1938.

[17]"Getting Down to Earth in the Brooklyn Field," Broadway Subway and Home Borough Car Advertising Company, Ltd., New York, 1920, pp. 14-15.

[18]*Eagle*, January 31, 1933.

[19]*Eagle*, February 2, 1933.

[20]Norval White, Elliot Willensky, eds., *AIA Guide to New York City* (New York: Macmillan, 1968), pp. 248-249.

[21]*The Brooklyn Navy Yard, A Plan for Redevelopment* (New York: Institute for Urban Studies, Fordham University, May 1968), pp. i-ii.

[22]*Brooklyn Communities*, vol. 1 (New York: The Community Council of Greater New York, 1959), pp. viii, xiv-xv.

[23]Interviews with John Dean, June 18, 1970; Sidney Frigand, David George, Stephen Hill, on October 23, 1970.

[24]Interview with David George, October 23, 1970. George was then Long Island editor of the *Eagle*.

[25]*Eagle*, February 28 to March 17, 1949; a TNS memo, September 8, 1952 refers to the Caccavajo article as a "fiasco."

A NOTE ON SOURCES

A recent comprehensive journalism history, Sidney Kobre's *Development of American Journalism* (1969), mentions the *Eagle* only to note that in the period of the popular penny press, 1830-1865, many "serious" writers, such as Edgar Allan Poe on the *Southern Literary Messenger* and Walt Whitman on the Brooklyn *Eagle*, temporarily turned their talents to journalism. Frank Luther Mott's classic *American Journalism* (1962) devotes a few lines to the *Eagle*'s founding, its Civil War controversy, its great reputation under St. Clair McKelway, and its brief and tragic membership in the Gannett chain, while Edwin Emery's excellent social history *The Press and America* (1962) covers the same ground, adding that the *Eagle*'s cartoonist Nelson Harding won the Pulitzer Prize twice, that the famous broadcaster H. V. Kaltenborn got his start at the *Eagle*, and that the *Eagle* died in 1955. Bernard A. Weisberger's survey *The American Newspaperman* (1961) understandably passes over the *Eagle*. There are no official published institutional histories of the *Eagle* such as Meyer Berger's *The Story of the New York Times* (1951) or Allan Nevins' *The Evening Post: A Century of Journalism* (1922), and neither of these fine books on New York papers pays any attention to the *Eagle*.

There are passing references to the *Eagle* in a few biographies, autobiographies, and recorded reminiscences of journalists who worked there for a while and then became more famous writers later on. *The Americanization of Edward Bok* (1930) gives glimpses of a cub reporter's life in the 1870s. The three biographies of New York's colorful Mayor William J. Gaynor, a former *Eagle* reporter, provide background on the *Eagle*'s war against Brooklyn bossism in the 1890s. They are Louis Pink's *Gaynor: The Tammany Mayor Who Swallowed the Tiger* (1931), Mortimer Smith's *William Jay Gaynor: Mayor of New York* (1951), and Thomas Lately's *The Mayor Who Mastered New York, the Life and Opinions of William J. Gaynor* (1969). The humorist Don

Marquis, an alumnus whom the *Eagle* always proudly described as a "mighty good reporter, the acme of praise among working newspaper people," neglected to mention his *Eagle* job in his own account of his life. The most recent biography of Don Marquis is Edward Anthony's *O Rare Don Marquis* (1962).

The *Autobiography of Emma Bullet* (1906), the *Eagle*'s turn-of-the century Paris correspondent, is largely a self-help inspirational tract, and William Cadwalader Hudson's *Random Recollections of an Old Political Reporter* (1911) includes his reflections on Cleveland, Blaine, etc., but says little about the *Eagle*.

The most renowned graduates of the *"Eagle* school of journalism," of course, were Walt Whitman, H. V. Kaltenborn, and Cleveland Rodgers. Although a number of scholarly articles have discussed the *Eagle* phase of Whitman's journalistic career, the most complete available study is Thomas L. Brasher's *Whitman as Editor of the Brooklyn Daily Eagle* (1970), superceding Gay Wilson Allen's definitive biography *The Solitary Singer* (1967). Allen's study of these years is based primarily on the Whitman anthologies edited by Cleveland Rodgers and Emory Holloway. *The Gathering of Forces: Editorials, Essays, Literary and Dramatic Reviews and Other Material Written by Walt Whitman as Editor of the Brooklyn Daily Eagle in 1846 and 1847* (1920), edited by Rodgers and John Black, and Holloway's *Uncollected Poetry and Prose of Walt Whitman* (1932), helped to reestablish Whitman's journalistic reputation. There are several small anthologies of Whitman's other journalistic writings, but the complete critical edition, *Walt Whitman, Journalistic Writing*, eds. Herbert Bergman and William White, in the series *The Collected Writings of Walt Whitman*, is scheduled for publication by New York University Press.

H. V. Kaltenborn has recorded some of his early *Eagle* experiences in his conversational autobiography *Fifty Fabulous Years: 1900-1950* (1950) and has elaborated on this material in his *Reminiscences* for the Columbia University Oral History Project. He has also been the subject of two Ph.D. dissertations, Giraud Chester's "The Radio Commentaries of H. V. Kaltenborn: A Case Study in Persuasion" (University of Wisconsin, 1947) and David Gillis Clark's "The Dean of Commentators: A Biography of H. V. Kaltenborn" (University of Wisconsin, 1965). Cleveland Rodgers has also recorded his life for the Oral History Project.

There is no up-to-date history of Brooklyn. The old multi-volume works by Henry R. Stiles, *A History of the City of Brooklyn* (1867, 1869, 1870) and

The Civil, Political, Professional, and Ecclesiastical History and Commercial and Industrial Record of the County of Kings and the City of Brooklyn, New York from 1683 to 1884 (1884), Stephen M. Ostander's *A History of the City of Brooklyn and Kings County* (1894), and Henry Isham Hazelton's *The Boroughs of Brooklyn and Queens, Counties of Nassau and Suffolk, Long Island, New York, 1609-1924* (1924), are primarily institutional and neighborhood histories with brief, generally uncritical biographies of prominent citizens, making little attempt to indicate the interaction of various forces in Brooklyn's history.

There are several antiquarian tracts devoted to keeping alive Brooklyn's respect for its old landmarks, and there are good histories of the original towns which became neighborhoods of the unified Brooklyn as well as histories of Brooklyn's various national and ethnic groups, such as the Jews of Williamsburg. Ralph Foster Weld's *Brooklyn Is America* (1948), which was originally written as a series of articles for the *Eagle*, is a popular study of the effect of immigration on Brooklyn. There is a good list of Brooklyn local histories in Weld's bibliography. Perhaps the two best books on Brooklyn are Weld's *Brooklyn Village 1816-1834* (1938) and Harold Coffin Syrett's *The City of Brooklyn 1865-1898* (1944), a study of the political movements which led to consolidation with New York. Finally, Alan Trachtenberg's interdisciplinary study *Brooklyn Bridge, Fact and Symbol* (1965) has a few important references to the *Eagle* in its footnotes and is the basis of part of my chapter on the bridge. The best book on this subject is David McCullough's *The Great Bridge* (1972).

The main source of information about the Brooklyn *Eagle* is the *Eagle* itself: its files, its morgue, its special publications, and especially the recollections of those who worked there. One forty-four page unpublished manuscript by executive editor Edwin B. Wilson summarizes the *Eagle*'s main campaigns, owners, famous editors and alumni and building moves. The *Eagle* was a very self-conscious paper in an extraordinarily self-conscious community. It was forever commemorating anniversaries, and on yearly intervals and other special occasions it reflected on itself and somewhat uncritically recorded its own and Brooklyn's progress. At the same time, its special publications have provided some of the most thorough and attractive popular histories of Brooklyn, i.e., *The Eagle and Brooklyn*, a two-volume illustrated history celebrating the *Eagle*'s move to its new plant in 1891; the *Consolidation Issue* marking the end of Brooklyn as an independent city January 1, 1898; Martin Weyrauch's *Pictorial History of Brooklyn* for the

Eagle's seventy-fifth anniversary in 1916; and *Historic Brooklyn*, the *Eagle*'s 1946 series of illustrated booklets covering the histories of Brooklyn's six original villages.

The almost complete *Eagle* file is on microfilm at the Brooklyn Public Library at Grand Army Plaza in Brooklyn and the New York Public Library Newspaper Annex. The Long Island Historical Society has scrapbooks with *Eagle* clippings, the New York Historical Society has bound volumes for 1913 and some special issues, and the archives of St. Francis College in Brooklyn has extensive *Eagle* material including the *Eagle* almanacs from 1891-1929 and bound volumes 1861-1864 and 1945-1955. The *Eagle* is indexed only from 1891-1902. The *Eagle* morgue, including clippings, photos, and library, is rotting in the basement of the Brooklyn Public Library. The files of the New York *Times* and *Editor and Publisher* have many references to the *Eagle*, especially its final year. Other very useful newspaper sources include the files of the New York Newspaper Guild's publications: *Frontpage, Guild Reporter, Eagle Reporter*, and strike bulletins.

Many people who worked for the *Eagle* are still alive, including the last publisher, Frank D. Schroth, although several, including Edwin Wilson, Jimmy Murphy, James Henle, Robert Grannis, and Colonel Preston Goodfellow have died between 1970 and 1973. I have corresponded with over sixty former *Eagle* employees and associates and have personally interviewed seventeen to get their impressions of the paper, their evaluations of its leading personalities, their judgment on the paper's relationship to its community, and their feelings about the events and forces that brought on the paper's demise.

The single most useful unpublished manuscript collection is that of *Eagle* former managing editor Thomas N. Schroth of Sedgwick, Maine. His papers include manuscript histories of the *Eagle* and the 1955 strike, his own office memos from 1952-1955, daily bulletins on strike negotiations, letters and addresses of Frank D. Schroth from 1940-1960, a complete collection of the *Eagle Eye*, and some scrapbooks and special issues of the *Eagle*.

BIBLIOGRAPHY

Manuscript Collections

Letters of Praise and Thanks from Brooklynites. In four large manila envelopes, *Eagle* morgue, Brooklyn Public Library basement.

Thomas N. Schroth papers, including some papers of Frank D. Schroth. As of this writing, these papers are in the possession of the author, Fordham University, Bronx, New York. They will be returned to Thomas N. Schroth, Sedgwick, Maine.

The Brooklyn *Eagle*

The original complete file of the *Eagle* has been put in storage by the New York Public Library system and is not available. The entire file (with a few issues missing), 1841-1955, is on microfilm at the Brooklyn Public Library, main branch, and at the New York Public Library, Newspaper Division. Some bound volumes, 1945-1955, are available at St. Francis College, Brooklyn, New York. The St. Francis College archives also have the complete file of the *Eagle* Almanac and a large collection of the *Eagle* postcard series.

The New York Historical Society has some *Eagle* special editions and the bound volumes for 1913.

The complete *Eagle* morgue, containing the files of *Eagle* writers, clipping files, photographs, and the *Eagle* reference library is in the basement of the Brooklyn Public Library, but it is poorly housed and uncatalogued.

285

Other Newspapers and Periodicals

The Eagle Eye, 1938-1939.
The Eagle Reporter, 1941-1955.
Editor and Publisher, 1954-1955.
Frontpage, 1954-1955.
The Guild Reporter.

Unpublished Material

Theses and Dissertations

Chester, Giraud. "The Radio Commentaries of H. V. Kaltenborn: A Case Study in Persuasion." Ph.D. dissertation, University of Wisconsin, 1947.
Clark, David Gillis. "The Dean of Commentators: A Biography of H. V. Kaltenborn." Ph.D. dissertation, University of Wisconsin, 1965.
Conlon, Timothy John. "The Death of the Los Angeles *Mirror*: A Study in the Effects of Suburbanization upon the Community Role of a Metropolitan Newspaper." Master's thesis, Stanford University, 1962.

Scrapbooks and Other Manuscripts

"A Decade Under the Guild, History of the Brooklyn *Eagle* Unit, Newspaper Guild of New York, from strike of 1937 to city-wide day in 1947 . . ." (Mimeographed.)
"Newspaper Comments Concerning the Seventy-Fifth Anniversary of the Brooklyn Daily *Eagle*, October 26, 1916." Thomas N. Schroth papers.
"Newspaper Comments, Letters, etc., concerning the Eighty-Fifth Anniversary of the Brooklyn Daily *Eagle*, October 26, 1926." Thomas N. Schroth papers.
Piper, Rick. Unpublished undergraduate paper on *Eagle* arbitration proceedings. 1966.
[Schroth, Thomas N.] "History of the Strike Between the Newspaper Guild of New York and the Brooklyn *Eagle*." (78 pp.) 1955. (Typed and photostated.)
[Wilson, Edwin.] "The History of the Brooklyn *Eagle*: 1841-1955." 1955. (Typed and photostated.)
Wirtz, W. Willard. "In the Matter of Arbitration Between Newspaper

Guild of New York and Brooklyn *Eagle*, Inc." Cook County, Illinois, February 2, 1959. (Typed and photostated.)

Interviews

Crowell, W. Frank. December 28, 1970. (Phone.)
Dean, John. June 18(?), 1970. (Phone.)
Deegan, John. June 17, 1970.
Frigand, Sidney. October 23, 1970. (Phone.)
Geller, Jules. June 18, 1970. (Phone.)
George, David. October 23, 1970. (Phone.)
Hamilton, Maxwell. July 2, 1970. (Phone and tape.)
Hill, Stephen. October 23, 1970. (Phone.)
Justin, Jules. January 4, 1971. (Phone.)
Kaufman, I. October 30, 1969; June 17, 1970.
Kelly, James A. June 30, 1970.
Moses, Robert. July 15, 1970.
Pilat, Oliver. June 18, 1970.
Salerno, Al. November 6, 1969.
Schroth, Frank D. November 27, 1969.
Schroth, Jr., Frank D. June 17, 1970.
Swain, Howard. December 28, 1970. (Phone.)
Weingarten, Victor and Violet. August 4, 1973.
Wilson, Edwin B. February 7, 1970.

Letters

Anthony, Richard H. January 30, 1970; June 6, 1970.
Avery, Lydia. February 1, 1970.
Barton, Helen M. February 9, 1970.
Bernhard, Andrew. January 26, 1970.
Bland, Ben. February 3, 1970.
Butler, Gwendeline E. January 25, 1970.
Chrisafides, Peter. January 26, 1970.
Cleary, Fanny F. Undated.
Coll, Helen Moran. February 10, 1970.
Cooper, Mrs. Arthur G. February 11, 1970.
Curtis, Joseph. March 6, 1970.
Danson, Harold L. February 2, 1970.

Dillon, Alice. January 27, 1970.

Dulac, Alicia Cogan. February 12, 1970.

Flynn, Marion Byrnes. February 1, 1970.

Fox, David. February 27, 1970; June 3, 1970.

Friedman, David. January 29, 1970; June 6, 1970.

Geller, Jules. January 26, 1970.

Goldstein, Stanley. February 3, 1970.

Goodfellow, M. Preston. January 27, 1970; May 20, 1970.

Gould, Ben. February 9, 1970.

Grant, Ellen M. February 9, 1970.

Gussak, John J. January 28, 1970.

Hamilton, Maxwell. January 27, 1970; June 15, 1970.

Henle, James. January 28, 1970; February 11, 1970; May 20, 1970.

Henry, Martin A. February 2, 1970.

Hillcourt, Grace. February 2, 1970.

Jex, Hope Satterthwaite. February 1, 1970.

Kilcoyne, Francis P. January 25, 1970.

Lasker, Joe. February 1, 1970.

Lein, Audrey M. Undated.

LeMieux, Cecelia W. Undated.

Libby, Violet K. January 31, 1970.

Lindenbusch, John H. February 5, 1970.

Livingston, J. A. May 20, 1970.

Luks, Gertrude. February 1, 1970.

McCormick, Kenneth. January 27, 1970.

McDonough, Marie. February 10, 1970.

Mangan, Stephen N. January 26, 1970.

Mannix, James A. January 26, 1970.

Moldenke, Harold N. Feburary 5, 1970.

Moses, Robert. July 7, 1970.

Mowbray, Arnold A. March 31, 1970; May 22, 1970.

Nevin, Barbara. January 26, 1970.

O'Connor, Veronica. Undated.

Okun, Blanche. January 26, 1970.

Parrott, Harold. March 2, 1970.

Pickman, Jerome. January 28, 1970; June 3, 1970.

Pilat, Oliver. February 2, 1970.

Postley, Maurice. January 26, 1970.

Quinn, Albert W. January 26, 1970.

Rankin, Amy C. February 3, 1970.
Rosenzweig, Seymour. February 10, 1970.
Silverman, George G. January 27, 1970.
Slocum, Milton J. M.D. February 10, 1970.
Sobel, Al. January 27, 1970.
Stanton, Alden O. (2) Undated.
Stern, Madeline B. January 30, 1970.
Summit, Macon. January 30, 1970.
Tiernan, Thomas J. February 18, 1970.
Vigman, Fred K. January 28, 1970; May 28, 1970; June 24, 1970.
Wolfe, Mrs. Bertram D. January 31, 1970.
Wolfe, Lawrence. February 4, 1970.
Zuger, Bernard, M.D. January 25, 1970.

Special *Eagle* Publications
(Listed Chronologically)

What the Eagle Thinks of the Governor and the Brooklyn Gang. (Undated
    pamphlet in New York Public Library, Local History section.)
Opening Ceremonies of the New York and Brooklyn Bridge, May 24, 1883. 1883.
Howard, Henry W. B., ed. *The Eagle and Brooklyn.* 1893.
Brooklyn Daily Eagle Almanac. 1896-1929.
Consolidation Number. 1898.
A Guide to New York City. 1899.
Peace Issue. January 1, 1899.
Bullet, Emma. *The Autobiography of Emma Bullet.* 1906.
*Program of the Dedication Ceremonies of the Prison Ship Martyrs' Monument, Fort
    Greene Park, Brooklyn, New York, Sat., November 14, 1908 and History of
    Prison Ship Martyrs.* 1908.
How a Modern Newspaper Is Made. 1911.
Development Series. 1912.
Hudson, William C. *Between the Lines, Random Recollections. Eagle* Library
    No. 177, Vol. 28, 1913.
Seventy-Fifth Anniversary, Brooklyn Daily Eagle. October 26, 1916.
Weyraugh, Martin H. *The Pictorial History of Brooklyn.* 1916.
Brooklyn and Long Island in the War. 1919.
Newsroom Handbook. 1919.
Wilson, Edwin B. *The Eagle Grand Canyon Dedication Tour.* 1920.
Col. William Hester, 1835-1921. 1921.

Brooklyn Today, Eightieth Anniversary Issue of the Brooklyn Daily Eagle, 1841-1921. 1921.

Programme, Eighty-Fifth Anniversary Celebration of the Brooklyn Daily Eagle. October 26, 1926.

Ninetieth Anniversary and Long Island Ten Year Plan Edition, Brooklyn Daily Eagle. October 26, 1931.

Forward, Long Island, 1636-1936. 1936.

Centennary Issue, 1841-1941. 1941.

Brooklyn's Relationship to the City of New York. Dr. Harold W. Dobbes, Chairman. Princeton Survey, Princeton University; Brooklyn *Eagle* Press. 1942.

Juvenile Delinquency in Brooklyn. 1944.

The Brooklyn War Memorial. 1945.

Staging Area—Brooklyn. 1945.

History of Brooklyn's Six Original Tours. 1946.

The Battle of the Big Stench. 1948.

Agreement Between the Brooklyn Eagle and Newspaper Guild of New York. November 30, 1952.

Oral History

"The Reminiscences of H. V. Kaltenborn." 2 vols. Oral History Research Office, Radio Unit, Columbia University, New York, 1950.

"The Reminiscences of William O'Dwyer." Taped by Mr. John Kelly, 1960-1962. 8 vols. Oral History Research Office, Columbia University, New York.

"The Reminiscences of Cleveland Rodgers." 2 vols. Oral History Project, Columbia University, New York, 1950.

"The Reminiscences of John Heffernan." Oral History Project, Columbia University, New York, 1950.

Books

Allen, Gay Wilson. *The Solitary Singer: A Critical Biography of Walt Whitman.* New York: New York University Press, 1955.

Anthony, Edward. *O Rare Don Marquis.* Garden City, New York: Doubleday and Company, 1962.

Berger, Meyer. *The Story of the New York Times, 1851-1951.* New York: Simon and Shuster, 1951.

Bok, Edward. *The Americanization of Edward Bok: The Autobiography of a Dutch Boy Fifty Years After.* New York: Charles Scribner's Sons, 1930.

Brasher, Thomas L. *Whitman as Editor of the Brooklyn Daily Eagle.* Detroit: Wayne State University Press, 1970.

Brooklyn Communities, Population Characteristics and Neighborhood Social Resources. 2 vols. New York: Bureau of Community Statistical Services, The Community Council of Greater New York, 1959.

The Brooklyn Navy Yard, A Plan for Redevelopment. New York: Institute for Urban Studies, Fordham University, May 1968.

Brooklyn Progress. Annual Report. Hon. John Cashmore, President, Borough of Brooklyn. 1951; 1955-1956.

Callender, James H. *Yesterdays on Brooklyn Heights.* New York: Doland Press, 1927.

Characteristics of the Population by Health Area, New York City: 1950. New York: Welfare and Health Council of New York, 1953.

Christie, George V. *The Brooklyn Daily Eagle.* Washington, D.C.: By the author, 1955.

Christman, Henry M. *Walt Whitman's New York.* New York: Macmillan Company, 1963.

Churchill, Allen. *Park Row.* New York: Rinehart and Company, 1958.

David, Henry. *The History of the Haymarket Affair.* New York: Collier, 1963.

Downtown Brooklyn. New York: Department of Church Planning and Research, Protestant Council of the City of New York, 1955.

Ellis, David M., Frost, James A., Syrett, Harold C., and Cannan, Harry J. *A History of New York State.* Ithaca: Cornell University Press, 1967.

Ellis, Edward Robb. *The Epic of New York City.* New York: Coward McCann Inc., 1966.

Emery, Edwin. *The Press and America: An Interpretative History of Journalism.* 2d ed. Englewood Cliffs: Prentice Hall, 1962.

Glazer, Nathan, and Moynihan, Daniel Patrick. *Beyond the Melting Pot.* Cambridge: M.I.T. Press, 1963.

Handlin, Oscar. *The Newcomers: Negroes and Puerto Ricans in a Changing Metropolis.* New York: Anchor, 1962.

Hazelton, Henry Isham. *The Boroughs of Brooklyn and Queens, Counties of Nassau and Suffolk, Long Island, New York, 1609-1924.* 6 vols. New York-Chicago: Lewis Historical Publishing Company, Inc., 1925.

Historic Brooklyn. New York: Brooklyn Trust Company, 1941.

Hofstadter, Richard. *Anti-Intellectualism in American Life.* New York: Alfred A. Knopf, 1966.

Hohenberg, John. *The New Front Page*. New York: Columbia University Press, 1966.

Hudson, William C. *Random Recollections of an Old Political Reporter*. New York: Cupples and Leon, 1911.

Janowitz, Morris. *The Community Press in an Urban Setting: The Social Elements of Urbanism*. 2d ed. Chicago: University of Chicago Press, 1967.

Juergens, George. *Joseph Pulitzer and the New York World*. Princeton: Princeton University Press, 1966.

Kaltenborn, H. V. *Fifty Fabulous Years 1900-1950: A Personal Review*. New York: G. P. Putnam's Sons, 1950.

Klein, Alexander, ed. *Empire City: A Treasury of New York*. New York: Rinehart and Company, 1955.

Kobre, Sidney. *Development of American Journalism* Dubuque: Wm. C. Brown Company, 1969.

Kranzler, George. *Williamsburg: A Jewish Community in Transition*. New York: Phillipp Feldheim, Inc., 1961.

Lancaster, Clay. *Old Brooklyn Heights*. Rutland, Vermont, and Tokyo, Japan: Charles E. Tuttle Company, 1961.

Lately, Thomas. *The Mayor Who Mastered New York, The Life and Opinion of William J. Gaynor*. New York: William Morrow and Company, Inc., 1969.

Leab, Daniel J. *A Union of Individuals: The Formation of the American Newspaper Guild, 1933-1936*. New York: Columbia University Press, 1970.

Lee, James M. *The Daily Newspaper in America*. New York: Macmillan Company, 1937.

Liebling, A. J. *The Press*. New York: Ballantine, 1964.

Lindstrom, Carl E. *The Fading American Newspaper*. Garden City, New York: Doubleday and Company, 1960.

Lowe, Jeanne. *Cities in a Race with Time: Progress and Poverty in America's Renewing Cities*. New York: Random House, 1967.

Lyle, Jack. *The News in Megalopolis*. San Francisco: Chandler, 1967.

McCaque, James. *The Second Rebellion: The Story of the New York City Draft Riots of 1863*. New York: Dial Press, 1968.

McCullough, David. *The Great Bridge*. New York: Simon and Shuster, 1973.

McKelvey, Blake. *The Urbanization of America, 1860-1915*. New Brunswick: Rutgers University Press, 1963.

Mott, Frank Luther. *American Journalism: A History, 1690-1960*. 3d ed. New York: Macmillan Company, 1962.

Nevins, Allan. *The Evening Post: A Century of Journalism*. New York: Boni and Liveright, 1922.

————, and Krout, John A., eds. *The Greater City: New York, 1898-1948*. New York; Columbia University Press, 1948.

New York As It Is; containing a general description of the City of New York; lists of offices, public institutions, and other useful information: including the Public Officers, etc., of the City of Brooklyn. New York: T. R. Tanner, 1840.

New York City Planning Commission. *Plan for New York City: Brooklyn*. New York: City Planning Commission, 1969.

New York Panorama. Federal Writer's Project. New York: Random House, 1938.

Ostander, Stephen M. *A History of the City of Brooklyn and Kings County*. 2 vols. Brooklyn: By subscription, 1894.

Our Brooklyn. Brooklyn: Kings County Trust Company, 1955.

Perkin, Robert L. *The First Hundred Years: An Informal History of Denver and the Rocky Mountain News*. Garden City, New York: Doubleday and Company, 1959.

Pink, Louis. *Gaynor: The Tammany Mayor Who Swallowed the Tiger*. New York: International Press, 1931.

Price, Warren C. *The Literature of Journalism: An Annotated Bibliography*. Minneapolis: University of Minnesota Press, 1959.

Reid, Ed. *The Shame of New York*. New York: Random House, 1953.

Rice, William B. *The Los Angeles Star, 1851-1864: The Beginnings of Journalism in Southern California*. Berkeley and Los Angeles: University of California Press, 1947.

Rodgers, Cleveland, and Rankin, Rebecca. *New York: The World's Capitol City, Its Development and Contributions to Progress*. New York: Harpers, 1948.

Rodgers, Cleveland. *New York Plans for the Future*. New York: Harper and Brothers, 1943.

"St. Clair McKelway" *Proceedings of the Fifty-First Convocation of the University of the State of New York*. Albany, 1915.

Seldes, George. *Freedom of the Press*. New York: Bobbs-Merrill, 1935.

————. *Lords of the Press*. New York: Messner, 1938.

Shaplen, Robert. *Free Love and Heavenly Sinners: The Story of the Great Henry Ward Beecher Scandal*. New York: Alfred Knopf, 1954.

Smith, Mortimer. *William Jay Gaynor: Mayor of New York*. Chicago: Henry Regnery Company, 1951.

Steinman, D. B. *The Builders of the Bridge: The Story of John Roebling and His Son*. New York: Harcourt Brace and Company, 1945.

Stiles, Henry R. *A History of the City of Brooklyn, Including the Old Town and Village of Brooklyn, the Town of Bushwick, and the Village and City of Williamsburgh*. 3 vols. Brooklyn: W. W. Munsell and Company, 1867, 1869, 1870.

————., ed. *The Civil, Political, Professional and Ecclesiastical History and Commercial and Industrial Record of the County of Kings and the City of Brooklyn, New York, from 1683 to 1884*. 2 vols. New York: W. W. Munsell and Company, 1884.

Swanberg, W. A. *Citizen Hearst*. New York: Bantam, 1963.

Syrett, Harold Coffin. *The City of Brooklyn, 1865-1898*. New York: Columbia University Press, 1944.

Tebbel, John. *The Compact History of the American Newspaper*. New York: Hawthorn Books Inc., 1963.

Trachtenberg, Alan. *Brooklyn Bridge: Fact and Symbol*. New York: Oxford University Press, 1965.

Villard, Oswald Garrison. *The Disappearing Daily: Chapters in American Newspaper Evolution*. Freeport: Books for Libraries Press, 1944.

Waskow, Arthur I. *From Race Riot to Sit-In: 1919 and the 1960's*. Garden City: Anchor, 1966.

Weisberger, Bernard A. *The American Newspaperman*. Edited by Daniel J. Boorstin. The Chicago History of American Civilization. Chicago: University of Chicago Press, 1961.

Weld, Ralph Foster. *Brooklyn in America*. New York: Columbia University Press, 1950.

————. *Brooklyn Village, 1816-1834*. New York: Columbia University Press, 1938.

Whitman, Walt. *The Gathering of Forces: Editorials, Essays, Literary and Dramatic and Other Material Written by Walt Whitman as Editor of the Brooklyn Daily Eagle in 1846 and 1847*. Edited by Cleveland Rodgers and John Black. New York and London: Putnam, 1920.

————. *The Early Poems and Fiction*. Edited by Thomas L. Brasher. The Collected Writings of Walt Whitman. New York: New York University Press, 1963.

————. *The Uncollected Poetry and Prose of Walt Whitman*. Edited by Emory Holloway. New York: 1929.

Wyllie, Irwin G. *The Self-Made Man in America, The Myth of Rags to Riches*. New York: The Free Press, 1954.

Pamphlets

Bird, Robert S. "Whatever Happened to Brooklyn?" *New York Herald Tribune*, February 15, 16, 19, 20, 21, 1962.

Rodgers, Cleveland. *Voicing Brooklyn: What the Brooklyn Eagle Has Meant Through the Years*. Brooklyn: Kings County Trust Company, 1955.

Schroth, Thomas N. *The Responsibility of the Newspaper and How It Can Best Serve Its Community*. Chattanooga, Tennessee: Southern Newspaper Publishers Association, March 14, 1953.

Who Killed the Brooklyn Eagle? New York: The Newspaper Guild of New York, 1955.

Articles

"Brooklyn and Queens." *Fortune* 20 (July 1939): 145-47.

Brown, Howard J. "Some Comments on Arbitration in the Newspaper Industry." *Journalism Quarterly* 34 (Winter 1957): 19-31.

de Pue, Stephanie. "Brooklyn Waterfront: Berths or Boondoggle?" *The Village Voice* (December 17, 1970): 22.

Hamill, Pete. "Brooklyn: The Same Alternative." *New York* 2 (July 14, 1969): 24-33.

Harding, Earl. "Death for the Guilded Eagle." *Partners* 9 (June 1955): 20-26.

Idzerda, Stanley J. "Walt Whitman, Politician." *New York History* 54 (April 1956): 171-184.

Josephson, Earl. "Are New York Dailies Losing Readers?" *News Workshop* 5 (December 1953): 1.

Judd, Jacob. "A Tale of Two Cities: Brooklyn and New York, 1834-1855." *The Journal of Long Island History* 3 (Spring 1963): 19-35.

Kazin, Alfred. "The Bridge." *New York Review of Books* (July 15, 1965): 6-8.

Ledlie, Joseph M. A. "Another Lost Image." *America* (September 5, 1970): 122-124.

Malafronte, Don. "Brooklyn *Eagle* Blends Optimism and Economy." *News Workshop* 5 (December 1953): 4.

Martin, Fred J. "Anatomy of a Failing Newspaper." *Montana Journalism Review* No. 11 (1968): 13-21.

Miller, Charles Grant. "The Making of Better Citizens in Brooklyn." *Editor and Publisher* (February 12, 1921): 1.

"Negroes Are City Folks." *Commonweal* (November 26, 1943): 132.

Moore, Samuel B. "Brooklyn—Past and Present." *Brooklyn Life* 51 (May 29, 1915): 36-72.

Nixon, Raymond B. "Who Will Own the Press in 1975?" *Journalism Quarterly* 32 (Winter 1955): 10-16.

Rose, William T. "The Eagle Strike." *The New Republic* (September 29, 1937): 210-211.

Rosten, Norman. "The Meaning of Brooklyn." *Holiday* (March 1960): 70-136.

Schlesinger, A. M. "The City in American History." *Mississippi Valley Historical Review* 27 (1940): 43-66.

Shaw, Irwin. "Brooklyn." *Holiday* (June 1950): 34-60.

Simon, Donald E. "Brooklyn in the Election of 1860." *The New York Historical Society Quarterly* 51 (July 1967): 249-262.

Sorrentino, Gilbert. "No Radical Chic in Brooklyn." *New York Times* (January 17, 1971): 29.

"The Death of the World." *The New Republic* (March 11, 1931): 84-85.

White, William. "Walt Whitman: Journalist." *Journalism Quarterly* 39 (Summer 1962): 339-346.

Wilson, Edmund. "A Bad Day in Brooklyn." *The New Republic* (April 22, 1931): 263-266.

Zunder, Theodore A. "William B. Marsh: The First Editor of the Brooklyn Daily Eagle." *American Book Collector* 4 (August 1833): 93-95.

INDEX